# Introduction to Special Educational Needs, Disability & Inclusion

Sara Miller McCune founded SAGE Publishing in 1965 to support the dissemination of usable knowledge and educate a global community. SAGE publishes more than 1000 journals and over 800 new books each year, spanning a wide range of subject areas. Our growing selection of library products includes archives, data, case studies and video. SAGE remains majority owned by our founder and after her lifetime will become owned by a charitable trust that secures the company's continued independence.

Los Angeles | London | New Delhi | Singapore | Washington DC | Melbourne

# Introduction to Special Educational Needs, Disability & Inclusion

## A Student's Guide

## Alexandra Sewell & Joanne Smith

Los Angeles | London | New Delhi
Singapore | Washington DC | Melbourne

Los Angeles | London | New Delhi
Singapore | Washington DC | Melbourne

SAGE Publications Ltd
1 Oliver's Yard
55 City Road
London EC1Y 1SP

SAGE Publications Inc.
2455 Teller Road
Thousand Oaks, California 91320

SAGE Publications India Pvt Ltd
B 1/I 1 Mohan Cooperative Industrial Area
Mathura Road
New Delhi 110 044

SAGE Publications Asia-Pacific Pte Ltd
3 Church Street
#10-04 Samsung Hub
Singapore 049483

Editor: Delayna Spencer
Editorial assistant: Orsod Malik
Production editor: Nicola Carrier
Copyeditor: Tom Bedford
Indexer: Adam Pozner
Marketing manager: Lorna Patkai
Cover design: Wendy Scott
Typeset by: C&M Digitals (P) Ltd, Chennai, India
Printed in the UK

**Library of Congress Control Number: 2020934666**

**British Library Cataloguing in Publication data**

A catalogue record for this book is available from the British Library

ISBN 978-1-5264-9483-2
ISBN 978-1-5264-9482-5 (pbk)

At SAGE we take sustainability seriously. Most of our products are printed in the UK using responsibly sourced papers and boards. When we print overseas we ensure sustainable papers are used as measured by the PREPS grading system. We undertake an annual audit to monitor our sustainability.

Dr Alexandra Sewell: To my excellent husband, Dave Brown. Thank you for your unending love and belief in me.

Joanne Smith: In memory of Granny Maggie, who taught me to be persistent and strong, secure in the knowledge that education can make a difference.

# CONTENTS

# LIST OF FIGURES AND TABLES

# ABOUT THE AUTHORS

**Dr Alexandra Sewell** is a HCPC registered Practitioner Psychologist, and prior to embarking on a career in academia held positions as an educational psychologist and trainee educational psychologist across the West Midlands, UK. She completed her Doctorate degree in Applied Educational and Child Psychology at the University of Birmingham in 2016. Alexandra joined the University of Worcester in July 2018 as a lecturer and researcher in Special Educational Needs, Disability and Inclusion. Her research interests range from social development in primary school to promoting student voice to enhance inclusive educational practice in higher education. She has published her research in numerous peer reviewed international education journals and has presented at educational psychology conferences in the UK. In her spare time, she enjoys reading for pleasure and going for long Sunday walks with her husband and two dogs, Monty and Mouse.

**Joanne Smith** was a Primary School Teacher and Inclusion Manager for 15 years. She studied for her MA in Special and Inclusive Education at the University of Worcester, joining the academic staff initially as an associate lecturer before securing a permanent position in 2017. Joanne is the course leader for the BA (Hons) Special Educational Needs, Disability and Inclusion programme and teaches across many courses within the Department of Education and Inclusion. She also owns a childcare business which was established in 2013. Her research interests lie within curriculum development, focusing on the incorporation of student voice across all phases of education, from early years to HE. Joanne has published articles in national educational journals and has presented at local specialist education conferences. She is starting her PhD study in October 2020. She is a busy mum of three children and enjoys family adventures and engaging with the arts in her spare time.

# 1

# AN INTRODUCTION TO SENDI: MODELS AND DEFINITIONS

Joanne Smith (with contributions from Dr Alexandra Sewell)

---

### Introduction

This book offers a comprehensive introduction to Special Educational Needs, Disability and Inclusion (SENDI). There are many models and definitions of SENDI, so this chapter will:

- Introduce you to differing definitions, theories and models of educational 'inclusion'.
- Explore current terms and concepts in relation to the understanding of 'special educational needs/disability'.
- Start to identify implications for practice.

# Definitions of special educational needs

Throughout this book we will consistently refer to inclusive practice that involves Children and Young People (CYP) with Special Educational Needs and/or Disabilities (SEND). This is in line with terminology used in current legislation: *The Special Educational Needs and Disability Code of Practice, aged 0–25 years* (DfE and DoH, 2014: 4, 5):

> A child or young person has SEN if they have a learning difficulty or disability which calls for special educational provision to be made for him or her. A child of compulsory school age or a young person has a learning difficulty or disability if they have a significantly greater difficulty in learning than the majority of others of the same age, or has a disability which prevents or hinders them from making use of facilities of a kind generally provided for others of the same age in mainstream schools or institutions.

A child under compulsory school age has SEN if they are likely to fall within the definition above when they reach compulsory school age or would do so if special educational provision was not made for them (Section 20 Children and Families Act 2014). Post-16 institutions often use the term Learning Difficulties and Disabilities (LDD). The term SEN is used in the Code across the 0–25 age range but includes LDD.

Many CYP who have SEN may have a disability under the Equality Act (2010) – that is '…a physical or mental impairment which has a long-term and substantial adverse effect on their ability to carry out normal day-to-day activities'. This definition provides a relatively low threshold and includes more children than many realise: 'long-term' is defined as 'a year or more' and 'substantial' is defined as 'more than minor or trivial'. This definition includes sensory impairments such as those affecting sight or hearing, and long-term health conditions such as asthma, diabetes, epilepsy, and cancer. CYP with such conditions do not necessarily have SEN, but there is a significant overlap between disabled CYP and those with SEN. Where a disabled child or young person requires special educational provision, they will also be covered by the SEN definition.

This book will explore current research and practice within the area of SEND, with some necessary reference to the historical context, particularly discussed in the next chapter. We (the authors) introduce you to some aspects of 'need' including specific learning difficulties and mental health difficulties. We discuss implications for practice, particularly in an educational context, and will look at the varied roles and contexts for a SEND practitioner. We will look at more global perspectives of SEND and consider implications for further research, returning to shared understandings of inclusion in the final chapter.

Throughout the book we will be referring to concepts of **inclusion** and **inclusive practice**. Inclusion, as you will discover, and our concept of it, is ever-evolving. We will be exploring models of inclusion in more depth in the final chapter, but characteristics of inclusive (educational) practice involve considering the needs of all learners, requiring educational settings to adapt provisions, resources, methods and implementations of curriculum. It could be a tool for promoting equality, underpinned by the Code of Practice as a framework. We will encourage you throughout this book to reflect on your experiences, personal beliefs and values, whilst developing your knowledge and understanding of differing models of SENDI.

---

  Time to Reflect

What is inclusion?

What does it mean to you?

When we talk about educational inclusion where does this come from?

What is inclusive practice?

---

# 'The inclusion framework'

Historical changes to inclusive practice will be explored in the next chapter. However, for us to understand inclusive policy frameworks, we must look at recent key developments in legislation:

- 2001 – Special Educational Needs and Disability Act (SENDA) and the SEN Code of Practice (DfES, 2001).
- 2010 – Equality Act.
- 2011 – SEN Green Paper (DfE, 2011b).
- 2013 – Children and Families Bill (DfE, 2013).
- 2014 – SEND Code of Practice (DfE and DoH, 2014).

## SENDA (2001)

SENDA strengthened the right of children with SEN to attend mainstream school, unless their parents chose otherwise, or this was incompatible with 'efficient education' for other children and there were no reasonable steps that could be taken to prevent that incompatibility. Legislation ensured that pupils were not placed at 'substantial disadvantage' in comparison to non-disabled peers. There was a legal duty not to treat a person with disabilities 'less favourably', without justification, for a reason relating to their disability, and an anticipatory duty to make '**reasonable adjustment**'. Public sector organisations are required to provide reasonable adjustments to 'avoid as far as possible by reasonable means the disadvantage which a disabled student experiences because of their disability'. The reasonable adjustments duty is explored in more depth in Chapter 6, and you can go to www.equalityhumanrights.com/en/advice-and-guidance/what-are-reasonable-adjustments for more information.

The SEN Code of Practice (DfES, 2001) stated that:

> A child with SEN should have their needs met, and these needs will normally be met in mainstream schools with the views of the child considered. There should be full access to a broad, balanced and relevant education, with 'all teachers being teachers of children with SEN'.

The CoP (DfES, 2001) identified that teaching children with SEN was a whole-school responsibility. A child had 'SEN' if they required provision which was different from, and additional to, that made for most pupils. Provision was made in a graduated approach. The terms *School Action* (SA) and *School Action Plus* (SA+) were used to identify, provide, and monitor provision for children with SEN. A *Statutory Assessment* was requested if there was 'significant cause for concern', which may or may not have led to a 'Statement of Special Educational Need'. This was when the local authority (LA) considered that the special educational provision necessary to meet pupils' needs could not be reasonably provided with resources normally available to mainstream schools. A statement specified longer-term objectives and SEN provision. The New Labour period emphasised SA and SA+ and discouraged LAs from linking all additional resources with statements. Statements were later dissolved or replaced with Education and Health Care (EHC) plans as discussed further on in this chapter.

## The Equality Act (2010)

The Equality Act (2010) brought together several pieces of older legislation. In relation to disability, the objectives of the Equality Act are therefore the same as the Disability Discrimination Act (1995) and SENDA (2001). The purpose is to avoid as far as possible, by all reasonable means, the disadvantage a student experiences through having a disability. Reasonable adjustments must be made for pupils with disability – if needed – whether they have a special educational need or not. The duty is proactive. The 'disability equality duty' means that public bodies must have due regard (for example) to the need to promote equality of opportunity and promote positive attitudes towards disabled persons. These duties are explored further in Chapter 6.

## The 2011 SEN Green Paper, *Support and Aspiration: A New Approach to Special Educational Needs and Disability* (DfE, 2011b)

The coalition government stated a 'lack of the right help ... system is bureaucratic and bewildering ... culture of low expectations ... limited choices' (DfE, 2011b: 4) for pupils with SEN and their families. The Green Paper drew on the Bercow (2008), Lamb (2009), Salt (2010) and OfSTED (2010) reports.

Proposals included 'tackling' the over-identification of SEN (DfE, 2011b: 10) and replacing SA and SA+ with a single SEN category (p.4). There would be a single assessment process and education, health and care (EHC) plan to replace statements 'with the same **statutory protection**' (p.5). This statutory protection means it is a legal requirement that any professional body named on the document must demonstrate an attempt to carry out the recommendations in the EHC plan that they are responsible for. Failure to adhere to the recommendations demonstrated within the EHC plan can result in legal action (see www.ipsea.org.uk for further information on legal duties).

There would be an option of a personal budget with pilots to assess whether this may extend to school-based provision. The paper suggested 'giving parents a real choice of school', mainstream or special (p.5). There would be provision for special school academies and potential for 'free' schools. It was suggested that special schools should share expertise and services (p.58).

## Children and Families Bill (DfE, 2013)

The Children and Families Bill included an extension of the SEN system from birth to age 25. The implementation of EHC plans meant that LAs and health authorities needed to work together more closely. This collaborative practice is explored further in Chapter 9.

## Special Educational Needs and Disability Code of Practice (DfE and DoH, 2014)

The 2014 Code of Practice refers to 'one fifth' of pupils with SEND. There is now a single category ('Additional SEN Support'). There is a single assessment process and EHC plans have replaced statements. Academies and free schools can be approved to admit pupils permanently who do not have an EHC plan in order 'to increase access to specialist provision'.

---

 **Time to Reflect**

- What do you mean by inclusion?
- What does your school/college/establishment/service mean?
- What do other people mean?
- What makes you feel included?
- When do you feel excluded? How does the legislation and policy (above) translate into practice?
- How does SEND policy relate to the wider educational context?

---

# Models of disability

Throughout this book we will repeatedly refer to various models of disability. A model of disability is made up of a set of assumptions about what disability is and how it occurs. Each model has a different perspective on what constitutes disability and provides differing reasons for how it occurs. Therefore, we can adopt each model of disability to support and develop our understanding of SEND and inclusion.

The two dominant models of disability are the medical model and social model. Each of these is covered across the chapters of this book. However, they are introduced below to support your learning.

## Medical model of disability

The medical model of disability takes a scientific approach to understanding difference. It posits that any behavioural variations that differ from the perceived norm can be categorised together based on clusters of symptoms.

Clusters of symptoms that appear to consistently co-occur across individuals are ascribed a label to become a condition or disorder. Diagnosis of this condition or disorder can then be accurately made.

This approach clearly places the cause of disability 'within' the person. This means that causes of disability are organic phenomena, being the result of something different with an individual's biological functioning, whether that is something different with their physical body, cognitive processing or behaviours.

Linked to both premises of a scientific approach and an emphasis on within-person causes, the medical model often takes the approach of seeking treatment and even cures for disability. There is an emphasis on professionalism in the belief that those in accredited professions with accredited qualifications are best placed to diagnose and treat those with a range of disabilities, with the aim of curing them.

Time to Reflect

How does the Code of Practice (DfE and DoH, 2014) process reflect a medical model?

**Note:** The *biopsychosocial model* founded by Engel (1977) views disability as arising from a combination of factors at the physical, emotional and environmental levels and is mainly linked to health concerns including mental health difficulties.

## Social model of disability

The social model of disability can be placed in direct contrast with the medical model (see Table 1.1). Instead of placing the causes of disability within a person it looks for external causes in the environment, including political and social causes. It refers to any element of difference that affects a person's functioning as an **impairment**, rather than difference and difficulty with daily functioning being an automatic indicator of disability.

From this perspective, impairments don't automatically lead to disability but are exacerbated by how an environment is designed. For example, a person may have a physical difference that leads to potential difficulties with moving in an environment depending on how it is designed. Such as, if the environment is so designed that it is difficult for them to access public buildings, e.g. a building having stairs but no lifts, then this external factor will exacerbate their impairment and cause then to be perceived as 'disabled' – in contrast with a normative sample of society for whom most environmental and social structures are designed. The subject of accessibility is further explored in Chapter 6 and our duties in terms of the social model are discussed in Chapter 12.

**Table 1.1**  Medical vs social model

| Medical model | Social model |
| --- | --- |
| Sam has a bilateral sensori-neural hearing loss. | Sam cannot hear the tutor because he keeps moving around, turning away and mumbling into his beard. |
| Max has a rare medical condition which causes them to lose concentration very easily. | Max needs lessons that are short, with a range of activities and opportunities for everyone to re-cap, catch up or practise. |
| Billy has dysgraphia and cannot write fast, especially under any sort of pressure. | Billy needs a laptop in some classes and an amanuensis for exams. |
| Mo has special needs and needs 1:1. | Mo needs some additional support in class. |
| Kim needs professional help. | What can we do (as a class/school/university) to support Kim? |
| We need a physiotherapist to advise us on how Ayo will manage in the nursery toilets. | We will ask Ayo/Ayo's mum about what Ayo needs to access the toilets. |
| Tam needs to be taken out of class because they cannot keep up with the numeracy lessons. | We will provide Tam with support for the numeracy lessons. This may take place in class and outside it. |
| All pupils will learn in a class of 30. Those who need extra help will be taken to a smaller group. | All pupils will work in and outside of their class group, in groups of varying sizes and in various ways at different times. |
| Pip's needs are too great to be met in mainstream school. | Mainstream schools in this area are not yet sufficiently adapted to meet Pip's needs. |
| Jamie's behaviour is upsetting the other children. | The school is not able to manage Jamie's behaviour without the other children becoming upset. |

 Spotlight on Research: The Affirmation Model

Swain and French (2000) argue that a new model of disability is emerging within the literature by disabled people and within disability culture, known as the affirmative model. This is a non-tragic view of disability and impairment which encompasses positive social identities, both individual and collective, for disabled people grounded in the benefits of lifestyle and life experience of being impaired and disabled. This view has arisen in direct opposition to the dominant personal tragedy model of disability and impairment (medical model) and builds on the liberatory imperative of the social model. The affirmation model addresses the limitations of the social model through the realisation of positive identity encompassing impairment as well as disability.

The above model links to our discussions on social justice explored in Chapter 12.

# Dimensions of need

Dimensions of need refer to categories of SEND that can be used to classify the needs of CYP. These have developed and changed over the course of the 20th and 21st century (see Chapter 2 which charts this development). The SEND Code of Practice (DfE and DoH, 2014) currently classifies dimensions of needs as follows.

## Communication and interaction

CYP who have difficulty in communicating with others. They may have difficulty saying what they want to, understanding what is being said to them or do not understand or use social rules of communication. CYP who may have difficulty with one, some or all the different aspects of speech, language or social communication at different times of their lives. CYP with Autism Spectrum Condition (ASC), including Asperger's syndrome and autism, are likely to have difficulties with social interaction. CYP who may have difficulties with language, communication and imagination, which can impact on how they relate to others.

## Cognition and learning

CYP who may be learning at a slower pace than their peers, even with appropriate differentiation. This category includes moderate learning difficulties (MLD) and severe learning difficulties (SLD) – CYP who are likely to need support in all areas of the curriculum and associated difficulties with mobility and communication. Also, CYP with profound and multiple learning difficulties (PMLD), who are likely to have severe and complex learning difficulties as well as a physical disability or sensory impairment. Specific learning difficulties (SpLD) may affect one or more specific aspects of learning. This encompasses a range of conditions such as dyslexia, dyscalculia and dyspraxia.

## Social, emotional and mental health difficulties

This may include CYP who are becoming withdrawn or isolated, as well as displaying challenging, disruptive or disturbing behaviour. This may reflect underlying mental health difficulties such as anxiety or depression, self-harming, substance misuse, eating disorders or physical symptoms that are medically unexplained. CYP with social, emotional and mental health (SEMH) difficulties may have disorders such as attention deficit disorder, attention deficit hyperactive disorder or attachment disorder.

## Sensory and/or physical needs

Refers to a disability which prevents or hinders CYP from making use of the educational facilities generally provided. These difficulties can be age-related and may fluctuate over time. This can include a vision impairment (VI), hearing impairment (HI) or a multi-sensory impairment (MSI) which requires specialist support and/or equipment for the CYP to access their learning or rehabilitation support. CYP with an MSI have a combination of vision and hearing difficulties. Also, a physical disability (PD) requiring additional ongoing support and equipment to access all the opportunities available to their peers (DfE and DoH, 2014: 85, 86).

These four dimensions are viewed as creating barriers to learning that need support to be overcome. This is covered in depth in Chapter 4.

 Time to Reflect

Consider the language of 'needs and impairment', referring to Chapter 3 in Thomas and Loxley (2007).

# The wave model of SEND intervention

In response to the dimensions of need as described above, educational settings may put in place 'Waves of intervention' (see below) when considering **provision mapping**. Provision mapping is used for schools and other institutions to 'map out' their provision for planning and auditing purposes. Refer to Wearmouth (2016) for further information and examples.

Wave 1 focuses on Quality inclusive teaching, accounting for the learning needs of all the pupils in the classroom. It includes providing differentiated work and creating an inclusive learning environment. It could be evaluated through regular lesson evaluations and professional dialogue with support staff and peers. It may also be monitored through work scrutiny and learning walks conducted by the school leadership team.

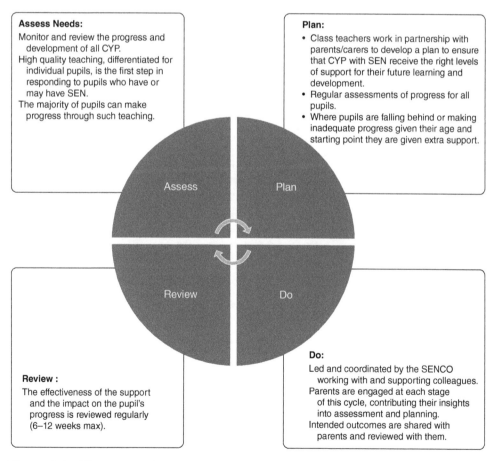

**Assess Needs:**
Monitor and review the progress and
   development of all CYP.
High quality teaching, differentiated for
   individual pupils, is the first step in
   responding to pupils who have or
   may have SEN.
The majority of pupils can make
   progress through such teaching.

**Plan:**
- Class teachers work in partnership with
   parents/carers to develop a plan to ensure
   that CYP with SEN receive the right levels
   of support for their future learning and
   development.
- Regular assessments of progress for all
   pupils.
- Where pupils are falling behind or making
   inadequate progress given their age and
   starting point they are given extra support.

Assess     Plan

Review     Do

**Review :**
The effectiveness of the support
   and the impact on the pupil's
   progress is reviewed regularly
   (6–12 weeks max).

**Do:**
Led and coordinated by the SENCO
   working with and supporting colleagues.
Parents are engaged at each stage
   of this cycle, contributing their insights
   into assessment and planning.
Intended outcomes are shared with
   parents and reviewed with them.

**Figure 1.1** The graduated response

Wave 2 is more specific; additional and time-limited **interventions** provided for some pupils who need help to accelerate their progress to enable them to work at or above age-related expectations. They are often targeted at a group of pupils with similar needs. Group **provision maps** may assist in evaluation, where a red, amber and green (RAG) system is implemented. Children are assessed against expected outcomes and highlighted: red – not achieved; amber – working towards; green – achieved. This monitors the individual progress as well as the success of the intervention. These outcomes could inform pupil progress meetings as part of the **graduated response** (see Figure 1.1).

Wave 3 is targeted provision for a minority of pupils where it is necessary to provide highly tailored interventions to accelerate progress or enable children to achieve their potential. Targets are reviewed on a child's **individual provision map** at the end of each term (e.g. see Table 1.2). Parents and children should be involved with this review and new target setting, as well as forming part of the graduated response.

**Table 1.2**  Extract from an example individual provision map

| | Name: B | Autumn term | |
|---|---|---|---|
| | Date of birth | | |
| Year | Summary of needs/ agency involvement | Plan/do | Assess/review |
| 6 | PD/SLCN OT SALT | To use red/yellow cards to signal feelings of frustration or when time out is needed. | Discussed with B and agency use of cards. Cards have been requested/asked B to use as and when. |
| | | To use alternative methods of recording including a laptop for extended writing and a scribe for planning. | B uses an alternative method of recording which in most instances will be a laptop. This is not only for extended writing but also for planning and general class learning. |
| | | To use s / sh / ch sounds in words. | Not achieved. B's speaking is still unclear at times. |
| Signed (when reviewed) | | Parent: | Pupil: |

## Time to Reflect

What are your experiences/knowledge of inclusive practice so far? Refer to Chapter 9 regarding LAs' duty in terms of information, support and advice – 'the local offer'.

# A note on the language used in this book

Language is important. The language used in this book has been carefully considered to be as inclusive and representative of diversity as possible. This is a critical consideration in our increasingly global and diverse collective society. However, language and the social perspectives rooted in language are always developing. We acknowledge that despite our attempt to make considerate language choices we may not be fully inclusive and representative of all. As such, we hope to model the need for continual consideration of inclusive language use and the challenges this presents.

## Gender pronouns

All case studies have gender neutral names and are referred to using gender neutral pronouns. This was chosen as a small act of advocacy and support for those who self-identify on a broader spectrum of gender identification than traditional binary classifications of male/female. However, it was also chosen as gender bias is present for those with certain experiences of SEND and we wish to attempt to counteract this. For example, with Autism Spectrum Condition (ASC) where there is a bias in educational research which includes more male participants than female; a reflection of the gender bias present in diagnosis of ASC. By using gender neutral names and pronouns we are making the point that any condition, such as a SpLD, or any presentation, such as challenging behaviour, shouldn't be subject to gender bias.

## Referring to disabled people

The UK Government gave clear guidance for the correct collective terms and phrases to use when writing about disabled people (see: www.gov.uk/government/publications/inclusive-communication/inclusive-language-words-to-use-and-avoid-when-writing-about-disability). It is important to emphasise each individual through use of the word 'people' so large groups are not collectively referred to as their condition or disability. As such, in this book we refer to 'disabled people' or a specific condition and then *people*, such as dyslexic people.

Key Points

- We have introduced you to differing definitions, theories and models of educational inclusion.
- We have explored current terms and concepts in relation to the understanding of 'special educational needs/disability'.
- We have started to identify implications for practice.

 Final Reflection Questions

- What would you add or remove from the current Code and why?
- What interests you within the area of SENDI?
- What might you like to research further? (See Chapter 11.)

# Further reading

This article provides a critical overview of the changes to the SEN Code of Practice since 1994:

Lehane, T. (2017). 'SEN's completely different now': Critical discourse analysis of three 'Codes of Practice for Special Educational Needs' (1994, 2001, 2015). *Educational Review, 69*(1), 51–67.

This interesting piece of research explored how parents will use either the medical or social model of disability to challenge the stigma that their children with disabilities may face:

Manago, B., Davis, J.L. and Goar, C. (2017). Discourse in action: Parents' use of medical and social models to resist disability stigma. *Social Science & Medicine, 184*, 169–177.

This research investigated 2813 outcomes from EHC plans and found that most outcomes were low quality. This is a good read if you are looking for research that critiques EHC plans:

Castro, S., Grande, C. and Palikara, O. (2019). Evaluating the quality of outcomes defined for children with Education, Health and Care plans in England: A local picture with global implications. *Research in Developmental Disabilities, 86*, 41–52.

# 2

# THE HISTORY OF DIFFERENCE AND DISABILITY

Dr Alexandra Sewell

---

## Introduction

It is possible to become caught up in contemporary debate about how we conceptualise and understand disability and Special Educational Needs (SEN). A historical perspective of education, disability and SEN is important as it helps us to examine these assumptions. This chapter will:

- Explore the historical development of the concepts of disability and special educational needs.
- Outline the language and cultural practices of significant historical eras that contributed to historically situated understandings of difference and disability.
- Chart the rise of educational opportunities for those with difference and disability in England and the role of policy and legislation in this.

# Historically situated social constructions of difference and disability

When exploring historical contexts, it is important not to assume that previous cultures regarded difference and disability under the same linguistic and theoretical frameworks as we do today. 'Disability' and 'SEN' are modern terms. What we understand these to mean has not been historically constant.

Historians seek to develop an accurate picture of the norms and attitudes of each historical culture. They approach their analysis of historical sources by attempting to put aside modern-day assumptions about difference and disability. Disability is viewed as a **social construct** (Corker and Shakespeare, 2002). This is where perceptions of what disability is are shaped through communal use of language and societal practices. Historians take the view that 'disability' is not an organic phenomenon but one which is constructed and re-constructed throughout human history (Avalos et al., 2007).

The following sections are structured to designate historically situated cultural practices and the language used to define difference and disability for each era. This will allow you to make your own analysis of how language used to define those with difference and disability has evolved, along with educational opportunities.

# Pre-1900s

## Language

Good body, bad body, maimed, mutilated, ugliness, weakness, idleness, avarice, wantonness, vice

## Societal values and attitudes towards difference and disability

### Mesopotamia

The approach of lifting the cultural veil on the history of difference and disability is apparent in historian Walls' (2007) study of the ancient culture of **Mesopotamia**. Mesopotamia was an ancient historical region that existed 6000 years ago in West Asia where Iraq, Kuwait and sections of Syria and Turkey are located today.

Artefacts from Mesopotamia demonstrate the earliest written accounts of those with difference and disability. Evidence of the categorisation of different physical body types is found in the myth of the gods Enki and Nimah, where Nimah states that 'man's body can be either good or bad' (Jacobsen, 1987: 152, as cited in Walls, 2007) and goes on to create 'bad bodies' from clay. These include bodies that have impaired hands and legs, blindness, deafness, mental disability, incontinence, infertile women and eunuchs (Walls, 2007).

Walls (2007) relates societal attitudes towards these 'good' and 'bad' bodies to wider Mesopotamian cultural values. Mesopotamian creation myths hold a central value that humans were given life to labour on the land so that the gods could live a life of pleasure (Dalley, 1998). Purposeful human labour was valued by society. In the myth of Enki and Nimah each 'bad' body is assigned an act of labour. For example, those with impaired legs are assigned to be a silversmith and those who are blind are given a role in the musical arts at court. Walls (2007) concludes that this 'communicates a social ideology of inclusion for people with differing abilities' (p.31). This could be viewed as a **community model of disability** where anyone with physical difference was incorporated into existing social structures by being assigned meaningful labour.

## Ancient Greece

**Ancient Greece** is an ancient civilisation that existed about 2,500 years ago. Historians who have studied Ancient Greece have also sought to understand social attitudes towards difference and disability by analysing texts and artefacts in relation to what is already known about wider cultural values and practices. Examples of painted Ancient Greek pottery display individuals with physical impairment or difference, such as obesity being laughed at as a form of entertainment (Garland, 1995). Kelly (2007) relates this act of public humiliation to Ancient Greece's wider cultural value for beauty and symmetry. Holding physical beauty in high esteem would explain why those who did not possess it would fall into a position of ridicule. Evidence for this is also found in literary texts which refer to physical difference with use of language such as 'maimed', 'mutilated' and 'ugliness' (Kelly, 2007).

Similarly, the Ancient Greeks prized thinking, reason and speech as the highest of all skills (Johnstone, 2012). Rose (2006) relates this general cultural value to the Ancient Greeks' societal attitudes towards deafness, which was conceptualised as being akin to muteness. An impairment in an ability to communicate was perceived as an impairment in reason with deafness viewed as the worst affliction to befall a human (Rose, 2006).

We see here an absence of modern-day categorisations of intellectual disability and learning difficulty. This highlights the importance of assessing historical accounts within their own historical–cultural contexts.

## Ancient Rome

**Ancient Rome** is an ancient civilization that existed over 2000 years ago. In Ancient Rome the lawful practice of killing babies (infanticide) who were born with a physical impairment, present from the 5th century BCE, is often taken as evidence of the historical roots of prejudice and discrimination against those with disability (Carroll, 2018). However, this too can be viewed as an appropriation of modern concepts leading to the misrepresentation of a historical era.

Wallace-Hadrill (1988) describes how hierarchy was tightly imbedded within Roman social practices. A particular element of this hierarchy was the Romans' preference for physical strength and good health, and a dislike of physical 'weakness', as optimal for expansion of the Roman Empire (Clarke and Rose, 2013). The practice of infanticide can be sensitively analysed for meaning when explored in this context of the wider cultural norm of social stratification. It would have been unlikely for such a social practice, deemed discriminatory by today's society, to have been questioned by contemporary Romans.

## Medieval period

The **medieval period** began after the fall of the Roman Empire and lasted 1000 years. Disability and difference in this period have attracted pronounced analysis and scholarship. Eyler (2016) argues that when studying the medieval era even the modern notion of '**impairment**' should be put aside. An impairment can be defined as possessing a physical or mental state that is diminished or damaged. Instead, Eyler (2016) argues that medieval societal attitudes towards general bodily difference should be investigated.

Christianity flourished in the medieval period and this formed the cultural basis for how difference and disability were constructed (Schuelka, 2013). A religious focus on moral superiority meant that those with bodily difference were perceived as morally corrupted (Eyler, 2016). Fictional narratives portray villains as receiving their moral comeuppance when struck by an impairment as a result of their evil actions (Orlemanski, 2016). Hsy's (2016) analysis of medieval literature demonstrates a trend where deafness is taken as an indication of sin and social stigma

(Hsy, 2016). The connection between bodily difference and morality is further exemplified with the connection of those with physical difference to acts of witchcraft (Pearman, 2010).

However, other indicators of identity, such as social class, could act as a buffer to such conceptualisations. O'Tool (2010) investigated the lives of individuals living in Quinze-Vingts hospital for the blind, set up by Louis IX in the 13th century. In the 13th and 14th century those of a lower class who were blind were stereotyped as suffering moral inflictions of 'idleness', 'avarice' and wantonness'. However, the individuals of Quinze-Vingts were members of the Parisian bourgeoise and were engaged in economic work in the textile industry. This indicates that bodily difference itself was not enough to exemplify moral deficiency; this stereotype emerged when combined with poverty (O'Tool, 2010).

## Summary

The historical periods explored here demonstrate how modern linguistic practices of 'disability' and 'disabled' can be viewed as anachronistic when understanding historically situated social constructions of difference and impairment. We must view historical social constructions of difference in relation to wider societal attitudes, cultural values and cultural practices of the time.

# Educational opportunities for those with difference and disability

Prior to the 19th century formal schooling for those with difference and disability was very limited. This was in part due to a wider lack of educational opportunities for the many. Historically, formal education has been the preserve of the elite, those with wealth and high social status (McCulloch, 2011). Only a small minority of schools, in comparison to today, were available for individuals from a less wealthy background (McCulloch, 2011).

Towards the end of the 18th century, urbanisation and a rapidly expanding population led to increased rates of infant disability, infanticide and child abandonment (Honeyman, 2016). Foundling hospitals were developed from 1740 onwards in response to the growing social problems, the purpose of which was to house children with a range of social needs until they could be given apprenticeships (Mathisen, 2015). Despite a lack of formal education, charitable apprenticeships, such as those provided by the London Foundling Hospital, served as a form of welfare for children with an impairment (Levene, 2008; Mathisen, 2015). They were trained in work that would allow them to join a rapidly expanding labour market.

Within this historical context, we can trace the beginnings of the practices of institutionalisation and providing apprenticeships. **Institutions** and **asylums**, gaining prominence in the early 19th century, developed to segregate individuals with a range of difference and disability. As we will examine more closely in the next section, they often 'employed' residents in what were deemed to be suitable work tasks. This was the most prominent form of provision for those with difference and disability running parallel to the wider movement towards compulsory schooling for all.

# 19th century

## Language

Deaf, dumb, cripple, inmate, mentally defective, imbecile, educable/ uneducable, handicapped

## Societal values and attitudes towards difference and disability

Warnock (1978) states that 'the middle of the 19th century had seen a stirring of social conscience over the plight of the disabled' (p.10). **The Industrial Revolution** had increased instances of physical impairment as a result of industrial work accidents. Urbanisation had exacerbated societal problems such as destitution, crime and begging. Church organisations, such as the Methodists and Evangelists, organised charitable support and relief for both types of societal ills (McCulloch, 2011). The attitudes of help and charity were closely aligned with religious conviction. For example, puritanism compelled Methodists to engage in charitable work and Evangelists' belief in the requirement to save the individual propelled them towards such acts.

Wider societal attitudes to disability can be related to ideas of strict social stratification. The Victorian society held views about an individual's place within a pre-proposed social hierarchy. Much opposition was made to the development of education for all, with many in the higher classes holding the view that it would lead the lower classes to wish to change their status and revolt (Lawson and Silver, 2013). This attitude also meant that those with a disability or difference were expected not to question their social place. There was a notion that each man should be educated according to his place and his labour tasks. It was this societal attitude that underpinned practices such as separating those with difference and disability from the society of others, for example through segregation in institutions.

## Educational opportunities for those with difference and disability

During the 19th century the Industrial Revolution altered the fabric of society. A new industrial class of wealth owners developed, known as the industrialists, as well as an underclass of factory workers (Morrish, 2013). As the United Kingdom's (UK) industrial economy bloomed so grew the need for a skilled workforce. The movement towards education for all began in 1867 when the Birmingham Education League was founded, paving the way for the National Education League in 1869. The league was made up of powerful industrialists who campaigned for elementary education for all, free from the voluntary education system still controlled by the churches (Aldrich, 1982; Lawson and Silver, 2013). Their main argument was that compulsory education would ensure a skilled workforce which would help the UK keep a competitive edge in the world market.

As a result of campaigning the *1870 Forster Education Act* became the first UK legislation to directly indicate how Children and Young People (CYP) should be educated (Aldrich, 1982). Voluntary church schools could continue but a system of non-denominational school boards was established which would create and oversee new schools in places that required them. Whether school boards should or should not educate those with disability and difference was not specified or considered in the legislation.

However, further progression towards compulsory schooling soon encountered the need to educate those with a disability or difference. The subsequent *1880 Education Act* made school attendance compulsory for children between the ages of five and ten, this age being lifted to 12 in 1899. In tandem with these changes, the *Elementary Education Act of 1893* made schooling compulsory for blind and deaf children. This was followed by the *Elementary Education of Defective and Epileptic Children's Act in 1899* which made education compulsory for children with a physical impairment (Aldrich, 1982; Morrish, 2013).

Before the effects of compulsory education took hold in the 20th century, institutions provided one of the few forms of educational provision available for those with difference and disability. Some of the first institutions were developed in the late 18th century and the beginning of the 19th century for individuals classified as blind and dumb. Mr Braidwood's Academy for the blind was set up in 1760 for paying pupils and by 1870 six further institutions had been established (Collins, 1995). These were followed by the first institutions developed specifically to house individuals with a physical impairment, The Cripples' Home and Industrial School for Girls in 1851 and another for boys in 1865 (Morrish, 2013).

Only a rudimentary education was offered. The 'educable' received basic lessons, but class sizes were large and teachers untrained (Collins, 1995). Residents were engaged in manual work and most received a form of education that gave them a trade or skill, such as basket weaving. Their wares were often sold as those from poor backgrounds were required to earn their keep. Nejedly (2017) reports evidence that children as young as five were separated into different workshops so they could contribute to their own economic welfare.

Pritchard (1963) made a social history of this practice and found that residents were incarcerated for long periods. They only left on certain occasions, such as to attend Church. He gives an example of a school for the blind where pupils were only allowed to send one letter a month to a friend or relative. This type of educational practice of separate physical spaces for those with difference and disability is known as **segregation**. It became the dominant model of specialised education in the 19th century. As we will explore in the next section, this model of educational practice gave way to **integration** and **inclusion** in the 20th century.

## Spotlight on Theory: Intellectual Ability and Intelligence Testing

In the late 19th century Sir Francis Galton formed the concept of intellectual ability where ability in cognitive and sensory skills, such as perception and memory, was seen to indicate the degree of a person's intellectual capacity. This is known as individual differences. Inspired by Charles Darwin's theory of evolution, he reasoned that the strength of intellectual ability differs between individuals and that it is inherited from parents. Galton and his theory of intelligence were at the forefront of the eugenics movement. The movement postulated that if intelligence was hereditary then humans' mental ability could be improved through selective breeding. The eugenics movement has been heavily critiqued for being elitist and based on existing racial prejudices (G.E. Allen, 2011).

Alfred Binet developed the first modern tests of intellectual ability in the late 19th century when the French Government commissioned him to develop an assessment that would help distinguish which pupils would benefit from regular education and those who would require a special arrangement. Binet calculated a subject's mental age by standardising his tests of increasing difficulty to see what individuals of each age could achieve. An individual's score would indicate their mental age. In the early 20th century Lewis Terman standardised Binet's tests on an American sample. Alongside this work he developed the concept of Intelligence Quotient (IQ). An IQ score was arrived at by dividing mental age by chronological age and multiplying by 100. Terman was also an advocate of the eugenics movement.

# 20th century

## Language

Integration, inclusion, equality of access, human rights, disability rights, special educational needs, provision, universal education

## Societal values and attitudes towards difference and disability

Societal attitudes towards difference and disability in the 20th century present a story of two halves. The first is typified by a scientific approach to understanding and classifying disability and difference, which gave rise to the **medical model of disability**. The second is exemplified by a movement towards understanding those with difference and disability as individuals, bringing individual nuance to the fore and challenging oppression, which gave rise to the **social model of disability**. An example of these attitudes in action is the **Disability Civil Rights Movement**.

The medical model of disability was previously outlined in Chapter 1. Here we will explore the attitudinal and societal shifts that gave rise to its development. The late 19th century gave birth to **modernism**, which flourished in the early 20th century as a way of viewing, thinking about and understanding the world and its phenomena (Childs, 2016). Modernism posits that the application of reason and the scientific method are important for human betterment (Childs, 2016). Humans should use their reason, along with repeated observation and objective measurement, to develop true knowledge about the world. This philosophical approach was initially applied to the physical world and influenced the Industrial Revolution through an increase in and application of scientific understanding; for example, an increased scientific understanding of electricity and the invention of the lightbulb by Edison in 1879.

As scientific interest turned from the physical world and machines to the social world and humans, modernism was applied again. This influenced the medical model of disability, as causes for physical impairment were assumed to be biological, and 'within person' (Fisher and Goodley, 2007). The scientific approach of observation and measurement was applied to generate categories of disability which would then be used to further understanding through diagnosis. Also applied was the notion of 'progression', that through increased scientific understanding humanity could be positively transformed. In the case of impairment, curing or improving an individual's difficulty was a central attitude (Childs, 2016; Fisher and Goodley, 2007).

The latter part of the 20th century saw the emergence of a second narrative for those with difference and disability, which challenged the dominance of the medical model perspective and its roots in modernism. The practice of segregation was questioned and biological, within-person reasons for disability were rejected. Alternative focus was placed on the environment, highlighting how society was designed for the 'typical majority' which was viewed as causing and exacerbating disability in those with impairments. These shifts in attitudes came to be formulated as the social model of disability (see Chapter 1).

This new attitude towards disability originated from the disabled community themselves, hand in hand with the Disability Civil Rights Movement (Scotch, 1989). The Disability Civil Rights Movement developed in the 1960s in the wake of the African-American Civil Rights Movement (Fleischer, 2001). Within the movement, individuals with difference or disability challenged and protested against oppressive societal structures. This generated momentum for public environments to be re-designed to be inclusive for a wider range of individuals. For example, as a form of protest wheelchair users would smash up pavements to highlight how they were designed with only individuals who walk in mind (Fleischer, 2001).

The movement transferred to the UK and led to several decades of activism (Shakespeare, 2006). New disability rights organisations developed such as The Union of the Physically Impaired against Segregation, and the Liberation Network of People with Disabilities. These groups engaged in multiple forms of activism, such as developing magazines. The quote below is taken from 'In From the Cold: The Liberation Magazine for People with Disabilities', published in June 1981. It exemplifies the fight to change societal attitudes so that people with difference and disability are viewed not as separate entities but as individuals with equal rights to participation:

> 'In From the Cold': we chose this title after much soul searching because it best conveys the feelings many of us had... The feeling most of us seemed to share was relief at no longer being isolated, we had been 'out there', each fighting the whole world on our own, and were suddenly 'inside' a group of people with similar ideas. The 'battle' became an exciting and enjoyable challenge. (p.2)

## Educational opportunities for those with difference and disability

With significant shifts in societal attitudes towards difference and disability, dramatic changes in educational opportunities followed suit. This can be broadly characterised as a movement from segregation towards integration, followed by the rise of inclusive educational practice.

In 1944 the *Butler Education Act* made the first step towards establishing equal rights to education for those with disability and difference in the 20th century. For the first time Local Education Authorities (LEAs) had a statutory duty to provide education for primary, secondary and at further levels for CYP (Morrish, 2013). This was extended to 'handicapped' children in Section 33 and 34 of the Act, where LEAs had a statutory duty to assess which children would require a different type of education due to difference or disability. To support assessment ten categories of 'handicapped' children were created in the 1959 *Handicapped Pupils and Special Schools Regulations Act*.

---

### Reflection Activity

1959 – Handicapped Pupils and Special Schools Regulations Act

10 categories of 'handicapped' children:

1. Blind.
2. Partially sighted.
3. Deaf.

*(Continued)*

4. Partially deaf.
5. Educationally sub-normal.
6. Epileptic.
7. Maladjusted.
8. Physically handicapped.
9. Speech defect.
10. Delicate.

The year is 1945 and you are a professional working for an LEA. You have recently been employed to meet the statutory requirement to assess CYP who may be 'handicapped' and require a different type of education. How would you go about this task? What information would you need? Do you think these 11 categories would help or hinder your assessment?

Although a step in an inclusive direction, it wasn't until the *1972 Education Act* that legislation was passed giving all children an equal entitlement to education despite difference or disability. This is encapsulated by the abolishment of the phrase 'uneducable child', replaced with the ethos of 'universal education' (Lawson and Silver, 2013). This was soon followed by the establishment of the *Committee of Inquiry into Education of Handicapped Children and Young People* in 1974. The inquiry had the significant task of investigating and advising how those with difference and disability could be supported to equally access education.

The inquiry took four years to complete this investigation and resulted in the *Warnock Report (1978)*. This was a ground-breaking document which laid out 225 recommendations for the government. Arguably, the most influential change was the introduction of the term *Special Educational Needs (SEN)* and how this reconceptualised our understanding of educating those with difference and disability. The new term acknowledged the role of environmental factors in improving or exacerbating disability and learning difficulty. In turn, it rejected the word 'handicapped' and a deficit approach. Instead, SEN was positioned as occurring when, in order to successfully learn, an individual requires educational provision that is different from and/or additional to what is typically available. An individual possessing an impairment or disability therefore would not automatically mean they would have SEN. They would be assessed by their response to typical educational practice available and the potential requirement for additional or different provision in order to succeed.

The report also suggested that the 10 existing categories of SEN were too specific and suggested four broader categories:

1. Speech and language disorders.
2. Learning difficulties.
3. Social and behavioural difficulties.
4. Visual and hearing difficulties.

A new system of assessment of SEN was initiated known as the **statementing process**. This process was to be run by LEAs. A **statement** was to be a legal document that recognised a child's SEN, as assessed by a qualified professional. It would also state what additional and special educational provision a child would be legally entitled to as a form of safeguarding their learning and educational progress.

The *1981 Education Act* implemented many of the suggestions including the four new categories and the retirement of the term 'handicapped' for SEN, and issued a new system of statements for SEN. This cemented Warnock's ideas and radically altered educational practices for individuals with disability and difficulty.

---

 Spotlight on Theory: Human Rights and Disability Rights

From the middle of the 20th century onwards the concept of human rights has strongly taken root in western cultures with a perceived global 'breakthrough' in the 1960s and 1970s (Hoffmann, 2016; Jensen, 2016). Human rights are defined as rights that are applicable to all human beings regardless of any personal status such as gender, race, disability or religion (United Nations, 2019). All people are entitled to rights such as the right to education, work and freedom of speech without discrimination (United Nations, 2019). Human rights therefore provide a legal protection for those with disabilities to ensure they access their rights without hindrance. The following is a timeline of key dates for the development of human rights.

1948 – The Universal Declaration of Human Rights

This document (United Nations, 1948) set a common standard for human rights for the first time which were to be universally supported around the world. Many of the rights set out were of significant relevance to disabled individuals, including the right not to be treated in an inhumane way, respect for a private life, the right to life and not to be discriminated against (British Institute of Human Rights, 2006).

*(Continued)*

1989 – UN Convention on the Rights of the Child

The principle of human rights was extended to children (United Nations, 1989). Of importance are the ideas that children have the right to life and survival, non-discrimination and that the child's best interests must be top priority for decisions made about them.

1994 – The UNESCO Salamanca Statement

Representatives from 92 global governments called for inclusion to be the norm for children with disabilities. There was a clear focus that a child should have the right to attend the 'neighbourhood' school regardless of their needs (United Nations, 1994).

2006 – Convention on the Rights of Persons with Disabilities

This is an international human rights treaty which seeks to ensure that people with disabilities gain full access to their human rights. There are eight guiding principles of autonomy and personal choice in decisions, non-discrimination, inclusion in society, that difference is accepted, equal opportunities, accessibility, gender equality and that children with disabilities are given respect for the development of their identities (United Nations, 2006).

# 21st century

## Language

Excellence for all, quality-first teaching, partnership working, discrimination, equality, pupil participation, partnership working

## Societal values and attitudes towards difference and disability

Societal values and attitudes towards disability and difference in the first twenty years of the 21st century have not stagnated; continual debate, new conceptions and understandings have taken root. After the 20th century's period of relative increase in disability rights, discrimination and segregation are still proposed to exist, if more subtly. Murphy (2005) argues that individuals with a disability are still barred from equal access to work opportunities. Whilst not apparent in an overt way, individuals with a disability are only allowed to take up certain roles if the job requirements match what is positioned as their 'unique potential'. This sets limits on the types of job opportunities that they have access to.

Stapleton et al. (2006) echo this idea, exploring subtle discrimination in disability support services and legislative policy. They state that recent policy has been paternalistic, meaning that it makes those with disability and difference dependent on state support and intervention. In doing so, it has created a 'poverty trap' for those with disability and difference. These societal attitudes demonstrate a potential emergence of a **charity model of disability**. This is where those with disability and difference are viewed as objects of pity as they are victims of unlucky circumstance (Retief and Letsosa, 2018). This leads to the view that it is the role of the able-bodied to provide supportive policies and legislation, services and job opportunities. However, despite the view that such intentions are admirable, Retief and Letsosa (2018) argue that this creates a harmful stereotype that those with disability and difference are 'helpless, depressed and dependent' (p.6).

## Educational opportunities for those with difference and disability

The 21st century has seen both consolidation and progression of policy and legislation supporting equality for those with difference and disability in the form of the *Disability Discrimination Act (2005)* and the *Equality Act (2010)*. These, along with other pertinent legislation, will be further explored in Chapter 6.

*The Children and Families Act (2014)* and the *Special Educational Needs and Disability Code of Practice* (DfE and DoH, 2014) instigated significant changes to how educational institutions support individuals with SEN and disability, after a period of review held by the coalition government during the early to mid-2010s. Statements of SEN were replaced with education, health and care (EHC) plans. Like statements, EHC plans were proposed to provide statutory protection for those with additional learning needs who would require educational provision that is additional to or different from that which is typically offered. The age at which a child/young person could have an EHC plans was extended to 25 to provide support for their transition into adulthood.

EHC plans were to have increased focus on partnership working, including multi-agency working and improved partnership working with parents and CYP (this is further explored in Chapter 9). To aid this process it was proposed that parents would be given a 'personal budget', where direct payments could be made to them to help secure prior agreed provision. In addition, it was now advised that the voice of the child and opinions of parents were to be prioritised as a part of an EHC plan assessment. Termed 'co-production', parents, CYP were to be equally involved with the creation of meaningful and functional outcomes, which were to be recorded in the final EHC plan.

As well as supporting the transition to EHC plans, LEAs were given a new statutory obligation to publish a 'local offer'. This was to be a document, often available online, detailing what services and support they provided for CYP with SEN and disability. As part of this, and to encourage 'joined up working', both health services and LEAs were expected to commission services jointly.

Within school settings, the previous wave approach to supporting SEN (see Chapter 1) was adapted, with the categories of 'school action' and 'school action plus' removed. Instead, one single category of 'SEN support' was developed. The rationale given for this change was an increasing over-identification of SEND as a result of the wave model (Curran, 2015). Focus was placed on quality-first teaching as a way of including all learners and so reducing the need for individuals to require additional provision, hence requiring the label of SEN (Curran, 2015).

The implementation of changes proposed in The Children and Families Act (2014) has been critiqued as having mixed success. Lamb (2018) observes that the involvement of parents in co-production of EHC plans has been limited in practice due to the context of reduced budgets for health services and LEAs. This analysis is further supported by research exploring parents' views reporting high levels of stress associated with perceived difficulty in having their children's SEN recognised and gaining appropriate educational support (Holland et al., 2018).

From a school perspective, the changes initially caused confusion. For example, the removal of the categories of school action and school action plus meant that Special Educational Needs Coordinators (SENCos) found that what constituted SEND was not clearly defined (Browning, 2018). Quality-first teaching, along with children who were originally placed on the school action register not being moved to the new SEN register, seemed to have pushed a culture change in schools where teachers take more responsibility for SEN learning at the classroom level (Browning, 2018).

Lastly, Castro et al. (2019) reviewed 236 EHC plans comprising 2813 outcomes to assess quality. Quality outcomes were defined as targets which were SMART (Specific, Measurable, Attainable, Relevant and Time-framed) and functional. This means they relate to the life skills pupils should learn. They were also concerned with whether outcomes had become more participant-focused by including the parent and child/young person. They reported that after rating all outcomes the data showed that quality of outcomes was generally low, with limited participant focus.

Such research demonstrates the difficulties associated with the implementation of the Children and Families Act (2014). The proposed changes can be critiqued for not being successfully implemented. It may be argued that further support, in the form of resource and financial input, is required from the government to secure their desired changes for the assessment and education of individuals with SEN.

### Time to Reflect

Marketisation is the application of market forces to the education system in an attempt to improve school services and outcomes. This is achieved by creating competition between schools, for example by creating league tables which compare exam results and reducing governmental control.

How do you think marketisation of the education system has potentially affected those with SEND?

### Key Points

- Difference and disability have been socially constructed and reconstructed throughout different historical periods.
- In the 20th and 21st century there has been a general move towards adoption and implementation of the concepts of inclusion and human rights.
- Difficulties in inclusive and equal educational practice for those with SEND still exist in the 21st century.

Final Reflection Questions

Changes in language show us how difference and disability has been continually re-constructed through time. Look at the language used in each era and consider the following questions:

- How has language been used to designate and describe those with difference and disability changed throughout history?
- How does language reflect societal attitudes towards difference and disability?

# Further reading

This book challenges existing ways of understanding the history of difference and disability:

Burch, S. and Rembis, M. (2014). *Disability Histories*. Baltimore, MD: University of Illinois Press.

This journal article provides commentary on how the field of disability studies has developed to consider history from different perspectives:

Kudlick, C.J. (2003). Disability history: Why we need another 'other'. *The American Historical Review*, *108*(3), 763–793.

Mary Warnock wrote a great chapter in her seminal review that covers the history of SEND in the UK:

Warnock, M. (1978). *Special Education Needs: Report of the Committee of Enquiry into the Education of Handicapped Children and Young People*. London: HM Stationery Office.

# 3

# INTRODUCING SPECIFIC LEARNING DIFFICULTIES

## Dr Alexandra Sewell

### Introduction

In this chapter each Specific Learning Difficulty (SpLD) will be explored in turn. The strengths and difficulties of each will be presented in the form of a case study as it allows the reader to link theory to practice. This chapter will:

- Introduce the concept of SpLD.
- Explore how definitions of SpLDs are arrived at.
- Outline key strengths and difficulties associated with each condition through case studies.

# Defining specific learning difficulties

Cognitive skills are core information processing skills that occur as a result of brain function and enable us to learn. Everyone has areas of cognitive strength and relative cognitive weakness. The cognitive abilities of most are described as 'average'. This means that in terms of their effectiveness for engaging in a learning activity they *perform* at a similar rate of success compared to most of the population of the same age. The term **neurotypical** has been coined to refer to the most common ways that the brain learns (Kapp et al., 2013).

In contrast, **neurodiversity** is a term that identifies those who learn in a different way to the perceived norm; their range of cognitive skills differ from the 'typical' way that cognitive skills enable a person to learn (Kapp et al., 2013; Moll et al., 2016). For example, when given a learning task they may perform at a different rate of success compared to most of the population at the same age, either taking more time or being able to complete it more quickly.

Neurological researchers have identified patterns of difference in cognitive skills for learning across the population (Moll et al., 2016). Identified patterns of difference in cognitive skills have been grouped and defined as a collection of SpLDs. SpLDs have been defined as 'problems with classroom learning which cannot be attributed to the pupil's intellect or motivation' (Stuart-Hamilton, 2007). This broad definition can be developed to include the notion of neurodiversity; SpLDs are a collection of identified diversities in cognitive skills for learning found in clustered sub-groups of the population; those who fall within these sub-groups learn differently to the perceived neurotypical norm.

It is arguable that a more culturally attuned terminology for this phenomenon would be specific learning differences or specific learning diversities. Such language would potentially reduce the stigma associated with the idea of having personal 'difficulty' with learning. However, as SpLD is the widely recognised term it shall be used in this chapter. SpLD is an umbrella term which refers to a range of different learning difficulties. These are termed dyslexia, dyscalculia, dyspraxia, dysgraphia, Attention Deficit Hyperactivity Disorder (ADHD) and Autism Spectrum Condition (ASC).

# Defining dyslexia

The term dyslexia is arrived at from the Greek 'dys', meaning difficulty, and 'lexia', meaning with words. It is an SpLD that affects how an individual learns to read, write and comprehend written (and sometimes verbal) language. Dyslexia has a high profile as a condition, meaning that is generally well-known by educationalists and has a substantial body of research exploring it. As such, there are numerous definitions.

In the UK, the Rose Report (2009) provides one of the more widely accepted definitions, especially by professionals involved in assessment. The report outlines six elements for how dyslexia should be defined. An overarching characterisation is that individuals with dyslexia have difficulty recognising and reading words at the whole word level, meaning that they find reading individual words challenging (Rose, 2009). Diversity in cognitive learning skills means that individuals must also show difficulties with phonological awareness (recognising sounds), verbal memory and verbal processing speed (Rose, 2009). Dyslexia is conceptualised by Rose (2009) as existing on a continuum, with some experiencing more severe forms of it.

A crucial element put forward by the Rose Report (2009) was that assessment of the severity and persistence of the condition must be based on analysis of how well an individual has responded to intervention. If an appropriate learning intervention for literacy has been put in place but limited progress has been made then this is a key indicator for the presence of dyslexia. This differs from the historical discrepancy model of dyslexia where it was thought that an individual must have high overall general intelligence, contrasted with a marked difficulty with literacy skills (Aaron, 1997). Rose (2009) clearly stated that 'Dyslexia occurs across a range of intellectual abilities' (p.9).

The British Dyslexia Association offers a definition for dyslexia which confirms the majority of Rose's (2009) conceptualisation of the condition. It differs in one aspect where it further acknowledges difficulty with visual and auditory processing (British Dyslexia Association, 2019). Another important source for a definition is the *Diagnostic and Statistical Manual of Mental Disorders* (DSM-5; American Psychiatric Association, 2013) which labels dyslexia as a 'specific learning disability'. Like Rose's (2009) definition it also takes a deficit model approach where significant difficulty with literacy needs to have been present over time, despite whether the individual has high or low general intellectual ability.

---

 ## Case Study: Dyslexia

Andy is eight years old and attends a mainstream primary school. Andy found learning to read challenging from a young age. Their class teacher

*(Continued)*

noticed that when listening to stories their comprehension was good, but they struggled to read individual words. Andy was referred for a learning assessment and was given a diagnosis of dyslexia.

Andy's difficulties at the whole word level occur because reading a single word successfully involves being able to visually recognise the form of the word and attach the correct language sounds to its visual representation (Shaywitz et al., 2004). Different areas of the brain are implicated in these two processes.

When recognising a word we use our brain's **visual processing skills**, the cognitive ability to accurately process visual information, and areas such as the left posterior inferior temporal area are activated (D'Mello and Gabrieli, 2018; Neudorf et al., 2019; Shaywitz et al., 2004). When attaching the correct phonological sounds to the visual representation of the word we use our brain's **phonological processing skills**, the cognitive ability to accurately process basic units of language (Shaywitz et al., 2004; Yates and Slattery, 2019). Areas associated with phonological processing, such as Broca's area, are activated (D'Mello and Gabrieli, 2018).

Bravo (2014) summarised the research literature and concluded it provided clear evidence that when individuals with dyslexia attempt to read a word there is less activation in these areas of the brain associated with visual and phonological processing. This explains why one of the significant features of Andy's learning needs is difficulty reading at the whole-word level.

Andy also has difficulty with reading fluency. Fluency has been described as being able to perform a skill with accuracy and speed (Wolf and Katzir-Cohen, 2001). Andy may read a text with some accuracy but will also make errors. Andy does this at a slow speed characteristic of dyslexia. Brain imaging research has shown that there is a region of the brain that enables us to recognise the whole form of words and quickly attach phonological sounds and word meaning – the left occipito-temporal region (Dehaene and Cohen, 2007). This is also sub-activated in individuals with dyslexia, most likely explaining difficulty with reading fluency.

Andy's parents have noticed that they are creative and produce novel ideas for creative tasks. Research evidence shows that individuals with dyslexia are good at 'connecting tasks' where they have to come up with unusual ideas and make connections between divergent ideas (Bigozzi et al., 2016; Cancer et al., 2016; Tafti et al., 2009)

# Defining dyscalculia

Dsycalculia is an SpLD that influences an individual's ability to comprehend and manipulate numerical information. Its etymology is also from the Greek word 'dys' meaning difficulty and 'calculia' meaning with numbers. Dyscalculia has a smaller profile than dyslexia meaning that it is not as well-known to educationalists and fewer research studies have been conducted to understand it.

The DSM-5 (American Psychiatric Association, 2013) previously termed the condition 'mathematics disorder' but it is currently classified as a specific learning disability in mathematics. To reach a diagnosis an individual must show problem with numbers, a sustained inability to acquire mathematic skills and severe difficulty in learning mathematical concepts and computations.

Within the research literature a couple of further definitions have been put forth. Historically, Kosc (1974) identified that mathematical abilities had to show a delay relative to expected age-appropriate number skills. In addition, it was clarified that there should not also be a simultaneous delay in general intellectual ability present. Kucian and von Aster (2015) summarised the literature and stated that difficulty with number processing was resultant of difficulties with several precursor cognitive and number skills. Deficits in precursor skills to number processing include **innate number sense**, an ability to differentiate between smaller quantities and larger quantities, and **subitising,** the ability to accurately estimate quantity without counting. Deficits in **number skills**, the basic skills that enable us to process numbers accurately, include **counting difficulties** (forwards and backwards), **mapping of number representations** (assigning correct symbols to each quantity) and the **place–value system** (not understanding that there is a system where each number/quantity has its place).

Each child with dyscalculia has a profile of individual strengths and difficulties with regard to number skills and pre-cursor skills (Bartelet et al., 2014). As such, dyscalculia should be defined as a heterogenous condition where the profile of individual differences around number processing will differ between children (Kucian and von Aster, 2015).

---

  Case Study: Dyscalculia

Amil is 12 years old and has always found mental arithmetic challenging, although sometimes Amil enjoys conceptual maths, such as symmetry.

*(Continued)*

Despite consistent intervention Amil still has difficulty with basic number skills. For example, when presented with a sum like 3+5, they take more time than others to recognise and name each number. This is because Amil has different cognitive skills to other children of a similar age. Research has found that the primary cognitive difference for those with dyscalculia is slow processing speed for naming numbers (Van Luit and Toll, 2018).

Amil also has difficulty immediately retaining and using information. This means they have poor working memory skills, also present for individuals with dyscalculia (Van Luit and Toll, 2018). In a classroom situation this means that too much information given at once can hinder engagement with a learning task. In addition, research has shown that the cognitive profile of dyscalculia includes non-verbal reasoning skills, specifically planning skills. Difficulties in the cognitive skill of attention were found to occur the least in those with dyscalculia. Research has consistently found this range of differences in cognitive skills (Gliksman and Henik, 2019; Paul et al., 2019; Rotzer et al., 2009).

However, a dominant theory is that these cognitive differences belie a core, domain-specific difficulty with number processing that impacts all other cognitive abilities associated with dyscalculia (Laurillard and Butterworth, 2016). This has been termed **number sense** and refers to an individual's basic ability to process numbers. Because of their poor number sense Amil finds basic number discrimination tasks challenging, such as quickly estimating how many dots are on a screen or quickly discriminating the larger group of quantities out of two options (Reeve et al., 2018; Von Aster and Shalev, 2007; Wilson and Dehaene, 2007).

Amil's difficulties with number sense have been present from birth. Amil's parents noticed that when they used to play counting guessing games Amil found this hard and showed frustration through crying. Evidence that these difficulties are present from birth provides impetus for the notion that number sense is a core difficulty of dyscalculia (Laurillard and Butterworth, 2016). As such, cognitive difficulty with number sense, as opposed to more general cognitive difficulties with processing speed, working memory etc., distinguishes dyscalculia as an SpLD from general **calculation dysfluency** – difficulty with completing mathematical calculations (Laurillard and Butterworth, 2016).

When Amil entered secondary school, they used their free time to develop artistic skills. As with dyslexia, there is anecdotal evidence that those with dyscalculia thrive with creative, hands-on subjects. However, there is currently no research evidence to support this and further research is required to explore it and other strengths of dyscalculia.

# Defining dyspraxia

As with the etymology of the other conditions, the 'dys' comes from the Greek for difficulty; 'praxia' means with movement. The World Health Organization (2014) refers to the condition more generally as specific developmental disorder of motor coordination, but also acknowledges the terminology dyspraxia as well as clumsy child syndrome and developmental coordination disorder. The condition is said to occur when a child experiences consistent impairment in their motor skill coordination (World Health Organization, 2014). That is, the successful movement and organisation of body parts to achieve a planned physical action is delayed in comparison to what would be typically expected of a child their age. This must be to such a marked extent that it negatively intervenes with their ability to engage in daily activities. Impairments in motor movement must not be the result of a medical condition.

The National Health Service (2019) provides a definition that supports the notion that physical co-ordination must be affected to a degree that it significantly impacts daily living. They add that this can lead a child to 'appear to move clumsily'. In the UK, the Dyspraxia Foundation (2019) confirm the main elements of each of these definitions but also highlight that dyspraxia occurs across the range of intellectual functioning. The organisation also makes the distinction of difficulties arising in both **fine motor skills** (motor planning that uses smaller movements) and **gross motor skills** (motor planning that uses larger movements).

---

 Case Study: Dyspraxia

Aang is 16 years old and studying for their A-levels. Since starting at sixth form college Aang has experienced some challenges. They have been getting lost in the corridors between lessons, even though they follow the same route each time. They have also found it difficult to plan how to effectively use their free periods. Aang is experiencing difficulty

*(Continued)*

with thinking and planning, which is a common difficulty for individuals with dyspraxia (Gibbs et al., 2007).

Since starting college Aang has found making new friends difficult. They accidently bump into those around them and can sit too close to others. Research shows that individuals with dyspraxia have difficulties with social skills. Poor spatial awareness can mean that it can be difficult to negotiate the physical expectations of social interaction (Saban and Kirby, 2019). De Oliveira and Wann (2010) found evidence that difficulties with spatial awareness are related to difficulties with integrating new visual information. To move successfully through an environment, new visual information needs to be successfully assimilated with existing visual information to understand the changing physical space. This is where the difficulties lie, leading to reduced spatial awareness (de Oliveria and Wann, 2010). This makes it challenging for Aang to anticipate how to move successfully through a space without bumping into others.

In their lessons Aang struggles with writing and uses a laptop. This arises from difficulties with fine motor skills that are characteristic of dyspraxia. Aang also experiences working memory difficulties (Jeffries, 2007). Aang has taught themself how to use Word during a lesson to take notes. This helps with their short-term memory processing.

Despite these persistent difficulties, Aang has done well at school and they are predicted good grades for their A-levels. They have strong Maths and English skills thanks to early intervention that took a multi-sensory approach to teaching basic skills. Research has shown this to be a more inclusive approach for those with dyspraxia (Abdulkarim et al., 2017; Newman, 2019; Pedro and Goldschmidt, 2019). Support from their family has also helped Aang to develop their personal strengths (Payne, 2015).

# Defining dysgraphia

Dysgraphia has the smallest profile; educationalists are the least aware of it and it has one of the smallest accompanying research literatures. Its etymology again links to the Greek 'dys' meaning difficulty and 'graphia' meaning 'marking letter by hand'. The ICD-10 (WHO, 2014) classifies it as a disorder of written expression and the DSM-5 (American Psychiatric Association, 2013) as a specific learning disorder with an impairment in written expression. Both focus on the principle that motor co-ordination delay must be specific to the skill of writing.

However, a common misunderstanding of the condition is that it simply manifests as illegible handwriting. Feifer (2001) outlined four variants of dysgraphia:

1. *Phonological*: Difficulty with writing and spelling words.
2. *Surface*: Over-reliance on visual representation of words and spellings.
3. *Phonological/surface mixed*: Confusion over many different types of spelling rules.
4. *Semantic/syntactic*: Difficulty joining the right words together to form a coherent sentence.

---

 Case Study: Dysgraphia

Lesley is five years old and is learning to write for the first time. The reception class teacher has noticed that they are finding refining their handwriting skills to be difficult and that they take longer to learn the correct spelling for basic words. Since nursery school, Lesley's parents have noticed they have difficulty with mark-making and forming the correct shapes when creating letters on a page.

The class teacher thinks that Lesley may have dysgraphia. They view Lesley as having neurodivergent cognitive skills. There is some evidence to support their assumptions. Van Hoorn et al. (2013) reviewed the literature of neuro-imaging studies and concluded that dysgraphia is associated with differences in functioning in multiple and wide-ranging areas of the brain. They also found that minor neurological dysfunction was correlated with the severity of dysgraphia.

---

The class teacher originally thought that Lesley may have dyslexia. Research into cognitive skills and differences associated with dysgraphia has found significant overlap with dyslexia. Döhla et al. (2018) put forward the need for finer graded assessment of the differences between the two conditions. They concluded that distinct difficulties with two cognitive processes distinguish dysgraphia from dyslexia: **auditory processing skills**, being able to process auditory information, and **visual magnocellular functions**, the pathways in the brain associated with processing visual information. In addition, Rapp et al. (2016) found that individuals with dysgraphia present with **orthographic working**

**memory difficulties**, which are difficulties with working memory for three-dimensional visual information.

Lesley's teacher encourages the development of personal learning strategies. This is mainly based on personal testimony from online blogs, such as Richards (2019) and Winter (2019) who both claim that those with dysgraphia can develop learning strengths, such as having a 'strategies list' for how to write an assignment. There is a need for further research exploring the strengths of dysgraphia.

# Defining attention deficit hyperactivity disorder

The most widely recognised definition of Attention Deficit Hyperactivity Disorder (ADHD) is that in the DSM-5 (American Psychiatric Association, 2013). The DSM-5 lists a range of symptoms across two diagnostic categories of inattention and hyperactivity/impulsivity. Depending on the age of the child a set number of symptoms for each category must be present for a diagnosis. The pattern of these symptoms must be present for more than six months and should significantly interfere with daily functioning.

**Inattention** is difficulty with selecting what is relevant and maintaining attention on the selected object long enough for successful achievement of a task outcome. Those who have difficulties with inattention find it hard to decide what to focus on and when attempting to focus become easily distracted. **Hyperactivity** can be defined as an excess of energy. This can make behavioural self-control difficult and can lead an individual to engage in behaviour without sufficient prior planning or consideration of the outcome, which is a definition of **impulsivity**. The DSM-5 (American Psychiatric Association, 2013) cites behaviours symptomatic of hyperactivity such as a child being fidgety and talking excessively. Example behaviours that may be indicative of impulsivity are difficulty with turn-taking and blurting out answers in class.

There are three distinct presentations to ADHD. A predominantly inattentive presentation is where more symptoms of inattention are observed. A predominantly hyperactive–impulsive presentation is where more symptoms of hyperactivity/impulsivity are observed. A combined presentation refers to a child that presents with symptoms from both diagnostic categories (American Psychiatric Association, 2013).

These common ADHD differences are known as **executive functioning difficulties** (Geurts et al., 2020; Welsh and Pennington, 1989). This includes difficulties with working memory, **cognitive flexibility** (shifting thinking between aspects of a task) and **inhibitory control** (being able to inhibit a desire to shift attention to distracting stimuli). As a result of

Case Study: ADHD

Valeska is 15 years old and has had a diagnosis of ADHD since they were seven years old. They take medication and attend a resource base attached to a mainstream secondary school. This means they receive extra support in lessons from a learning mentor and takes some of their classes in a smaller group.

Valeska shows the same difficulties throughout the day no matter what the school subject or activity. They have difficulty paying attention to learning instructions but also find it hard to retain any information. They especially find independent work difficult when a task involves more than one activity component and requires shifting attention between different task components. Lastly, Valeska finds it hard to filter out irrelevant information and is often off-task.

the impact of executive functioning difficulties Valeska is a few grades behind the age average. Research has found Children and Young People (CYP) to be at risk of lower academic achievement (Biederman et al., 2004).

A couple of Valeska's teachers have noted that communicating ideas verbally is a strength for Valeska. Valeska has been a prominent member of the debate team for a year. Research has suggested that a relative strength in ADHD can be **verbal processing** (Hartnett et al., 2004). This is where CYP possess the ability to reason and answer questions using language. Ek et al. (2007) found that a sample of people with ADHD possessed the strength of using language in a logical way, with high verbal reasoning skills.

Despite their difficulties, Valeska is beginning to make progress at school with the support given. Valeska has supportive parents, a secure home environment and a friendship group consisting of exemplary students. These are all known protective factors. Research has shown that a stable family life characterised by love and financial security and positive peer relationships can all mediate negative educational outcomes for CYP with ADHD (Climie and Mastoras, 2015; Mackenzie, 2018).

# Defining autism spectrum condition

The National Autistic Society (2019) broadly describes autism as a 'life-long, developmental disability that affects how a person communicates with and relates to other people, and how they experience the world around them'. This summarises the wider differences associated with the condition, that of atypical social communication skills and repetitive behaviour combined with sensory interests or sensitivities (DSM-5; American Psychiatric Association, 2013).

From 1981 to 2013 the condition was theorised as consisting of three diagnostic categories of impairments, known as the **triad of impairments** (Wing, 1981). These were difficulties with communicating effectively with others, repetitive interests and activities, and difficulties with social interaction. The related condition of **Asperger's Syndrome** was another diagnosis category. In the fifth iteration of the DSM in 2013 this was subsumed into the umbrella term Autism Spectrum Condition (ASC).

ASC is broken down into three levels of severity. Each level is categorised according to the amount of support required for the individual to successfully function in daily life. Level one requires *some support, level two substantial support and level three very substantial support*. One potential critique of these labels is that the words used are vague and descriptive. It is left to the practitioner and family to ascertain what would merit 'some', 'substantial' and 'very substantial' support.

The National Autistic Society (2019) describes differences in social communication as including difficulties interpreting nuanced social interactions, such as understanding jokes and sarcasm, delayed understanding of social conventions, such as conversational turn-taking, and difficulty interpreting and responding to the emotions of others through non-verbal cues such as tone of voice or facial expression. This may lead an individual to behave in ways that seem socially inappropriate or at odds with culturally defined social norms. Restrictive interests and repetitive behaviours are described as manifesting a preference for routine, dislike of sudden or unexpected changes to routine, engagement in repetitive forms of play, and highly focused interests in specific subjects.

Lastly, in the past decade there has been increased acknowledgement that individuals with ASC may respond to sensory information differently (Tavassoli et al., 2018). The DSM-5 (American Psychiatric Association, 2013) states that there can be either **hypo** or **hyper reactivity** to **sensory stimuli**. This means that sensory data, such as smells, tastes and visual information, can be unpleasant and upsetting for the individual or can be highly pleasant and sought out.

 Case Study: ASC

Alex was diagnosed with autism at 16 years old, significantly older than when most children are diagnosed. This is a common experience for girls

(Green et al., 2019). Alex is 18 and has just started at university. They are studying for a double honours degree in Biology and Chemistry. Alex is keen to make new friends but experiences social anxiety when meeting new people. It was their experience in secondary school that some of their sensory behaviours, such as flapping hands for comfort when upset (known as stimming), made them seem different. Alex can also experience very low mood for a few weeks at a time. Alex is not alone in these challenges; research has shown that people with autism are at greater risk of developing mental health conditions (Gillan, 2019; Hollocks et al., 2019).

Alex was diagnosed as having high-functioning autism. They have good general intelligence and comprehend the complexity of their university topics. However, Alex can find it difficult to keep up with what they experience as the quick pace of lectures. The cognitive profile of adults with high-functioning autism shows difficulties with processing speed and working memory, which is one of the likely reasons Alex experiences the presentation of information in lectures as too fast for adequate comprehension (Rabiee et al., 2019; Velikonja et al., 2019). Alex also has some difficulties comprehending verbal information, which makes the traditional lecture structure not the best form of learning for them. Again, research has shown difficulties with verbal processing (Velikonja et al., 2019). As a result, Alex sometimes misses lectures and prefers to study the material independently. They make the most of one-to-one tutorials. However, Alex is aware this limits their opportunities to make friends, potentially exacerbating experiences of low mood and social anxiety.

Alex has been reading about autism and has become interested in activism. They use their growing social media platform to debunk myths and promote neurodiversity. This reflects a protest movement which views those with an autism diagnosis as 'autists' rather than having a medical disability (Jaarsma and Welin, 2012). It has been posited that this could result in a fundamental transformation in how autism is understood (Bertilsdotter et al., 2019; Kapp et al., 2013).

 Spotlight on Theory: Social Constructionism

It is possible to take the knowledge presented in this chapter as undisputable truth. But it is also important to develop our understanding of

*(Continued)*

SpLDs from different theoretical perspectives. The majority of research into SpLDs is conducted from a medical/psychoneurological perspective. Social constructionism theory offers an alternative lens through which to conceptualise and understand difficulty and difference with particular learning processes.

Social constructionism contests that scientific experimental research leads to objective factual truth about SpLDs. Instead, it argues that we create, and re-create, what SpLDs are through everyday social interactions involving the use of language. For example, numerous conversations between parents, professionals and children with dyslexia will construct and re-construct what dyslexia is and how it is affecting the child.

## Key Points

- Each SpLD is characterised by its own distinct cognitive profile but there is overlap between conditions.
- SpLDs can be understood from a neurodeficit or a neurodiversity perspective.
- Further research is required to substantiate existing claims of cognitive strengths for SpLDs.

## Final Reflection Questions

- If a class teacher chose to view SpLDs from the perspective of neurodiversity how could this influence their teaching practice?
- Why is it important to have clearly defined definitions of SpLDs based on the research literature?

# Further reading

This recommended reading explores how neurodiverse individuals are best supported in the classroom context:

Armstrong, T. (2012). *Neurodiversity in the Classroom: Strength-Based Strategies to Help Students with Special Needs Succeed in School and*

*Life*. Alexandria, VA: Association for Supervision and Curriculum Development.

This reading will help you to further your understanding of social constructionism theory and how SpLDs can be understood from a different perspective:

Dudley-Marling, C. (2004). The social construction of learning disabilities. *Journal of Learning Disabilities*, *37*(6), 482–489.

This interesting piece of research explores the effect emotions have on academic achievement for individuals with learning difficulties:

Sainio, P.J., Eklund, K.M., Ahonen, T.P.S. and Kiuru, N.H. (2019) The role of learning difficulties in adolescents' academic emotions and academic achievement. *Journal of Learning Disabilities*, *52*(4), 287–298.

# 4

# SEND SUPPORT AND INTERVENTION: OVERCOMING BARRIERS

Dr Alexandra Sewell

---

### Introduction

Educational professionals seek to intervene and support those with SEND to help them overcome any barriers they may face to successful learning. This chapter will:

- Introduce the metaphor of 'barriers to learning' and key concepts of 'intervention' and 'learning strategies'.
- Explore a range of ways that 'barriers to learning' can be removed.
- Introduce critical debates regarding SEND support and intervention.

# Barriers to learning

In Chapter 2, the Warnock Report (1978) was presented as the document that introduced the term Special Educational Needs (SEN). Alongside this new definition emerged the idea that children with SEN experience 'barriers to educational progress' (Warnock, 1978: 126). Some individuals experience difference or disability which leads to them not being able to access typical educational practice and because of this they do not meet age-related academic and developmental expectations. As a result, they have experienced a **barrier to learning**.

# Overcoming barriers to learning

Barriers to learning can be reduced through the consistent application of additional and specialist provision which is tailored to meet a child's SEN. There are two key terms to distinguish between:

1. **Strategies**.
2. **Intervention**.

Of note, in the literature the terms strategy and intervention can be used interchangeably. In this chapter a clear distinction is made between the two and they are defined as follows:

> Strategies: A teaching strategy can be defined as the implementation of a discrete instructional action as part of wider teaching practice. For example, when teaching phonics to a child a teacher may use flash cards to present each phonic sound to the individual in turn; this would constitute the use of one teaching strategy. The teacher may then plan to present the flash cards to the child twice a day for ten minutes each time until the pupil has learnt all the phonic sounds; this would comprise use of another teaching strategy.

> Intervention: Within the field of applied psychology interventions consist of a set of planned discrete actions that seek to bring about a positive change for the individual. Drawing on this conceptualisation, teaching interventions consist of a planned set of strategies used together to promote learning. For example, the combined use of the two strategies previously outlined is an example of the learning intervention 'distributed practice'. This is where target information is repeatedly presented for shorter intervals over extended periods of time (Benjamin and Tullis, 2010).

Case Study: Andy

Andy is five years old and in Reception year at a mainstream school. Andy has delayed expressive and receptive language skills. They can use two words together to make some of their basic needs known. Andy can understand simple sentences when used by adults in a familiar context or routine, such as 'sit at the table' when they are in a kitchen.

Andy has started learning phonics at school and is not making the expected rate of progress. They can recognise some letters of the alphabet. Andy prefers to play alone and doesn't interact much with peers. Sometimes they get up and leave a group learning task without permission from the teacher, to pursue an activity of their own choosing. In certain contexts, such as being in the dining hall at lunch time, Andy can become very upset by the loud noises and intense food smells.

 Time to Reflect

Consider the previous case study of Andy. Sketch the outline of a wall on a piece of A4 paper, made up of individual bricks. Take some time to consider the potential barriers to learning that Andy may experience. Write them on each brick. Take some time to think of any learning strategies, interventions and educational provision arrangements that would help them to overcome these barriers. Write these next to the barriers so that you can see how the wall would be overcome as a barrier.

# Evidence-based practice

**Evidence-Based Practice (EBP)** is concerned with the process of how practitioners decide which interventions to use. EBP evolved from the concept of Medical-Based Practice (MBP) (Evidence-Based Medicine Working Group, 1992). The term was coined in the mid-1990s drawing on the central idea from MBP that use of any intervention should be based on current and valid research evidence (Haynes et al., 1996). Research evidence should demonstrate the effectiveness of the intervention for achieving its goals. The emergent model of EBP also placed emphasis on the importance of 'clinical judgement', the professional's expertise and opinions, as well as on patients' views (Sackett et al., 1996).

## EBP in the field of education

EBP has made its way into the field of education. For example, in the United States in 2002 the US Department of Education established the What Works Clearing House as part of the Institute of Educational Science (visit: https://ies.ed.gov/ncee/wwc/FWW). The organisation reviews research for educational interventions and strategies (referred to as 'programmes' and 'practices' in their own literature) and determines which can be labelled 'evidence-based' and effective.

In the UK, the coalition government published a report encouraging teachers to incorporate EBP into education (Goldacre, 2013). **Randomised Controlled Trials (RCTs)** were promoted as a valid research method for evaluating the effectiveness of interventions. An RCT is an experimental procedure where participants are randomly assigned to one of two groups, a treatment group and a control group. The treatment group receives the intervention and the control group doesn't. Changes in both groups over a specified period of time are recorded. If changes to the treatment group are significantly different from the control group in the desired direction, then the intervention is assessed as having been effective. Goldacre (2013) stated that there was only a limited amount of RCTs for testing educational interventions and that this needed to be increased to improve teachers' access to EPB. In response, the UK government developed 'What Works Centres' to assess research evidence for educational practices (Gough et al., 2018).

# Evidence-informed practice

The translation of EBP into education has been critiqued. One of the main critiques levied is an over-emphasis on 'scientific'-based data (Norcross et al., 2006). It is also argued that the process from research to publication is too long, so that by the time teachers access research findings they are already out of date (Webb, 2001). It has also been put forward that the promotion of evidence from an RCT research format is too fixed. Nevo and Slonim-Nevo (2011) claim that RCT evidence was only one form of valid evidence amongst many that practitioners could draw upon. They developed the concept of **Evidence-Informed Practice (EIP)** where empirical evidence is still valid but other sources of evidence, such as case studies and qualitative research reporting Children and Young People's (CYP's) perspectives, are equally useful. They argue that EIP offers more flexibility to teachers when seeking evidence on which to base educational choices.

EIP is supported by Nelson and Campbell (2017), who argue that the application of information from RCTs cannot purely be a technical activity where evidence is easily translatable into new and different educational contexts. They contend that even the application of empirical evidence is influenced by political agendas and culturally situated conceptualisations of what teaching and learning are. As such, the flexibility that EIP allows is welcomed by them. This is further supported by Flynn (2019) who argues that each school contributes a unique knowledge community, so there will be differing concerns with regard to which elements of the evidence base are most important for that setting. For example, some teachers may be less concerned with the minutiae of research design and more with the practical outcomes of the intervention. Brown and Zhang (2016) found this to be the case when they interviewed 696 teachers from 79 schools exploring their perspectives on EIP and EBP. Teachers reported the need for a school-wide systemic approach to examining and applying evidence-based interventions and strategies.

# Inclusive pedagogy

## Two ways of thinking about inclusively educating children with SEND

There are, broadly speaking, two differing theoretical viewpoints that can be adopted when seeking to remove SEND-based barriers to learning. This first is the view that effective teaching for those with SEND is also effective teaching for all pupils. From this viewpoint there is a need to develop inclusive teaching approaches that can be applied to the whole class. One theory which encapsulates this view is known as **inclusive pedagogy**. This stance argues that specific, specialised educational strategies and intervention for SEND are not required. The approach takes the stance that all needs can be met via good quality, general classroom teaching. It is important to note that inclusive pedagogy is not a term interchangeable with inclusive education or inclusive practice – it has been developed to designate this particularly theory.

The second view is that specific SEND disorders require specialist interventions and strategies, rather than a blanket pedagogical approach that is arguably supportive for all. This has been argued to be particularly the case for Specific Learning Difficulties (SpLDs) such as dyslexia (Lewis and Norwich, 2004). In the forthcoming sections, we will discuss inclusive pedagogy and then return to SpLDs and evaluate specialised interventions for specific difficulties. The reflection questions at the end of the chapter will help you develop your own views on whether you feel specialised, specific interventions are required or not for removing SEND-based barriers to education.

## What is inclusive pedagogy?

Inclusive pedagogy offers a theoretically distinct approach that places itself directly in contrast to the view that individuals with SEND are different from others and therefore require unique and additional educational intervention. Florian (2015) terms this form of traditional thinking about SEND 'bell-curve thinking'. This extends from the presumption that learning ability is innate and fixed. It is argued that this leads to the assumption that 'ordinary' educational practice meets the needs of the majority but those who are outliers will need something different.

Inclusive pedagogy claims that this makes those who receive specialist forms of educational intervention feel singled out and different. It also argues that such a view of what SEND is and how it should be supported pathologises difference; those who do not fall within the designated realms of 'ordinary' are automatically abnormal. Such thinking is said to lead teachers to believe that those who require something that is educationally different from the ordinary will find it hard to succeed. There is a risk that this becomes a self-fulfilling prophecy. Florian (2015) refers to the phenomena of disproportionality, where people from minority backgrounds are disproportionately represented in SEND groups, as evidence for this.

Inclusive pedagogy asserts that ability is not fixed and can be developed. Individual difference is argued to be a core component of the experience of being human. To enact inclusive pedagogy in their classroom practice a teacher must therefore 'work out what they can do to support the learner while maintaining a commitment to everybody and avoiding situations that mark some students as different' (Florian, 2015: 11). As inclusive pedagogy was developed from observing teachers who successfully achieved this it focuses less on *what* strategies or interventions are being used and more on *how* they are used (Florian, 2015).

## Critiquing inclusive pedagogy

The main critique that may be levied at inclusive pedagogy is that due to its theoretical positioning it does not specify exactly how it can be applied to teaching practice. If inclusive pedagogy is 'defined not in the choice of strategy but in its use' (Florian, 2015: 13), how do teachers make the jump from this conceptual notion to the practical task of achieving it in their classroom? It could be argued that teachers are essentially practical creatures; they are concerned with what they *do* in the classroom more than any theoretical assumptions of learning (Allan, 2003).

Rix et al. (2009) conducted a three-year systematic literature review of inclusive teaching practices. Whilst a range of practical teaching strategies emerged, such as scaffolding learning and carefully planned group work, the key finding was that such strategies are only effective when teachers acknowledge they have a responsibility to all learners. This draws parallels with inclusive pedagogy's central idea of making what is ordinary provision available for all. However, it could still be argued that this does not provide specific guidance for teachers for how they can achieve this.

Florian and Linklater (2010) turned their attention to how inclusive pedagogy could be integrated into initial teacher training in the Inclusive Practice Project funded by the Scottish Government. They found that if initial teacher training focused on moving trainee teachers' conceptualisation of SEND away from 'bell-curve thinking' then teachers began to feel they could support SEND based on their existing knowledge and practical expertise. There was no need arising for them to engage in additional training to learn a new set of specialist interventions or strategies.

In comparison to other approaches, the inclusive pedagogy approach does not offer as direct or exacting instruction for what teachers should do to help those with SEND overcome barriers to learning. However, initial research has shown that intervening at the level of teachers' theoretical knowledge and changing their beliefs about difference, rather than intervening at the level of teachers' tacit knowledge and instructing them in what to do, can lead to inclusive practice. Mintz and Wyse (2015) support this, arguing that theoretical knowledge should not be separated from pedagogy. In other words, *what* a teacher conceptualises SEND and inclusive practice as is just important as *how* they go about supporting the removal of barriers to learning.

## Reflection Activity

Visit Chapter 7 and read the section that introduces the theory of Universal Design for Learning (UDL). It could be argued that the central premise of UDL and inclusive pedagogy align. Create a mind map to compare UDL with inclusive pedagogy.

# Specialised interventions for specific learning difficulties

In the previous section we were introduced to two ideas; that SEND can be supported through the inclusive pedagogy approach or that there is a need to deliver specialised interventions, and strategies tailored to specific SEND categories and conditions. This second view can be aligned with more of a scientific, positivist approach to understanding difference and diversity (Mintz and Wyse, 2015). This takes the approach that difference can be categorised into discrete diagnostic categories. This medical model approach has been interested in the development of specific educational interventions for each diagnostic category (see Chapter 1 for a summary of models of disability). In this section, we will be taking a closer look at this stance by using SpLDs as a focus. The SpLDs of dyslexia, Attention Deficit Hyperactivity Disorder (ADHD) and Autism Spectrum Condition (ASC) have been chosen for this as they have the largest range of specialised interventions with accompanying research evidence.

## Dyslexia

There is an abundance of specialised interventions targeted for dyslexia and a range of specific teaching strategies that are advised based on research evidence. However, not all can be said to be evidence-based, or even evidence-informed. Snowling (2013) cautions that 'the field of dyslexia is plagued with supposed "cures" that have no proper evidence base' (p.12). With regard to teaching strategies, the Rose Report (2009) stated that any strategies should be phonics-based and concentrate on supporting pupils with dyslexia to learn to decode words. Snowling and Hulme's (2011) review of the literature supports this, showing that there is a good evidence base for phonics-based intervention and a smaller evidence base for oral language-based interventions.

Specific learning interventions for dyslexia have typically been compared to a collation of general strategies. For example, Storey et al. (2017) compared the Headsprout Early Reading intervention with typical SENCo delivered strategies for improving reading skills for learners with SpLDs. Headsprout combines the strategies of systematic instruction to target phonic sounds, clearly identified criteria for moving on to new learning targets and the generalisation of learnt skills. Storey et al. (2017) found that the procedural, systematic approach of Headsprout was more effective than a heterogenous collection of SENCo-delivered strategies.

## ASC

With ASC there can also be found a plethora of classroom-based strategies as well as specific interventions claiming the 'specialised' title. Strategies can be clustered into groupings with each group focusing on supporting a particular trait that someone with autism may present with in a learning setting. There is an underlying assumption, rightly or wrongly, that these traits can act as a barrier to learning in some way. Table 4.1 presents the main groupings and some example strategies.

**Table 4.1**   Autism groupings and strategies

| Autism traits | Groupings | Example strategies |
| --- | --- | --- |
| Rigidity of thinking (preference for routine) | Visual-/physical based strategies to support engagement in work tasks | Visual timetable and now/next boards |
| | | Task management boards/boxes |
| | | Individual work stations |
| Rigidity of thinking (special interests) | Harnessing and making use of special interests | Giving access to special interests as a reward for a specific learning behaviour |
| | | Adapting teaching and learning materials to include special interests |
| Emotional recognition and regulation | Understanding emotions/ regulating emotions | Emotion recognition activities such as: |
| | | 'The Incredible Five Point Scale' (Buron and Curtis, 2012) |
| | | Emotions chart |
| Social communication difficulties | Teaching social skills/ developing successful social interaction | Social scripts |
| | | Modelling and reinforcement for target social skills |
| | | Social stories and comic strip conversations (Gray, 1994) |
| Language expression and understanding | Supporting understanding and use of language | Use of signs and symbols |
| | | Visual timetable and now/next |

As with dyslexia, these strategies vary with regard to the amount and quality of research evidence that supports them. For example, the strategy of integrating special interests into the curriculum is based on a developing evidence base. Gunn and Delafield-Butt (2016) reviewed 20 studies and found that an integration of interests into the curriculum generally led to positive academic gains. Out of 91 participants only one showed a decrease in engagement. In addition, qualitative research into classroom-based strategies can be helpful for discerning pupils with ASC's preferences for certain strategies. For example, Trembath et al. (2014) interviewed pupils who had experience of visual timetables and found that they reported the timetables helped to plan their thinking for events.

An example of an intervention that targets specific traits is emotion facial recognition training. This seeks to rectify a difficulty in reading facial expressions to understand what another person is feeling by explicitly teaching various facial expressions and their associated emotions.

An example of a broader intervention is one drawn from behaviourist psychology principles, often referred to as **Applied Behaviour Analysis (ABA)**. Terminology should be considered carefully here, however. ABA is a branch of psychology that includes the application of Skinner's operant conditioning theory. As such, ABA is applied to a wide range of behaviours and conditions. When applied systematically to support the learning of those with autism it is more specifically referred to as Early Intensive Behavioural Intervention (EIBI) (Reichow, 2012). EIBI involves applying ABA principles of learning to develop the functional living skills and communication skills of children with ASC (Reichow, 2012). The literature states that the teaching processes should be intensive, at least 40 hours a week, and start from around two years of age (Reichow, 2012).

Controversy exists as to whether EIBI can be claimed to be evidence-based. Discussion mainly centres around the choice of research methodology used to evaluate effectiveness. In the field of ABA, **single-case research design** is predominantly used (Smith et al., 2007). This involves a small number of participants as it seeks to understand change in behaviour for one person in response to environmental influence (Smith et al., 2007). It is claimed that numerous productions of single-case design research have shown EIBI to be effective (Love et al., 2009). However, wider disciplinary reviews of the research evidence, such as Reichow et al. (2018), claim that there is weak evidence to support EIBI as single-case design studies do not typically conform to research 'gold standards', such as randomly assigning participants to intervention and control conditions.

## ADHD

As with the examples of dyslexia and ASC, there are an abundance of interventions for ADHD, but it is the concept of EBP that is mainly applied to decide which ones should be considered 'specialist' and therefore effective for the condition. The National Institute for Health and Care Excellence (NICE) develops clinical guidelines for intervention based on research evidence. Its guidelines for ADHD diagnosis and management clearly recommend certain interventions and intervention combinations (NICE, 2018).

NICE (2018) recommends that parents of children with ADHD should first attend a parenting group before medication is considered. An example of an evidence-based parent intervention is the 'Triple P: Positive Parenting Programme' developed by Professor Matt Sanders and his team at the University of Queensland. The programme draws on cognitive-behavioural and developmental psychology theory to teach parents new ways to interact with their children to support their development. The programme has consistently demonstrated significant improvements in both the child's symptoms of ADHD and parental stress associated with managing their child's condition (Aghebati et al., 2014; Charach et al., 2013; Hoath and Sanders, 2002). These findings have been replicated in countries that have a different cultural approach to a westernised form of parenting, such as in China (Au et al., 2014).

NICE (2018) also recommend that 'environmental modifications' be made before medication is trialled as an intervention. In an educational context, environmental modifications are any changes to the physical environment or teaching instruction that improve the day-to-day learning of a person with ADHD. There are many combinations of strategies that can be implemented but the following are some examples of those that are evidence-informed (DuPaul et al., 2011):

- Task switching: Providing two work tasks, or two distinct components to the same work task, so that a pupil can switch to another task when they find it difficult to concentrate on the other.
- Chunking work tasks: This involves having a pupil complete a specified 'chunk' of a work task, either a specified time or quantity of work, before being given a brief break away from the task completely. They then return to the task and complete another 'chunk' before being given another brief break.
- Activity order: Considering the order in which learning activities are placed throughout the day. For example, concentration can be better in the morning, so place activities that require more concentration first thing in the daily routine.
- Reducing distractions: Modifying the teaching environment to reduce distractions, such as seating a pupil close to the whiteboard and teacher to access information, and/or reducing the number of distracting wall displays.
- Movement breaks: Providing set breaks throughout the day where the pupil can move and expend energy.

- Reduce task demands/length of tasks: If a task is too long or complex then a pupil can lose concentration more easily. Shorter tasks or tasks that aren't so complex can support this.
- Task choices: Giving the option of two or more tasks so that the pupil can choose which one to do.
- Supporting verbal instructions with written instructions: Providing a visual aid for what is required in a learning situation.

The NICE (2018) clinical guidelines also make clear that families and CYP with ADHD should be advised on the positive effects of a healthy lifestyle, one which involves regular exercise. Exercise is known to increase executive functioning skills in children, including attention and concentration (Hill et al., 2011). There is also exciting evidence that routine exercise implemented as an intervention for ADHD from a young age could redirect the developmental pathway of ADHD (Wigal et al., 2013). This means that exercise would potentially change the physiology of those with ADHD and so reduce the intensity of the negative associated symptoms as the child develops (Archer and Kostrzewa, 2012; Halperin and Healey, 2011). Exercise as an intervention is easily implemented in the school environment as teachers already possess the expertise and equipment to run PE programmes (Pontifex et al., 2013). However, further RCTs are required for this line of intervention to be fully considered evidence-based (Ng et al., 2017).

# Provision mapping: Organising school-based SEND intervention

The final section of this chapter will look at how strategies and interventions for overcoming barriers to SEND can be practically implemented in educational settings through the example of provision mapping. As stipulated in the SENCoP (DfE and DoH, 2014) schools must provide a transparent record of a child's SEND needs, what interventions and strategies are put in place to support them and how these will support the learning of the pupil. A provision map is a document that provides this information. It is reviewed regularly to demonstrate learning progress, or lack of progress, in response to provision. NASEN (2014b) developed a four-step process to developing a provision map:

1. Auditing provision: Listing the provision the child receives and sharing key information such as the frequency of each intervention.

2. Collecting baseline data and setting targets: Baseline measures may be National Curriculum levels or other relevant data, such as phonics knowledge.
3. Measuring progress: Learning progress should be regularly updated in relation to key targets and recorded in the provision map.
4. Evaluating outcomes: By comparing progress data to baseline data a judgement can be made as to whether targets have been met.

In most schools the SENCo takes responsibility for the organisation of provision maps, but it is a document that all staff should regularly update and use (Cheminais, 2010). Provision mapping is most successful when the SENCo is given adequate time, resources and responsibility to complete the map (Ekins, 2012). The importance and significance of this task should not be underrated, and senior leadership should be realistic and generous about the amount of support given to SENCos to complete this task (Cowne et al., 2018).

## Key Points

- 'Barriers to learning' is a metaphor where SEND can prevent learning effectively, but barriers can be removed through additional and specialised educational provision.
- There are two theoretical standpoints that can be adopted for understanding how SEND should be supported in an educational setting. The first is that specialist intervention is required for each specific condition and need. The second is that teaching practice should be inclusive for all from the beginning.
- There is much debate around whether EBP or EIP is more appropriate for educational practice for SEND.

## Final Reflection Questions

Imagine you are a teacher who wants to implement a new educational intervention for teaching early years pupils with dyscalculia how to count.

*(Continued)*

- What types of evidence would you draw on to assess whether this will be effective for your class?
- How will you evaluate this evidence whilst also considering your understanding of the group of learners' strengths and difficulties?
- How could members of a school's senior leadership team develop a systemic, school-wide approach to implementing EIP in their school?

# Further reading

This book explores the theory of inclusive pedagogy in depth:

Deppeler, J., Loreman, T., Florian, L. and Smith, R. (2015). *Inclusive Pedagogy Across the Curriculum*. Bingley: Emerald Group Publishing.

This book will enable you to fully understand how the concept of EBP can be applied to the field of education:

Pring, R. and Thomas, G. (2004). *Evidence-Based Practice in Education*. London: McGraw-Hill Education.

This is a piece of research which has sought to give examples of specific school-based support for learners with an SpLD:

Ross, H. (2019) Supporting a child with dyslexia: How parents/carers engage with school-based support for their children. *British Journal of Special Education*, 46(2), 136–156.

# 5

# EXPLORING MENTAL HEALTH IN CHILDHOOD AND ADOLESCENCE

Dr Alexandra Sewell

## Introduction

To effectively learn a child or young person needs to be in an attentive mood, experience enjoyable emotions and be able to respond effectively to unpleasant emotions. The presence of a mental health condition can prevent this and act as a barrier to learning which requires additional educational provision. This chapter will:

- Introduce you to two ways that experiences of mental health can be conceptualised and also to some common mental health conditions and experiences.
- Build on your previous learning of the medical model of difference and disability.
- Outline and evaluate the various ways mental health is supported in an educational context.

# Psycho-medical model approach to mental health

The dominant approach to understanding experiences of mental health is the psycho-medical model (sometimes just termed medical model) introduced in Chapters 1 and 2 (Whooley, 2010). This model adopts what is known as a **nomothetic** approach to understanding any uncomfortable emotions that individuals experience and associated behaviours that may impact daily functioning. The nomothetic approach is concerned with looking at a large sample of people and seeking commonalities between them. This allows laws or rules to be established that can then be generalised to all humans (Leamy et al., 2011; Whooley, 2010).

With the phenomena of mental health, this involves studying clusters of people who may be having similar emotional, mental and behavioural experiences and then designating those experiences as **symptoms**. A symptom is a physical, behavioural or mental feature of a disease or condition that those with the condition are observed to possess (DeMatteo et al., 2010; Leamy et al., 2011). Clusters of symptoms form the basis of a mental health condition or disorder. For example, if you studied a selection of people who all experience a racing heart, sweaty palms and difficulty breathing you may label this collection of symptoms as 'anxiety'. With further research you will likely discover a whole range of symptoms common to this group of people, such as recurring thoughts about how they can keep safe from danger, difficulty concentrating and sensitivity to perceived threats (Beck et al., 2005). The psych-medical model approach has clustered these symptoms to form the condition Generalised Anxiety Disorder (GAD) (DSM-5; American Psychiatric Associaion, 2013; Beck et al., 2005).

The psycho-medical model of mental health places emphasis on professional knowledge in the domains of assessment and treatment for mental health conditions (DeMatteo et al., 2010; Leamy et al., 2011). In addition to researching what conditions exist, those with professional training in the field of psycho-medical mental health research and support also research tools and procedures that can be used to accurately identify the presence of symptoms leading to identification of a condition (Whooley, 2010). This is known as a diagnosis.

# DSM-5 and childhood psychopathology

The *Diagnostic and Statistical Manual – Fifth Edition* (DSM-5) is published by the American Psychiatric Association and outlines broad categories of mental health conditions for children and adults and their associated symptoms (American Psychiatric Association, 2013). It also makes recommendations for diagnosis and common treatment approaches. Disorders are divided into five dimensions:

1. Clinical symptoms: Experiences of mood disorders, anxiety disorders and eating disorders.
2. Personality and mental retardation: Long-term problems that influence effective life functioning, e.g. cognitive impairment and personality disorders.
3. Medical conditions: Any medical conditions that can worsen axis one, e.g. a brain injury.
4. Psychosocial and environment problems: Anything external to the individual that can worsen axis one, e.g. unemployment or homelessness.
5. Global assessment of functioning: Allows a professional to assess a person's overall level of functioning.

Experiences of clinical symptoms related to dimension one in those under the age of 18 are known as childhood psychopathology (Lewis and Rudolph, 2014). The most diagnosed forms of childhood psychopathology are behaviour disorders, including Oppositional Defiance Disorder (ODD) and Attention Deficit Hyperactivity Disorder (ADHD) (Maughan et al., 2004; Polanczyk et al., 2014). The DSM-5 reports ODD childhood rates occurring between 2 and 16% and ADHD rates occurring between 3 and 12% (American Psychiatric Association, 2013). ODD is characterised by persistent patterns of aggressive behaviours towards others coupled with a disregard for adult established behaviour rules. ADHD has been outlined in full in Chapter 4. The symptoms associated with these conditions are termed **externalising behaviours** (Lewis and Rudolph, 2014). The term refers to an externalisation of difficulties, symptoms that can be seen by others, i.e. observable behaviours.

Anxiety and mood disorders occur less frequently in childhood populations. GAD has a typical onset age of eight years old and a lifetime prevalence of 5% (Albano et al., 2003). It is the most common childhood mood disorder, with other mood disorders such as depression diagnosed less frequently in childhood (Albano et al., 2003). The symptoms associated with these conditions are termed **internalising behaviours**. Internalising refers to behaviours and experiences that can't be seen by others, such as thoughts and emotions, referencing unobservable behaviours.

In addition to the DSM-5 (American Psychiatric Association, 2013) the ICD-10 (WHO, 1992) defined a mental disorder as 'a clinically recognizable set of symptoms or behaviours associated... with distress' (p.3). The World Health Organization further defines mental health as a continuous experience of well-being which allows an individual to know their own abilities, manage stress, be productive in work and contribute to the wider community (World Health Organization, 2004). As such, mental health is conceptualised on a continuum ranging from being prevented from participating in daily activities to successfully participating in daily activities.

# An alternative approach to mental health

An **ideographic** approach to understanding human experience is concerned with individualised experiences of mental health. Rather than exploring common symptoms across individuals a nuanced view of emotional and behavioural difficulties and their impact on an individual's life is sought. This downplays the importance of professional knowledge and seeks a localised understanding of why the focus person may have developed the symptoms present. Individuals themselves are encouraged to develop their own theory for why their mental health experiences have occurred and develop their own solutions based on this.

Narrative therapy is an example of psychological theory that takes a strong ideographic approach to understanding people's experiences of mental health. It posits that all humans develop narratives of self that construct who they are and how they interpret their experiences (White and Epston, 1990). If they have developed one narrative about their mental health experiences, they can be supported to develop a new narrative, known as **re-authoring** (White and Epston, 1990).Through a process known as externalising conversations a person is supported to separate the 'problem' from themselves. They are then supported to re-author a new alternative narrative about their experiences of mental health.

---

 Spotlight on Research: Hannen and Woods (2012)

Hannen and Woods (2012) reported a case study where narrative therapy was used to help a 12-year-old girl who experienced self-harm, self-identifying as a 'self-cutter'. The ideographic approach allowed the girl and researcher to co-develop a nuanced, personalised view of why the 'problem' of self-cutting had begun and re-author a new narrative. The girl developed her own folk psychology theory that self-cutting happened when she felt a lot of anger. She perceived anger as some-thing that could take control of her and that she disappeared when it occurred. Through the process of re-authoring, this narrative changed where anger began to be seen not as a personality trait but something that could dissipate when she engaged in helping others. This is an example of how a localised understanding of mental health can be developed through use of alternative approaches to the medical model, such as with narrative therapy.

## Time to Reflect

In the SENDCoP (DfE and DoH, 2014) mental health falls under the cat-egory of 'Social, Emotional and Mental Health' and is defined as follows:

> Children and young people may experience a wide range of social and emotional difficulties which manifest themselves in many ways. These may include becoming withdrawn or isolated, as well as dis-playing challenging, disruptive or disturbing behaviour. These behaviours may reflect underlying mental health difficulties such as anxiety or depression, self-harming, substance misuse, eating dis-orders or physical symptoms that are medically unexplained. Other children and young people may have disorders such as attention deficit disorder, attention deficit hyperactive disorder or attachment disorder. (6.32)

Consider whether this definition takes more of a nomothetic or ideo-graphic approach in conceptualising and understanding mental health needs.

# School-based intervention: Targeted intervention and provision

Educational-based support for pupils experiencing mental health needs as a barrier to learning can be personalised and targeted. It can also involve whole-school systemic provision. Professionals supporting Children and Young People (CYP) tend to adopt both nomothetic and ideographic approaches to delivering support. They seek to apply evidence-based strategies and intervention gleaned from nomothetic research and balance this with their understanding of the individual characteristics and contextual factors of the pupil they are supporting (Rones and Hoagwood, 2000). Typical individual intervention is explored below for behavioural disorders and mood disorders.

## School-based intervention for behaviour disorders

School-based intervention for behaviour disorders has traditionally followed behaviour management principles derived from Applied Behaviour Analysis (ABA) (Cooper et al., 2007). ABA employs the principles of operant conditioning, that behaviour is either reinforced by consequences in the environment, increasing the likelihood of it occurring again in the future, or punished by consequences in the environment, decreasing the likelihood of it occurring again in the future (Cooper et al., 2007). Behavioural intervention methods for behaviour disorders have a strong literature that has explored their common use and efficacy (Ervin et al., 1998; Farmer and Xie, 2007; Gresham, 2004; Ingram et al., 2005; Lane at al., 2009; Lewis et al., 2004; Newcomer and Lewis, 2004; Sasso et al., 2001).

Functional behavioural assessment involves collecting data on behaviours associated with the disorders ODD and ADHD and generating hypotheses for what is causing them to occur (Ervin et al., 1998; Stahr et al., 2006). Hypotheses are developed based on what environmental consequences may be reinforcing the child's behaviour that is deemed socially unacceptable, such as aggression (Ervin et al., 1998). This information is then used to develop intervention strategies aimed at reducing unwanted behaviour and teaching new alternative behaviours. New behaviours are chosen to be socially acceptable (Ervin et al., 1998). This approach can be applied as a form of behaviour management and change promotion in the school environment. It can also be developed conjunctively in the home environment.

Educational practice in the 21st century has witnessed a movement away from the exclusive use of a behavioural management approach to supporting SEMH students with **externalising behaviours**. There is an argument that interventions should be appreciative of the emotional functioning aspect of behavioural disorders such as ADHD and ODD (Steinberg and Drabick, 2015). As a result, interventions that address such a need have been developed. These are often based on psychological theory that forefronts the importance of emotional regulation and relationships in promoting positive child development (Steinberg and

Drabick, 2015). For example, Attachment Aware Schools promotes supportive strategies based on the notion that all students will be mentally well if they have a secure attachment style (Attachment Aware Schools, 2020).

Emotion coaching is an example of an intervention for externalising behaviours that is gaining in popularity and traction. Emotion coaching is a universal approach that can be applied to all children. Its implementation is supported by Emotion Coaching UK (www.emotioncoachinguk.com). Gottman et al. (1996) developed emotion coaching by observing the behaviours of parents who were successful when intervening with their child's behaviour. He found that when parents repeatedly coached children positively it supported the child to learn to regulate their emotions and associated behaviours, such as aggressive and disruptive behaviour (Gottman et al., 2013). There are five steps to successful emotion coaching:

1.  Being aware of a child's emotions as they arise.
2.  Building intimacy with the child.
3.  Being empathetic and validating the child's emotional experience.
4.  Using words to support the child to label the emotion.
5.  Boundary-setting for behaviours associated with the emotion and helping the child to problem-solve.

## School-based interventions for mood disorders

School-based interventions for mood disorders can either be classroom adaptions, one-to-one input based on therapeutic intervention, or a blend of the two. Therapeutic-based intervention often involves following a procedure that has typically been developed through research. Classroom adaptions involve drawing on a range of strategies. These are tailored to the individual and their specific needs. However, there is a limited research base for the effectiveness of classroom-based accommodations and adaptions, with research mainly focused on supporting anxiety conditions (Killu et al., 2016; Schaeffer et al., 2005).

Killu et al. (2016) outlined four types of accommodations for supporting anxiety in a classroom setting: cognitive accommodations, socioemotional accommodations, behavioural accommodations and physiological accommodations. Cognitive accommodations should address difficulties with memory, attention and concentration. For example, a 'peer buddy' could be used to help a child stay on task and a reduced workload can help with memory processing. Socioemotional accommodations would seek to support difficulties with shyness, panic and worry at entering a new context, such as the classroom. For example, scheduling pre-arranged breaks to help with stress and anxiety. Behavioural accommodations can be put in place for difficulties like task avoidance, irritability and perfectionism. For example, developing both teachers' and students' skills to manage stress (Kazdin, 2000). Physiological accommodations aim to target somatic experiences of anxiety, such as a racing heart, muscle tension and dizziness. Recommended strategies include alternating stressful activities with physical activity and providing a quiet place for pupils to relax.

Therapeutic-based interventions often take a procedural form developed through research. This means they prescribe what the intervention consists of and how it should be delivered. School-based interventions can be delivered in one-to-one, small group and whole class formats. The most common therapeutic tradition for this method of support is Cognitive Behavioural Therapy (CBT). The FRIENDS programme is an example of a CBT evidence-based procedural intervention for supporting mood disorders in school that is used around the globe (Rodgers and Dunsmuir, 2015; Stallard et al., 2005). The programme has been shown to have positive outcomes for mood disorders, whether delivered by clinicians with training in the field of mental health or school staff without clinical training (Rodgers and Dunsmuir, 2015; Stallard et al., 2005). It is also preventative, meaning if delivered universally to all pupils, can prevent the later development of mood disorders (Stallard et al., 2005).

**Positive psychology** offers an alternative to dominant CBT models of intervention in an educational context. Positive psychology is concerned with scientifically studying human flourishing (Seligman et al., 2009). It seeks to discover the psychological mechanisms and environmental inputs that allow pupils to thrive with their learning and development (Seligman et al., 2009). As such, it is positioned as a movement away from the field of childhood psychopathology which focuses on when individuals are not functioning well.

Positive psychology has been applied to improving the mental health and emotional well-being of pupils. Intervention concentrates on fostering three cornerstones of flourishing. The first is the experience of positive emotions (Seligman et al., 2009). The second is the concept of engagement in life. This is exemplified by the experience of 'flow', where you are so consumed with the task at hand you lose a sense of time (Csikszentmihalyi, 1990). Lastly, it is important for pupils to have meaning in their lives. This can be found through connection with others or causes that a person cares about (Seligman, 2002). The Pen Resiliency Programme and the Strath Haven Positive Psychology Curriculum were both developed to be used by schools to foster the cornerstones of flourishing (Seligman et al., 2009). The research literature demonstrates that both are effective in producing improvements in pupils' well-being and mediating mental health difficulties (Seligman et al., 2009).

---

 Case Study: Lesley

Lesley has a diagnosis of GAD and ODD and is in Year Six. Their class teacher uses a blend of personalised and whole-school systemic strategies and interventions to support them. They have a SEND passport which outlines that the following has been put in place to support them.

Classroom adaptations

Access to a quiet and calming space after science and literacy-based activities that are known to be stressful to them.

After an hour of work a five-minute activity break is to be implemented. Activities are skipping, shooting basketball hoops and dancing.

A 'peer buddy' will be assigned during independent silent reading.

Behaviour management strategies

- A functional behavioural assessment found that aggressive outbursts were maintained by attention from peers and teachers.
- Whole class to be instructed to ignore behavioural outbursts (targeting reduction of unwanted behaviour) and selected peers supported to interact with Lesley when engaging in calm behaviour (targeting increase in desired behaviour).
- Emotion coaching training to be delivered to all school staff and used when it is apparent that Lesley is experiencing unpleasant emotions.

CBT intervention

Whole-class CBT intervention for stress and anxiety to be implemented.

---

# School-based intervention: Systemic intervention

Systemic intervention consists of a school-wide plan to change practice at multiple levels (Adelman and Taylor, 2007). When focusing on supporting the development of positive mental health in pupils this involves seeking school-wide practices that are implemented at the whole-class level for all pupils (Weare, 2000). It also involves a statement of intent from the senior leadership team with regard to a united focus on supporting and improving emotional development in addition to academic achievement.

The Social and Emotional Aspects of Learning (SEAL) programme is an example of a systemic intervention for pupil well-being and mental health that was widely adopted in the UK. It has been described as 'a comprehensive, whole-school approach to promoting the social and emotional skills that underpin effective learning, positive behaviour, regular attendance, staff effectiveness and the emotional health and well-being of all who learn and work in schools' (DCSF, 2007: 4). The programme is based on Goleman's (1996) theory of emotional intelligence which states pupils need to develop self-awareness, self-regulation of emotions, motivation for engagement in meaningful activities, empathy and social skills as a foundation for positive mental health and well-being.

It consists of a set of curriculum resources and an ethos that schools can adapt to implement widespread change. The following steps for whole-school change were recommended by the SEAL National Strategies (DfE, 2011a):

- SEAL is implemented as a part of a wider school framework seeking to raise standards in behaviour and achievement.
- The school ethos reflects a desire to provide a positive climate for developing social and emotional skills.
- The ethos also recognises the connection between social and emotional skills and learning.
- All children have a planned opportunity to learn how to develop social and emotional skills.
- Children who would benefit from small group intervention receive this.
- Pupils are involved in developing the SEAL programme.
- There is a good connection with other schools and the wider community.
- Teachers are also encouraged to improve their social and emotional skills.

Research into the effectiveness of SEAL reported mixed results. In a summative review Humphrey et al. (2010) reported that published case studies demonstrated a fragmentation in the way that different schools attempted whole-school implementation. A significant critique was that 'pockets of activity' (Humphrey et al., 2010: 3) were attempted rather than the adoption of true systemic change. Perhaps as a result of this, it was found that the programme did not impact individual pupils' emotional well-being, social skills and mental health (Humphrey et al., 2010). This issue was also found by Lendrum et al. (2013) in the secondary school context. Nine secondary schools also experienced a range of inconsistency with systemic change, postulated as a result of the 'goodness of fit' of the SEAL programme with existing school ethos. However, Hallam (2009) found that the majority of teachers and senior leaders who experienced SEAL in a primary school context felt it had been effective.

Despite the mixed, and somewhat disappointing, efficacy of SEAL for supporting the mental health of pupils, from a whole-school perspective it can be framed as one of the earlier innovative programmes in this area. With the increase of mental health difficulties in childhood there is renewed focus on the school context as means of systemic intervention (Lamb-Parker et al., 2008). In other western countries, such as Australia, whole-school programmes have been developed and trialed with successful outcomes (Wyn et al., 2000). Research continues to seek the best combination of foci for systemic change. This demonstrates a belief in the field that whole-school approaches hold promise, despite a general reduction in the implementation of SEAL and other early programmes.

Trussell (2008) outlined that teachers' perceptions of pupils' ability and temperament, positive school communities, well-managed classrooms, opportunities for positive social interaction and individualised curricula all contributed to supporting positive mental health development. As such, they were recommended as sites for intervention for the development of whole-school programmes supporting systemic change. Similarly, Cappella et al. (2008) located effective teaching instruction and classroom management as influential and highlighted the importance of parental involvement. As interest in this area of research grows, future whole-school interventions will consider these elements and those arising from future research when seeking to systemically support the mental health of pupils.

## Reflection Activity

Longstanding mental health difficulties are reported to have increased 4.8% since 1995, and there is concern that CYP are experiencing higher levels of emotional distress than previous generations (Pitchforth et al., 2019). Create a mind map of what might influence an increase in mental health difficulties in CYP. Consider how they relate to each other.

## Key Points

- Mental health needs can be conceptualised in different ways. A nomothetic approach seeks to look for common symptoms across individuals to form conditions that can be diagnosed. An ideographic approach explores a personalised experience of mental health and does not to seek to generalise to other individuals.
- Educational contexts offer important opportunities for effective intervention and support for CYP experiencing mental health difficulties. Intervention can be targeted and individualised for a pupil, focusing on classroom adaptations. Support can also be school-wide via planned systemic change.
- Mental health difficulties have been reported to have risen significantly in CYP. It is likely that the educational context will continue to be an important site for support and intervention.

## Final Reflection Questions

- If you were a teacher seeking to understand a pupil's mental health needs would you adopt an ideographic or nomothetic form of assessment? Why would you make this choice?
- What type of training do teachers require to be able to implement targeted interventions to support children with internalising and externalising difficulties?
- What barriers do schools face when attempting systemic school-wide support for supporting pupils with mental health needs? What can be done to help them overcome these barriers?

# Further reading

This book gives practical examples of how whole-school systemic intervention can support CYP's mental health:

Knightsmith, P. (2019). *The Mentally Healthy School's Workbook*. London: Jessica Kingsley.

This book supports teachers to support the mental health of pupils when limited budget funds are available:

Erasmus, C. (2019). *The Mental Health and Wellbeing Handbook for Schools: Transforming Mental Health Support on a Budget*. London: Jessica Kingsley.

This research paper explores how confident teachers typically feel in their ability to support the mental health of their students:

Askell-Williams, H. and Lawson, M.J. (2013) Teachers' knowledge and confidence for promoting positive mental health in primary school communities. *Asia-Pacific Journal of Teacher Education*, 41(2), 126–143.

# 6

# EQUALITY: ACCESS, PROVISION AND OUTCOMES

## Joanne Smith

---

### Introduction

In this chapter, we will explore the purpose of having equalities legislation and reflect upon whether specific groups of people are treated equally to each other. We will look at barriers to and enablers of equality, with a specific focus on educational experiences. This chapter will:

- Explore notions of difference and diversity, how these have implications for learners' educational experiences.
- Examine equality legislation and practice based on principles of equality of access, provision and outcomes.
- Consider other factors related to equality provision, such as culture, English as an additional language and looked after children.

# Equal, equality, equity: What is the difference?

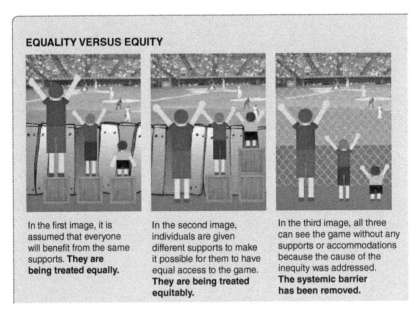

**EQUALITY VERSUS EQUITY**

| In the first image, it is assumed that everyone will benefit from the same supports. **They are being treated equally.** | In the second image, individuals are given different supports to make it possible for them to have equal access to the game. **They are being treated equitably.** | In the third image, all three can see the game without any supports or accommodations because the cause of the inequity was addressed. **The systemic barrier has been removed.** |

**Figure 6.1**   Equality vs equity

Source: Image adopted by unknown artist from original by Craig Froehle. Found on business disabilityinternational.org

---

          Time to Reflect

Consider Figure 6.1 in relation to an inclusive classroom: what would it look like in terms of equal access; would you strive to remove systemic barriers?

---

# The Equality Act (2010): Protected characteristics, concepts and definitions

The Equality Act (2010) replaced previous legislation (such as the Race Relations Act 1976 and the Disability Discrimination Act 1995) ensuring consistency in what employers and employees need to do to make their workplaces a fair environment and comply with the law. Every organisation must not discriminate against employees and people that use their services because of particular characteristics, known as the **protected characteristics**: age, **disability**, gender reassignment, marriage and civil partnerships, pregnancy or maternity, race, religion or belief, sex (gender) or sexual orientation (gay, lesbian or bisexual).

**Discrimination** is treating someone unfairly because of their characteristics. If organisations treat people differently because of these characteristics, then they could be acting unlawfully. This could result in the organisation being taken to court and sued for their actions (Equality and Human Rights Commission: www. equalityhumanrights.com). Refer to Chapter 10 for further discussion on discrimination.

Children and Young People (CYP) have equal protection for most of the protected characteristics. However, while a child is attending school there is no protection against age discrimination until they are educated post-16.

The Equality Act (2010) also includes the public sector equality duty. This means public bodies, like the police, schools and hospitals, not only have to take steps to stop discrimination, but also have to promote equality. Public bodies should promote equality of opportunity, for example, by ensuring girls and boys have access to the same apprenticeships, or disabled students have access to resources and support (see **reasonable adjustments**, discussed further on in the chapter). Public bodies should promote good relations, e.g. via anti-bullying policies and promotion of cultural understanding between different ethnic groups. The Act also allows 'positive action', which enables public bodies to provide additional benefits to some groups of people to tackle disadvantage, e.g. providing additional lessons for Gypsies and Travellers.

## The environment: Disability and inclusion

The Equality and Human Rights Commission report in relation to disability (2018) found:

Disabled people are not enjoying the progress experienced by other groups. Their right to an **inclusive education** is not being fulfilled. The proportion of disabled children at special rather than mainstream schools has increased, and they are more likely to be excluded from school. Disabled people earn less per hour on average than non-disabled people. They are more likely to be in low-pay occupations and this likelihood has increased. Disabled people are more likely to be in poverty. Those who cannot work rely on an increasingly restricted welfare regime that is projected to lower their living standards even further. They also face poorer health and lack of access to suitable housing. Safety is another major concern, as fewer disabled people have confidence that the criminal justice system is effective. Without the fundamental building blocks of good education, an adequate standard of living, and being safe and healthy, disabled people are often unable to participate fully in society. (p.6)

## Time to Reflect

What are the implications of these findings in current education provision?

**Table 6.1** Disabling and enabling environments

| Disabling environments | Enabling environments |
|---|---|
| (The World Health Organization, 2001: 241) | (www.cdc.gov/ncbddd/disabilityandhealth/disability-strategies.html) |
| A physical environment that is not accessible | Making products, communications, and the physical environment more usable by as many people as possible (e.g. Universal Design for Learning) |
| Lack of relevant assistive technology (assistive, adaptive, and rehabilitative devices) | Modifying items, procedures, or systems to enable a person with a disability to use them to the maximum extent possible (**reasonable adjustments**) |
| Negative attitudes of people towards disability | Eliminating the belief that people with disabilities are unhealthy or less capable of doing things (stigma, stereotypes) |
| Services, systems and policies that are either non-existent or that hinder the involvement of all people with a health condition in all areas of life | Getting fair treatment from others (non-discrimination) |

# Reasonable adjustments duty

The duty requires an educational organisation to take positive steps to ensure that disabled students can fully participate in the education and other benefits, facilities and services provided for students. This was introduced in the Disability Discrimination Act (1995) and taken forwards into the Equality Act (2010). When the DDA was first implemented it was recognised that many organisations were likely to 'do the minimum' to comply, rather than using this requirement to provide a truly enabling environment.

Organisations are required to take reasonable steps to avoid the provision, criterion or practice putting disabled students at a substantial disadvantage. They should also avoid any physical features that put disabled persons at a substantial disadvantage; this includes removing the physical feature in question, altering it or providing a reasonable means of avoiding it. Organisations cannot justify a failure to make a reasonable adjustment; where the duty arises, the issue is whether the adjustment is 'reasonable' and this is an objective question, which may be determined through relevant legal channels if necessary.

The duty is an anticipatory and continuing one that organisations owe to disabled students generally, regardless of whether they know that a student is disabled or whether they currently have any disabled students. Organisations should plan and anticipate the requirements of and adjustments for participants who are disabled. It is not an expectation that organisations anticipate the needs of every prospective student, but they are required to think about and take reasonable and proportionate steps to overcome barriers that may impede people with different kinds of disabilities. For example, while it may be appropriate for universities to install a hearing loop in lecture theatres to anticipate deaf students' needs, it is not an expectation to have a British Sign Language (BSL) interpreter on the payroll (see Table 6.1).

Where a provision, criterion or practice places disabled students at a substantial disadvantage in accessing education and any benefit, facility or service, the further or higher education institution must take such steps as are reasonable to take in the circumstances to ensure the provision, criterion or practice no longer has such an effect. This might mean waiving a criterion or abandoning a practice altogether but often will involve just an extension of the flexibility and individual approach that many education institutions already show to their students.

For example:

> A college has a strict policy that does not allow drugs on the premises. A student with a heart condition carries medication related to their condition. The college allows them to bring their medication with them to college. This is likely to be a reasonable adjustment to the college drug policy.

A competence standard is defined as an academic, medical or other standard applied by or on behalf of an education provider in determining whether a person has a particular level of competence or ability. It is not a provision, criterion or practice and therefore there is no duty to make reasonable adjustments in relation to the application of a competence standard. However, the duty does apply to the process of demonstrating that a person meets the competence standard.

For example:

A student with a visual impairment has their written exam provided in enlarged text. This would be an example of a reasonable adjustment to demonstrate meeting the competence standard.

When deciding whether an adjustment is reasonable you can consider how effective the change will be in avoiding the disadvantage the disabled person would otherwise experience, its practicality, the cost, the organisation's resources and size and the availability of financial support.

---

 **Time to Reflect**

Which of the following do you think would be an appropriate reasonable adjustment? Why/why not?

- Allowing and making provision for an employee or a student whose immunity is compromised (e.g. due to chemotherapy treatment) to work from home at times.
- Relocating a small private training business to new premises to enable wheelchair access.
- Providing a support worker for a worker or a student whose disability has caused a lack of confidence.

---

Moving on from reasonable adjustments, there are other influencing factors to consider when exploring equality practice. This practice is evaluated in the final chapter of the book; however, we can consider some of these aspects here.

# English as an Additional Language

There are more than a million children from 5–16 years old in UK schools who speak in excess of 360 languages between them in addition to English. The average proportion of English as an Additional Language (EAL) students in a school is 13.6%. Teaching EAL learners is sometimes controversial. Key debates often revolve around the question of whether it is better to immerse the learner in the 'new' culturally dominant language, or to allow or even encourage the learner to continue to speak their own language. Students from minority groups traditionally do less well at school than students from the dominant group – this is not just because of the language issue, but is also more pronounced when the minority student's culture and language are not valued by the school. Cummins (2014) argues that children with EAL learn better if they continue to develop their first language as well as their English – thereby arguing against the idea that only English should be spoken (immersion theory).

*BICS are Basic Interpersonal Communication Skills*; these are the 'surface' skills of listening and speaking which can be acquired quickly by many students; particularly by those from language backgrounds similar to English who spend a lot of their school time interacting with native speakers.

*CALP is Cognitive Academic Language Proficiency*, and, as the name suggests, is the basis for a child's ability to cope with the academic demands placed upon them in various subjects. Cummins states that while many children develop native speaker fluency (i.e. BICS) within two years of immersion in the target language, it takes between five and seven years for a child to be working at the same level as native speakers as far as academic language is concerned.

**Note:** Although, as inclusive practitioners, we do need to consider the needs of those with EAL, we cannot assume that these learners are not competent or virtually fluent. We have included EAL here as a consideration of a potential barrier to learning that practitioners may need to plan for.

# Gypsy, Roma, Traveller communities

(With acknowledgements to Lisa Smith, Global Leader for Young Children World Forum Foundation, The Advisory Council for the Education of Romani and Other Travellers)

The term Gypsy, Roma and Travellers (sometimes shortened to GRT) is an umbrella term for what is actually a very diverse ethnic group. In the UK the two main groups to whom legal status is afforded are 'Gypsy/ Roma' and 'Irish Travellers' but there are many other sub-groups. The term 'Gypsy' encompasses many groups with tribal and geographical associations, e.g. 'Vlach Rom', 'Rom', 'Kalderash', and 'Luri'.

To be recognised as an '**ethnic group**', a group (such as GRT) must have the following characteristics: long shared history; cultural tradition of their own; common geographical origin; and a common language.

In 2003, GRT were added to the school census so the government could start collating statistical data. Irish Travellers are a separate and distinct ethnic group originating from Ireland. They share some of the same cultural values as Romani Gypsies, such as a preference for self-employment and living and travelling in caravans or 'trailers', but there are also big differences. For example, many Irish Travellers are Catholic and their language – 'Cant' – is not related at all to Romani. British Romani Gypsies are English, Scottish and Welsh. There has been central and eastern European Roma migration to the UK and GRT are Europe's largest and fastest growing ethnic minority.

Knowles and Lander (2011: Chapter 7) say that:

> the law has served not only to radically affect the life and traditional culture of Gypsies, but also to criminalise it … Is it surprising that some members of society continue to assume that Travellers are unclean and unwanted? Indeed, it is not surprising that those who are physically forced to live on the margins of society are also metaphorically thought of and treated like detritus by society.

In 2012 the government found a 90% decline in Traveller Education Services since 2010. They reported that GRT experience some of the worst outcomes of any group, across a wide range of social indicators. For example, there is an excess prevalence of miscarriages, stillbirths and neonatal deaths in GRT communities. Around 20% of traveller caravans are on unauthorised sites. GRT communities are subjected to hostility and discrimination, and in many places lead separate, parallel lives from the wider community (report found at: https://assets.publishing.service.gov.uk/government/uploads/system/uploads/attachment_data/file/6287/2124046.pdf).

As a result of this report, 28 commitments were made to the GRT community to tackle these issues, including highlighting GRT pupils as a vulnerable group in the revised Ofsted framework. In response to high levels of exclusion, the government were to take steps to assess the impact of school-based commissioning, alternative provision and early intervention. Ofsted were to conduct a survey on prejudice-based bullying (www.tes.com/news/need-know-gypsy-and-roma-educational-inequality).

By 2017, after exam reforms, the overall percentage of pupils achieving the expected standard in reading, writing and maths at the end of primary was 61% on average, compared to 16% among GRT pupils; 59.1% of all pupils achieved Grade 4 or above in English and Maths while only 10.7% of Gypsy and Roma and 22% of the Travellers of Irish heritage achieved this. There were still also high levels of permanent and fixed-term exclusions. Department for Education statistics for 2016–17 show that while

2.29% of all pupils have one or more fixed period exclusions, this rises to 7.1% of Gypsy/Roma pupils and 7.3% of Travellers of Irish heritage.

Nine out of ten CYP from a GRT background have suffered racial abuse and nearly two thirds have been bullied or physically attacked (Lane et al., 2014). **Discrimination** can be intentionally or unintentionally racist in character on account of the lack of knowledge of legal minority ethnic status. As result of this, behaviour may not be identified as racist and consequently not taken seriously in schools. High exclusion rates were often a result of physical retaliation to these incidents (Traveller Movement, 2016). Gypsy, Traveller and Roma pupils are on average four times more likely to be excluded from school than the whole school population. Research also found that 100% of appeals against the exclusions of Gypsy, Traveller and Roma pupils were successful, suggesting that many exclusions were unfairly given. Bhopal (2011) found that despite race equality policies being in place, racism experienced by GRT pupils was not dealt with adequately or effectively. Some parents may have had a negative experience of formal education themselves and may be distrustful of the school's ability to ensure their children's safety and well-being.

Travelling is no longer an obvious reason for academic under-achievement, as many GRT families don't travel. Even for many pupils with stable attendance, attainment is significantly lower than those of their peers (Derrington and Kendall, 2008). Nationally, attendance for GRT pupils has increased and continues to do so. Although transition rates from primary to secondary school remain high, the majority of GRT pupils will not complete a high school education. Fragmentation of the school system and increased pressure to raise standards often contradict inclusion policies. Some schools are refusing to admit children from this group imposing discriminatory conditions on admissions or delaying registration. Parents may have a limited experience of the formal education system or how it works and may find it difficult to access supportive resources or know how to access support to challenge unlawful practice.

Ofsted (2014) have repeatedly reported unreasonably low teacher expectations. There is a severe lack of knowledge or recognition of GRT ethnicity and culture in many schools. Research shows that where pupils' identity is devalued, they do not go on to develop to their full potential. Roles involving economic independence, entrepreneurship and self-employment are of high value in the community. In high school, some teenagers may find the curriculum not relatable to the practical knowledge and skills needed for this type of role and parents may feel the curriculum is not flexible enough to offer appropriate support for this type of growth. Persistent disruptive behaviour was the most common reason given for school exclusions of children from these communities, which could point to unmet need. However, GRT pupils are often viewed as oppositional to educational achievement.

# Looked after children

Section 17 of the Children Act 1989 placed a duty on local authorities to safeguard and promote the welfare of children 'in need' and provide a range and level of services to meet their needs. **Children in need** are those who require local authority services to achieve or maintain a reasonable standard of health or development, who need local authority services to prevent significant or further harm to health development, or who are disabled.

Services for children identified as 'in need' can include: Family support (to help keep together families experiencing difficulties); leaving care support (to help young people who have left local authority care); adoption support; and disabled children's services (including social care, education and health provision).

**Looked after children (LAC)**: Children in the care of the local authority. Section 47 of the 1989 Children Act states that social services have a duty to investigate if informed that a child in their area is suffering or is likely to suffer significant harm. There are 72,670 LAC and the number of LAC has increased steadily over the last nine years (DfE, 2016/2017). Provision for LAC should be child-centred based on the child's needs (www.gov.uk/government/uploads/system/uploads/attachment_data/file/647852/SFR50_2017-Children_looked_after_in_England.pdf).

Statutory Guidance for Local Authorities July 2014 (www.gov.uk/government/uploads/system/uploads/attachment_data/file/335964/Promoting_the_educational_achievement_of_looked_after_children_Final_23-....pdf).

Children Act 1989: Local Authorities (LAs) have a duty to safeguard and promote the welfare of a child looked after by them. This includes a duty to promote the child's educational achievement, wherever they live or are educated. The authority must give attention to the educational implications of any decision about the welfare of those children. The LA and LEA/school should work together to ensure that, except in an emergency, appropriate education provision for a child is arranged at the same time as a care placement.

Director of Children's Services (DCS): Has professional responsibility for the leadership and strategic effectiveness of local authority children's services. Independent Reviewing Officer (IRO): Every LAC must have a named IRO who is appointed to participate in case reviews and monitor the local authority's performance in relation to a child's case. *The 'Virtual School Head'* should co-ordinate educational services for LAC within each LA area. Each school should have a *'designated teacher'* to oversee all LAC in the school. Children must have an appointed *social worker* and other support as required.

## Reflection Activity

**Primary experiences**

(www.youtube.com/watch?v=DAfxqer1UP4)

What are the issues that hold back LAC?

Are these issues to do with learning, social or psychological factors?

How does the school address them?

**Secondary experiences**

(www.youtube.com/watch?v=J7EgWVfMne4)

What are the views of the children? What needs to change?

How does this relate to how schools and society in general view LAC?

Do you think that schools create an 'enabling environment' for LAC? (Think about the social and medical models.)

What improvements can be made to increase success?

Now we have explored some of the factors that could affect a learner's educational experience, we also need to consider what happens if a learner has multiple influencing factors, i.e. intersectionality.

 ## Spotlight on Theory: Intersectionality

The interaction between gender, race, and other categories of difference in individual lives, social practices and cultural ideologies and the outcomes of these interactions in terms of power. (Davis, 2008: 68)

*(Continued)*

> Watch: Kimberlie Crenshaw: The urgency of intersectionality: (www.ted.com/talks/kimberle_crenshaw_the_urgency_of_intersectionality)
>
> Factors involved in intersectionality include power – intersectionality usually involves multiple-minority identities, which are often the least powerful groups– and multiple discrimination: intersectionality means that a person may be discriminated against on a number of different fronts. Often, intersectional experiences reveal that existing legal and policy mechanisms are stacked against people with a multiple minority identity. And these institutions may fail to account for critical cultural differences.
>
> Intersectionality refers to the hierarchal nature of power and how a person who belongs to many marginalised groups may have some of their issues from other identities ignored. Legal and political mechanisms generally think of all problems separately, which may leave out other identities. With intersectionality in place, legal and political mechanisms can look at the big picture, rather than separating a person's problems into small parts and ignoring some of these.

Moving on from mainstream education, which might not work or is not appropriate for some learners, we turn to considerations of alternative provision

# Pupil referral units

(www.independent.co.uk/news/education/schools/pupil-referral-units-the-children-beyond-mainstream-education-and-the-schools-that-turn-their-lives-a6713976.html)

The current incarnation of Pupil Referral Units (PRUs) came about in 1993 during John Major's government. There are now just under 400 in England and Wales. More than 20,000 pupils are catered for by 'alternative provision', the umbrella term under which PRUs fall. Because of the need for a high staff-to-student ratio, the units tend to be small, with some teaching just a handful of pupils.

A PRU is a school that accommodates the most (perceived) troubled and disruptive of pupils, fulfilling local authority obligations to educate all children, including those expelled from mainstream schools. PRUs also provide education for teenage mothers, and children with physical and mental health issues that prevent them attending mainstream school. The aim is to put as many pupils as possible back on an even keel and then reintroduce them to mainstream schools.

Often, children come to PRUs with unmet learning needs. Staff at PRUs may be trained in psychological diagnostic techniques – and pupils are frequently found to have communication or educational difficulties. In many cases, these children have adopted bad behaviour as a defence mechanism. By acting up they distract teachers from the fact that they do not understand what they are being taught. The Pendlebury Centre makes use of drama therapists, a cognitive behavioural therapist, a bereavement councillor, social workers, a family liaison worker, one psychotherapist for the children and another one for the staff.

> In their eyes, normal is just being able to come to school. These children are often here because they have had an emotional experience which they have struggled to come to terms with. Our job is to give them the space to do that while making sure their learning continues. (Janice Cahill, Headteacher – Pendlebury Centre)

Other alternative schools include:

- The Boxing Academy: Uses sport to help 'disruptive' young male students regulate their behaviour.
- Everton Free School: Uses football to re-engage excluded children with education.
- Family School: Strong emphasis on mental health therapies, bringing children's family members into the classroom.

# Special schools

Current English government policies identify a role for special schools in both transforming mainstream education and continuing to provide specialist support for individual needs (DfE and DoH, 2014: 28; Fredrickson and Cline, 2015: 82). Department for Education data on SEN provision shows that the proportion of pupils with statements/EHC plans attending special schools has been increasing since 2007. By contrast, the percentage attending secondary schools has fallen by a similar amount. The percentage attending primary schools has remained constant and there has been a small increase in the percentage attending other settings such as independent schools, alternative provision and non-maintained special schools.

## Time to Reflect

What does the data tell you about mainstream vs special/alternative provision in terms of SEND?

Note that some learners may have part-time placements, attend specialist units attached to mainstream schools, be home educated or have dual registration.

## Key Points

In this chapter you have:

- Explored equality legislation and its impact on inclusive practice.
- Looked at influencing factors that affect the learners' experience including disability, EAL, LAC and GRT.
- Considered the impact the learning environment may have on these factors, and gained an introductory understanding of alternative provision to mainstream education.

## Final Reflection Questions

- In your experience, are people treated equally? If not, why not?
- What are the barriers/enablers to equality?

# Further reading

This insightful chapter provides information on the effects of using creativity in prison education:

Taylor, S. (2017). Inclusion and the arts. In R. Woolley (ed.), *Understanding Inclusion: Core Concepts, Policy, Practice*. London: Routledge.

This book gives further insights into considerations for equality and inclusion within school settings:

Goepel, J., Childerhouse, H. and Sharpe, S. (2015). *Inclusive Primary Teaching: A Critical Approach to Equality and Special Educational Needs and Disability*. Northwich: Critical Publishing.

This book provides you with a deeper understanding of the concepts of 'family' and 'difference':

Knowles, G. and Holmstrom, R. (2013). *Understanding Family Diversity and Home-School Relations: A Guide for Students and Practitioners in Early Years and Primary Settings*. London: Routledge.

# 7

# ASSISTIVE TECHNOLOGIES IN PRACTICE

Dr Alexandra Sewell.

---

## Introduction

We live in a technology-rich society. Assistive technology can be fundamental in helping people access daily living and educational opportunities. This chapter will:

- Define what assistive technology is and outline how theory and legislation support its use.
- Explore various types of assistive technology that help with communication, support those with visual and hearing impairments, encourage social development and enable access in a classroom.
- Consider the impact of assistive technology use on identity development.

# What is assistive technology?

**Technology** is a term we are all familiar with as it permeates every aspect of our working and resting day. From a social science perspective, sociologist Bain's (1937) broad definition of technology is often referred to: this identifies technology as any item produced and used by a human being. This includes 'tools, machines, utensils, weapons, instruments, housing, clothing, communicating and transport devices' (Bain, 1937: 860). As such, technology is fully integrated with our modern human world; it is an essential aspect of how we live our lives. This integration has its antecedents in the historical invention and use of tools by humans.

**Assistive technology** has been more specifically defined as 'any item, piece of equipment, or product system, whether acquired commercially off the shelf, modified, or customised, that is used to increase, maintain, or improve the functional capabilities of a child with a disability' (Edyburn, 2004: 16). Edyburn (2004) points out that assistive technology can be absolutely anything and is positioned as being so if it is adaptive – that is if it modifies some aspect of the individual so they can perform daily life functions with the device, which they previously couldn't. In summary, it is not some formal property of the item or the device that classifies it as assistive technology, but whether it alters and modifies some aspect of the user's daily functioning.

# Classifications of assistive technology

Assistive technologies can be classified in one of two ways, by level of assistance or category of assistance. With level of assistance, the technology is classified by the degree of complexity which it encompasses (Bouck, 2015). This ranges from **no-tech, low-tech, mid-tech** to **high-tech**. For example, a timetable to organise your learning would be considered no-tech, use of visual communication systems would be low-tech, mobile apps would be considered mid-tech and a laptop or advanced technology such as eye gaze tracking would be considered high-tech.

Level of technology should not be confused with utility or impact of technology for producing meaningful change for the individual user. No-tech to low-tech can be just as impactful, if not more so, than high-tech. In a society characterised by exponential technology development, high-tech and new-tech can be automatically assumed to be superior. However, no-tech or low-tech is often favourable for being more cost-effective for individuals and institutions seeking access to assistive technology.

Assistive technologies can also be categorised according to their purpose. Bryant et al. (2010) outlined the following seven categories:

1. *Positioning* – technology that supports a person with seating or position.
2. *Mobility* – technology that assists movement and mobility.
3. *Augmentive and Alternative Communication (ACC)* – technology that assists communication and speech development.
4. *Computer access* – technology that supports access to computer use.
5. *Adaptive toys and games* – technology that supports access to leisure and play activities.
6. *Adaptive environments* – technology that supports daily living skills and functioning.
7. *Instructional aids* – technology that supports the development of learning skills, such as literacy or numeracy.

Categorising technology by function can benefit a community understanding of assistive technology. For example, when new devices are created their purpose can be clearly and easily communicated to the correct potential users. However, as assistive technology develops in line with wider technological improvements, we may see that demarcation by function isn't relevant. As technology is further integrated into daily living it is likely to fulfil a wider range of daily functions simultaneously.

# Legislation and policy

In the UK, Section 22 of the Chronically Sick and Disabled Person's Act (1970) paved the way for subsequent legislation that has implications for how technology and design should be implemented in improving the daily inclusion of those with disabilities. The Act stated that the local authority and schools had to ensure that buildings, including public facilities like toilets and recreational facilities like parks, would be accessible to all. This led to increased use of adaptive environments as they helped improve access to community spaces. Equally, public transport and transport to school had to be accessible to all, leading to technological innovation, such as the addition of hydraulic lifts to newly designed buses.

The Disability Discrimination Act (1995) and the Equality Act (2010) extended the duty to ensure that 'reasonable adjustments' are put in place to improve access for individuals with a disability. The first requirement refers to a 'provision, criterion or practice' that would put a person with a disability at a significant disadvantage. For example, a class teacher using only one type of teaching style to teach phonics without considering a reasonable adjustment of differentiation to support those with additional needs. The second requirement refers to that of a physical barrier, such as adding a ramp over steps to ensure a wheelchair user can access a school building. The third requirement is that, in cases where without the help of an auxiliary aid a disabled person would be disadvantaged, an auxiliary aid should be made available.

With increasing use and reliance on the internet to complete daily living functions, the Public Sector Bodies (Websites and Mobile Applications) Accessibility Regulations (2018) extended the duty of public sector bodies to ensure that their web pages are accessible for all, including via mobile phone apps. For example, photos on a website can be made accessible for someone with impaired vision via alt text captions. These describe the picture. Use of a screen reader can help access this information.

 ### Spotlight on Theory: Universal Design for Learning

Universal Design for Learning (UDL) is a useful conceptual framework for appreciating how each assistive technology device may support inclusion in a learning setting. UDL developed from the Universal Design (UD) movement in architecture in the 1980s (Rose, 2000). The main premise of UD is that design of a building, or design of any technology device, should be developed so it is usable and accessible by all individuals from the outset (Story, 1998). This is contrasted with a process of design where the design takes a normative approach and then is later adapted to be inclusive of difference and disability, known as retrofitting (Story, 1998). In addition, UD takes the approach that what is useful from a design perspective for those with difference and disability will generally benefit all users (Story, 2001).

UDL has extended these principles to the classroom setting. It too rejects retrofitting, stating that from a learning perspective this would be akin to strategies such as differentiation of a general lesson plan (Bracken and Novak, 2019; Rose, 2000). Instead, it puts forth the need to design learning experiences so that they are inclusive of all learners from the beginning. Bracken and Novak (2019) conceptualise UDL as a framework upon which both existing teaching practice and new strategies can be understood and reformulated to be inclusive. This framework consists of three aspects termed 'learning networks', each one with an accompanying principle (Stanford and Reeves, 2009).

Aspect one is the recognition network and the accompanying principal of offering multiple means of representation. This is considered the 'what' of learning and is concerned with how information is presented, i.e. what teaching strategies are used. Assistive technology that allows information to be presented in different ways would be related to this aspect. For example, if a teacher uses a whole-class visual representation of instructions, such as a visual timetable, this may benefit those with communication difficulties but will also be useful for all as it clearly outlines what tasks will occur during the lesson.

Aspect two is the strategic network and the accompanying principal of offering many means for action and expression. This is known as the 'how' of learning and references how individuals plan and execute learning tasks. It is about offering a range of ways for learners to express their ideas and what they know. Any use of assistive technology that allows for different ways for learners to do this would be said to fall under this aspect. For example, a student with visual impairment may use specific technology to write their assignment and may wish to submit electronically for this reason, even if a physical copy is required.

Aspect three is the affective network and the accompanying principal of multiple means of engagement. This is referred to as the 'why' of learning and explores the emotive and experiential side of learning, what engages and interests the student. An assistive technology device that taps into this aspect would provide enjoyment and interest. For example, there are a range of learning apps that utilise a bright and colorful interface, fun characters and a game element to engage their users. If a teacher made these available for all pupils, in addition to more traditional learning strategies, it would be in line with this aspect.

# Augmented and Alternative Communication (AAC)

Augmented and Alternative Communication (AAC) is any assistive technology device that supports an individual to communicate with others. This means making their wants, needs, opinions and desires known. There are three categories of AAC: *unaided, non-electronic aided* and *electronic aided*. Unaided refers to communication that is not external to the individual. For example, **British Sign Language** and **Makaton** involve a person learning to make signs with their hands and gestures to communicate.

Time to Reflect

Look at the picture in Figure 7.1 of an Italian train ticket. Consider how the design of the ticket would be inclusive for those with difference and disability but would also benefit all users. Consider how the information is presented and the use of symbols.

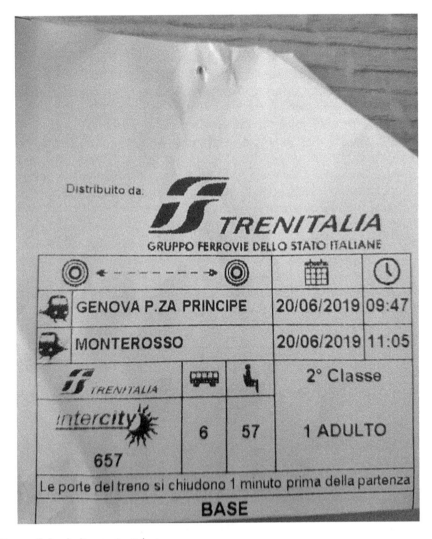

**Figure 7.1**   Italian train ticket

Non-electronic aided refers to the use of a device that is external to the individual but isn't electronic. A well-known example of this is the Picture Exchange Communication System (PECS). This system involves individuals learning to associate a picture printed on a card with the actual item or activity. They can point to or give the card to someone to communicate a desire for that item or activity.

There is a substantial literature exploring PEC's efficacy. Preston and Carter (2009) conclude that there is some limited evidence that PECS is easy to learn and improves **functional communication**, which is using communication to make wants and needs known to others. However, there is little evidence to ascertain if it leads to language development more generally. Hart and Banda's (2010) review also concludes that PECS improves functional communication but reported an additional positive effect of a reduction in challenging behaviour and some increases in use of speech. Further reviews have confirmed these findings (Sulzer-Azaroff et al., 2009).

Electronic AAC, also known as Speech Generating Devices (SGD) or Voice Output Communication Aids (VOCAs), are assistive technology devices external to the individual that would fall into the high-tech category. Such devices can vary in design, but typically follow the same underlying principles as PECS and other such systems/devices. With high-tech the way in which individuals access the communication system can differ, such as the use of eye gaze technology where a user focuses on a symbol or word with their eyes and the device will then select this as the communicative symbol they wish to use (Hutchinson et al., 1989).

In summary, AAC is a successful field of assistive technology which can lead to increased quality of life for a range of users (Caligari et al., 2013; Hamm and Mirenda, 2006; McNaughton and Bryen, 2007). After conducting a meta-analysis of the literature for AAC devices, O'Neill et al. (2018) found that AAC use can improve functional communication and expression for users. However, with regard to longer-term language development, they found that there was limited evidence and called for further research.

# Assistive technology for hearing impairment and visual impairment

The development and use of assistive technology for those with visual impairment has grown rapidly in the 21st century. Bhowmick and Hazarika (2017) demonstrate this growth by reporting a high increase in the number of scientific papers published on the topic, from 50 publications during the 1990s to 400 publications per year by 2014. Increased use has occurred across a range of activities in the contexts of learning, work and Leisure. The more common examples of assistive technology devices used by individuals with a visual impairment are:

- Service dogs: Specially trained to help an individual with a visual impairment complete a wide range of daily tasks such as fetching items, and navigating movement such as crossing the road safely.
- Canes: Individuals are trained to use a cane as a mobility aid to safely manoeuvre in new environments.
- Electronic mobility aids: These types of devices use ultrasonic waves to bounce off oncoming obstacles in the environment.
- Reading assistance: These constitute a range of devices that help an individual read words on paper or electronically. For example, the JAWS screen reader will take text on a computer screen and turn it into speech.
- Augmented and virtual reality approaches: These types of devices can support individuals who experience peripheral/tunnel vision loss, where glasses are worn and computer generated augmented and virtual reality images are projected to complete the missing field of vision.

In a teaching and learning context assistive technology can improve attainment and engagement in learning for individuals with visual impairment. Improved access to written materials and resources planned as part of a lesson or activity can improve reading and writing skills. For example, Kamali Arslantas et al.'s (2019) web-based vocabulary building programme aimed to be accessible for those with visual impairment and found that it led to substantial progress in vocabulary test scores. Use of assistive technology has also been reported to improve quality of school life by providing such a crucial facilitative role in the learning process (Hersh and Johnson, 2010). Barriers to assistive technology use in education include a lack of specialist advice and training for educational professionals, as well as limited access to computers and specialist technology (Alves et al., 2009).

Likewise, assistive technology has made a substantial contribution to educational access and improvement in quality of life for individuals with a hearing impairment. Typically, devices are concerned with conveying language-based information that would usually be communicated verbally to the individual. The most common examples of these are as follow.

## Devices to assist listening

- This group of technologies aim to assist with difficulty with hearing. One common example is the cochlear implant which is implanted surgically and improves the sense of sound for those with sensorineural hearing loss.
- A classroom-based example is an FM system which a teacher can wear. Sound emitted by the teacher wearing the system is sent via radio signals to the student's receiving device.

## Devices to present information visually

- Visual alerting devices alert a person to sound using a visual stimulus. For example, when a fire alarm sounds a light will also flash.
- Captioning is where verbal linguistic information is presented in visual language form for a range of media.

## Summary

As with assistive technology for visual impairment, the research literature has demonstrated that devices generally improve access to learning and raise engagement and attainment. Rekkedal (2012) found that students with hearing impairments who used assistive technology generally reported positive attitudes towards the devices and felt that they supported them to learn.

# Assistive technology and psycho-social intervention

The continual evolution of high-tech assistive technology has resulted in an interest in its application to psycho-social problems, such as experiences of mental ill health and difficulties with social interaction. Virtual reality has been at the forefront of this expansion into these areas of human difficulty. Whilst this area of technology and research into it can both be said to be in their infancy, the results of emergent studies are promising.

**Virtual Reality (VR)** environments have been developed to support individuals with social cognition difficulties, such as people with Autism Spectrum Condition (ASC), to practise their social skills in a way that is socially non-threatening (Kandalaft et al., 2013; Parsons and Mitchell, 2002; Politis et al.,

2019). Whereas social skills training has traditionally included practice with real people, VR allows practice within an augmented environment. This has the added advantage of promoting generalisation of new social skills to a range of contexts and has been shown to lead to improvements in emotional regulation and social understanding (Parsons and Mitchell, 2002; Kandalaft et al., 2013). **Participatory design** has been proposed to allow individuals with autism to also help design VR environments that will support them. Using this method, Politis et al. (2019) designed a VR environment to support the development of conversation skills.

Traditional therapies, such as Cognitive Behaviour Therapy (CBT), have also begun to utilise VR to reach therapeutic goals. For example, exposure therapy is used to treat anxiety disorders, such as specific phobias. The individual is gradually exposed to what causes their anxiety but is taught anxiety reduction and management techniques to meet the increasing level of challenge. The use of VR in exposure therapy has numerous advantages, including improved safety. Research has shown that exposure therapy conducted in VR environments is as effective as real-life environments, but not more effective (Carl et al., 2019). As such, it offers a valid alternative. This finding has been replicated with specific populations, such as individuals with autism who have specific phobias (Maskey et al., 2019). Similarly, VR has been used to expose individuals with Post-Traumatic Stress Disorder (PTSD) to virtual simulations of the traumatic event, guided by a therapist to support changes in thoughts towards the event. This technique has been shown to reduce post-traumatic symptoms in the moment which leads to a longer-term reduction in associated depressive symptoms (Peskin et al., 2019).

Clearly, the use of VR in psycho-social intervention is exciting as the results of current research are promising. Whilst widespread use by CBT therapists is not yet reported, surveys of CBT therapists' attitudes have found that VR is positively received and that as the financial cost of equipment has reduced the uptake of VR has increased (Lindner et al., 2019).

# Instructional aids: Assistive technology in the classroom

Instructional aids are assistive technological tools and devices that support learning. According to Bouck (2015) there are two categories of instructional aids: those concerned with access and achievement and those designed to support teaching delivery. The first category includes assistive technology that seeks to include individuals with SEND in learning opportunities and raise their achievement, and the second has a more general scope in enhancing teaching practice. Table 7.1 gives some examples from low-tech to high-tech for a few different skills.

**Table 7.1** Assistive technologies – low-tech to high-tech

|  | Low-tech | Medium-tech | High-tech |
|---|---|---|---|
| **Reading** | Using a piece of paper to cover most of the visual text and then revealing one line at a time to facilitate concentration and attention during reading | Audio books | A text-to-speech reading pen (see: 'C-pen exam reader' at www.readerpen.com) |
| **Writing** | A pencil grip | Access to a keyboard to type instead of write | Dictaphone |
| **Maths** | A number line or an abacus | Calculators | Apps such as 'photo math' where the phone's camera is used to take a picture of a sum and ideas for completing the sum are generated by the app (see: www.photomath.com) |

From looking at the examples above you have likely seen many everyday uses of instructional aids which are fully integrated into the modern classroom. Research seeking to assess the impact of instructional aids for learning initially analysed their effectiveness by exploring the extent to which they supported learners' recall of information (Haertel and Means, 2003). By the end of the 20th century, high-tech instructional aids that involved the support of a computer were viewed as a way of overcoming resource-based barriers to teaching, such as time dedicated to teaching. This was particularly so for pupils with SEND who often required interventions that consisted of time, intensity and consistency in instruction (Woodward and Rieth, 1997).

More recent research into instructional aids has continued to focus on the goal of knowledge retention. For example, Barnyak and McNelly (2016) assessed whether summer access to non-fiction eBooks would improve vocabulary scores in a sample of children, when compared to non-access. Access to summer eBooks did not improve vocabulary scores. However, in the early 21st century a wider scope of analysis for instructional aids has begun to be adopted. For example, Barnyak and McNelly (2016) collected data to see if access to eBooks would lead to an increase in positive reading attitudes, which it did. Smith (2000) outlined a range of further outcomes that the analysis of instructional aids could be based on.

Included in these were cost – not only to purchase but also in terms of how long it took a user to complete a learning task – the need for educational professionals to engage in further training or not, and users' views of how the device performed.

---

### Case Study: Maisy

Maisy McAdam is a higher education student studying for a degree in Special Educational Needs, Disability and Inclusion. She is blind and regularly uses assistive technology. Here she writes about her initial embarrassment with assistive technology and how she overcame it:

'I am a millennial, so I like avocado on toast and my phone. I got my first mobile phone at 10 years old and have had one ever since. I've always loved reading blogs and forums on my phone. When I lost my sight, I thought that was all going to be a thing of the past until I was introduced to the world of assistive technology. Like many disabled people assistive technology has greatly improved my ability to live an independent life. But my journey to accepting the use of assistive technology wasn't a smooth one.

I lost my sight aged 15 and at the time I and those around me had no idea about the technology that was available. For several months my mother was supporting me to get online. It isn't what any teenager wants. When I was told about the various types of speech software available it was a huge insight.

One of the biggest fears for my family was the cost of assistive technology. Luckily, all Apple products are built with software already installed called "Voice Over". In the early days of using Voice Over I was embarrassed to use it around my friends. It isn't especially discreet, and the voice is robotic and monotonous. This embarrassment began to change when I met a teacher of assistive technology. She was also blind and used her software so efficiently that it motivated me to become as good as her.

It wasn't long before I was able to use the Voice Over on my phone with the voice set to a high speed. It soon occurred to me that it was nothing to be embarrassed about, people generally are interested and impressed at the software and think it's amazing. Soon I was able to jump back into the online world, connecting with friends and family. Accessing online communities made up of other disabled people has become important and enjoyable for me.'

# Assistive technology and identity

In this chapter an understanding of assistive technology has been developed through the perspective of form and function; we have focused on the following questions:

- How are assistive technology devices designed?
- What task do they fulfil for the user?

Whilst the research literature for assistive technology is predominantly concerned with these questions, other researchers take an interest in the personal effects of technology use. Questions of concern are related more to the self and personal experience, such as:

- How does a person's use of assistive technology affect their sense of who they are?
- How does a person's use of assistive technology impact on how others view them and react to them?

Identity is how we view ourselves; how we socially construct who we are in relation to others. This notion is explored in Chapter 10 through the theories of positionality and social identity theory. Sometimes, we may notice that others have created an identity for us, based on both tangible and intangible characteristics they perceive us to possess. The identity they project onto us may be at odds with our own self-image and understanding of who we are. Research in the field of disability studies and critical theory often explores the process of 'othering' in reference to this experience. '**Othering**' is a useful concept through which to explore identity formation in individuals with disability and the role that assistive technology use plays in this.

'Othering' occurs when an individual is identified by their personal characteristics and features as falling outside of the socio-culturally defined parameters of a normative personhood (Clapton and Fitzgerald, 1997). For example, in a workplace setting research has shown that workers with a disability can be defined by their colleagues as being 'other' based on physical bodily difference and visual impairments (Mik-Meyer, 2016). Inherent in this 'othering' process is the risk of stereotyped and stigmatising judgements (Mik-Meyer, 2016). Clapton and Fitzgerald (1997) propound that this problematises the role of the human body in social interactions in their claim that 'our bodies write our stories' (p.1).

Assistive technology devices can be positioned as physical extensions of the body when worn by users. Ravenberg and Söderström (2017) term them 'identity markers' as they play a role in showing difference to a perceived norm as part of the 'othering process'. This pivotal role in the making of identity can impact assistive technology use, such as the abandonment of the device because it makes the user feel like they 'stand out' in social situations (Ravenberg and Söderström, 2017).

Lupton and Seymour (2000) explored this by interviewing 13 individuals with a disability who used assistive technology. The positives of technology were highlighted, such as allowing social integration with others, which was said to occur if the technology was 'invisible'. In this case it would not make a user stand out from others, and thus its role as an 'identity marker' was reduced. However, assistive technology could make those interviewed feel 'different' if it was large, obvious and led them to engaging in daily tasks in a different way to a perceived norm. This raises important questions about assistive technology design; not only should it aim to improve access to daily life tasks but should consider social integration as well.

Assistive technology can also offer an introduction to and inclusion in social spaces and activities previously not accessible to users. This enables users to form social relationships in a wider community. Williams (1993) argues that this leads to new opportunities for identity formation. In this context, research has found that the obviousness of the assistive technology device to others is downplayed in favour of social relationships and the impact these have on how identity is constructed and understood. This was also found to be the case by Øien et al. (2015) who interviewed nine 5 to 6 year olds with cerebral palsy who used assistive technology devices in the classroom. The positive view reported was that the devices enabled children to engage in a wider range of classroom activities. This enhanced selfhood through the opportunity to enact culturally valued versions of social play previously inaccessible to them.

 Key Points

- Assistive technology is clearly defined not by formal properties but the extent to which it helps a person access educational and daily living activities not accessible to them without the device.
- Assistive technology can be categorised by the level of tech involved and by function.

- Assistive technology can support users in a wide range of domains including communication, supporting those with visual and hearing impairments, encouraging social development and enabling access in a classroom.
- Identity-formation is impacted by assistive technology use. If a device is conspicuous it can make a person with a disability feel 'othered'. However, devices can also improve access to social situations and so indirectly affect identity.

 Final Reflection Questions

- As technology and assistive technology are fast-growing fields of research, what areas of learning and functional living skills should be prioritised?
- Consider the assistive technology devices and tools reviewed in this chapter; which aspects of the UDL framework would they potentially map onto?

# Further reading

This book gives a comprehensive introduction to UDL and explores how it can make higher education teaching and learning more inclusive:

Bracken, S. and Novak, K. (2019). *Transforming Higher Education through Universal Design for Learning: An International Perspective*. London: Routledge.

This interesting research paper describes how AAC systems can be designed so specific speech phrases are made available in certain geographical locations by using GPS, such as 'can I have a coffee please' being made available on a device when a person is in a coffee shop:

Hossain, M.S., Takanokura, M. and Nakashima, K. (2018). Design of a location-aware augmented and alternative communication system to support people with language and speech disorders. *Journal of Alternative Medicine Research*, *10*(1), 81–88.

This journal article outlines the range of assistive technology that can be used to enhance classroom teaching:

Netherton, D.L. and Deal, W.F. (2006). Assistive technology in the classroom. *The Technology Teacher*, 66(1), 10.

# 8
# SEND: A GLOBAL PERSPECTIVE

Gareth Dart

## Introduction

It is estimated that there are 150 million Children and Young People (CYP) living with a major disability in the world today (WHO, 2011), the great majority of whom live in low- and middle-income countries (LMICs). This chapter explores the ways in which their disability makes it far less likely that they will attend school and/or achieve a good quality education (UNESCO, 2013), as well as various policy and practical responses to this challenge. In this chapter you will:

- Explore information from key sources that provide data about the situation of learners with SEND in **low- and middle-income countries** (LMICs).
- Use this data to consider the challenges facing learners with SEND, considering the notion of 'intersectionality'.
- Become familiar with various international declarations and conventions that help shape policy and practice regarding provision for SEND globally.
- Consider what evidence exists for good practice in such contexts.

### Case Study: The Chief Part A

An American friend of the author, Ron, with years of experience of special education and disability rehabilitation in various African and Asian countries, was working with Kenyan colleagues in a rural area of the country. They had managed to open a rehabilitation centre for children with disabilities and were very excited because it was the first service of any sort for people with disabilities in that area. They had been visiting the local villages letting the communities know about this excellent new resource. As they entered one remote village Ron saw two children with microcephaly coming down the path. He and his colleagues eagerly sought out the chief of the village to inform him of the new possibilities for these two children.

### Time to Reflect

What might have been the possible responses of the chief to their news and offer?

### Case Study: The Chief Part B

The chief welcomed them warmly to the village and listened carefully to the news about the new rehabilitation centre and Ron's suggestion that this would be an excellent opportunity for the two children with microcephaly. The chief thought for a while and then told his visitors the following. He said that he was glad to hear the news of the centre and grateful that they had come to tell the community. However, these two children had an important role in the village as they helped fetch water each day. This meant that they were valuable members of the community and that they were treated with great respect by the village. What would happen if they went to the rehabilitation centre each day? They would lose their purpose in the village and the village would lose valuable members of the community.

### Time to Reflect

What are your thoughts on the response of the chief?

We return to this story later in the chapter, but it is a useful starting point as it illustrates many of the key issues that we will explore and discuss here.

# General picture: Education

Special and inclusive education takes place in the broader context of education in general and it is worth briefly considering the great changes that have swept through this sector globally over the last three decades. Although media reports and academic texts often seem to focus on the challenges and failures of the development of formal education, the truth is that extraordinary progress has been made in providing access to basic education globally (World Bank, 2018). The number of children not in school in the world 'almost halved between 2000 and 2011, dropping from 102 million to 57 million' (Howgego et al., 2014: 3). Much of this can be attributed to the abolition of school fees in response to the agenda of Education for All, a global agreement dating back to 1990 (UNESCO, 2013).

Challenges of course remain. The UNESCO (2015) global monitoring report notes that some parts of the world have fared better than others: the picture in sub-Saharan Africa remains challenging, there have been huge questions regarding the quality of education that children are receiving whilst they are at school, and such enormous increases in school attendance put massive strains on the supply of qualified teachers, adequate classrooms and other resources. Moreover, to bring us to the focus of this chapter, children with disabilities are the group least likely to have benefitted from this increased enrolment and least likely to benefit from education even if they do attend school (UNICEF, 2013).

# General picture: Disability

Again, before we focus on issues of SEND at the school level, let us take a broader view and examine the status of people with disabilities more generally in LMICs to better understand the context within which education operates.

## Prevalence

The World Report on Disability (WHO, 2011) is viewed as providing the most reliable source currently available on disability data and statistics (Al Ju'beh, 2015: 12). It claims that worldwide there are over a billion people with a form of disability, approximately 15% of the world's population. Rohwerder (2015: 7) notes that Mitra and Sambamoorthi (2014: 940) reach a similar figure (14%) using the same data though using a different methodology. Rohwerder (p.7) reports that both sources:

> ... also find that disability prevalence is: higher in low- and middle-income countries than in high-income countries; among people aged 65 and above (39 per cent) than among working age adults (12 per cent); and among women (18.5 per cent) than men (12.1 per cent).

Of particular interest is the assertion from the WHO report (2011) that prevalence rates are set to rise and that of these 1 billion people, around 93 million children under the age of 14 years old have a severe or moderate disability, and four out of every five children with disabilities live in LMICs. Research demonstrates that not only are children with disabilities less likely to go to school than children without, but they are also more likely to drop out if they do go (EFA, 2015: 11).

## Difficulties with estimating numbers

However, consistent, comparable, accurate data is extremely difficult to come by and so figures need to be treated with caution (Singhal, 2019: 42). Take this example from the Kingdom of Jordan, an LMIC, as presented by Al Jabery et al. (2012). They report that a survey of the general population in 2004 revealed a rate of disability of 1.3%. This contrasts dramatically with the WHO (2011) general global estimate of 15%.

---

   Time to Reflect

- What might account for this discrepancy?
- Why might accurate data on the prevalence of disability in LMICs in general be difficult to come by?

---

Compare your thoughts on this with those of the authors, who consider that this is probably a major underestimation and explain the discrepancy thus:

> Several factors make estimating prevalence rates extremely difficult. These include... lack of formal definitions, societal attitudes, lack of qualified

professionals, limited diagnostic and assessment tools… A main reason may be the survey's ignorance of high prevalence disability categories… (Al Jabery et al., 2012: 197–198)

As you probably noted in your discussion above there are many challenges to the collection of good-quality data on the prevalence of disability in LMICs. These include a lack of personnel trained in such methods, the necessary resources to carry out such surveys, a lack of political will and commitment to such endeavours (a country might be struggling with very basic development needs such as the supply of clean water, electricity, basic schooling etc.; UNICEF, 2014), the low status of people with disabilities in society, different conceptions of what it means to be disabled, and crucially the lack of simple, usable tools or instruments to gather such data in a manner that allows for the agglomeration of such data across different national contexts.

Regarding this point it is worth noting that there have been positive developments over the last decade. **The Washington Group** have developed a set of diagnostic tools that are simple to use and assess disability and functioning as an outcome of the interaction between the local environment and a person's health conditions (Disability Africa, 2018; Singhal, 2019). Examples of the tools are worth studying and can be found by searching online for 'The Washington Group Short Set of Questions on Disability'.

## Position in society

Great care has to be taken in making global claims about the position of people with disabilities in various societies as there is no 'single story'. The concept of disability can be viewed in many ways depending on the impairment, societal norms, individuals' beliefs, and current contexts (Rohwerder, 2015: 1). Take the story that opened the chapter. In that rural Kenyan village, the two young people were not defined in terms of their impairment (microcephaly) but rather in terms of their role in the community (valued fetchers of water). Modern, literacy-based schooling has created a whole new category of 'learning disabled' students whose disability would have been entirely invisible in a traditional pre-literate society. Indeed, it is possible that the diverse thinking skills that many of these children appear to display might have been a real asset in such societies.

Nevertheless, it is true that people with disabilities worldwide often face discrimination, misunderstanding, rejection and lack of opportunities. The charity Disability Africa (2018: 4) notes that:

… disabled people have been 'left behind' principally due to a lack of under-standing about disability and associated negative attitudes, not so much due to impairments themselves. Whilst this issue is absolutely not unique to LMICs, studies have found that social attitudes towards disabled people in LMICs can be more extreme and the degree of stigma and shame can be greater than in higher income contexts.

---

 Spotlight on Research

Consider this extract reporting on research from Andhra Pradesh, a state in India:

> Research … in the early 2000s asked people about whether disabil-ity was a punishment or curse of God. The researchers found around 40 percent of respondents agreeing that it was, with the share of people holding such views increasing with age, being higher among women, higher for lower socio-economic groups, and higher for those who were illiterate. Interestingly, there was not a major difference in such views between urban and rural respond-ents… (World Bank, 2007: 2.3)

---

 Time to Reflect

What might be the impact on people with disabilities and their families if they are viewed as being 'punished by God'? How might this impact on their ability to access education?

---

It should be stressed that this is not the case for all children or all con-texts, and indeed such views were also common in many western countries until relatively recently, but such interpretations are common across many LMICs and can lead to children being kept or even hidden at home. As Disability Africa note:

> … negative attitudes and stigma surrounding disability ultimately result in disabled children being comprehensively deprived of their fundamental needs. Disabled children who are excluded from their communities are likely to be deprived of healthcare, education, social interaction and even food. (Disability Africa, 2018: 2)

## Factors intersecting with disability

It is important to recognise when discussing disability in the context of LMICs that there are often other factors intersecting with disability that compound the challenges that children and their families face. Poverty, undernutrition, poor health and an unsafe, or insanitary, home environment may impact a child's cognitive, motor and social and emotional development, putting them at greater risk of disability and educational exclusion (Howgego et al., 2014; WHO, 2011). Other factors that interact with disability include gender, geographic location and the impact of natural and man-made disasters. Lynch et al. (2014) report that girls with albinism in Malawi are less likely to attend resource centres than boys, and Mitra et al. (2013: 1) report on a study covering 15 different countries which found that 'disability was significantly associated with higher multi-dimensional poverty as well as lower educational attainment, lower employment rates, and higher medical expenditures'.

## Access to schooling

Research indicates a major challenge surrounding inclusive education in LMICs is the dearth of good quality research regarding it. Price (2018) notes that:

> Although there has been an increase of research in the last 5 years, robust, empirical evidence for low- and middle-income countries is still lacking, and difficulties around clear definitions of inclusive education and comparability of data on education of children with disabilities, makes it difficult to assess to what extent they are being left behind.

The last 30 years has seen significant development in terms of the international response at a policy level to the needs of people with disabilities in general and in education in particular. Some of the key protocols are addressed in brief below. For a more in-depth discussion of these and other similar initiatives see Rose (2019). It is worth stressing that international agreements do not in themselves ensure that such policies and directions are followed at the national level. But they do indicate an agreed direction of travel, and countries who are signatories are compelled to provide regular progress reports as to how the issues are being addressed. They also provide a valuable tool for various pressure groups within countries to hold their governments to account. As Rose (2019: 38) notes, 'Ultimately the success of any of these global frameworks will be whether and how they impact on the education experiences of children with disabilities'.

Mariga et al. (2014: 14) note that multiple barriers exist to providing an education that includes children with disabilities and learning difficulties. They posit, among other issues:

- The stigma and shame associated with disability that still persists in many cultures, communities and countries.
- The negative attitudes of some parents arising from having a child with disabilities. They may feel it is not worth investing in education for a disabled child.
- The negative perceptions of professionals and policy makers. They too may feel that disabled children cannot learn...
- Protection of professional interests. Teachers may feel that having disabled children in school would mean too much extra work for them and may show up their lack of expertise as teachers...
- Officials with limited knowledge of educating children with disabilities...
- Limited resources allied with insufficient preparation and inadequate planning.
- A lack of political will to make changes to existing systems.

Having briefly delineated the position generally for people with disabilities and the challenges of meeting their educational needs, we will go on to discuss current responses to these issues first of all from a global policy perspective and then at a practice-based level.

# Response: Global policy

The misery, suffering and disruption caused by the two World Wars in the first half of the 20th century saw a response at an international level that led to the setting up of a number of international organisations, most notably the United Nations, and various statements of intent and charters designed to protect and promote access to various aspects of life, including education, for individuals and groups (Park, 2018). Chief amongst these was the United Nations Universal Declaration of Human Rights (UDHR) (Article 26) which set out the principles for free and compulsory education for all.

The notion of education as a human right has permeated the various (and at times rather bewildering array of) UN-led declarations that have sought to enact the vision of the UDHR. Key among these has been the Education for All (EFA) framework of 1990. This helped shape the six EFA goals of 2000 (UNESCO, 2000) and the more recent Incheon Education 2030 framework (UNESCO, 2015). Le Fanu (2013: 40) notes how the notion of inclusive education as a means for achieving the right of an education 'has acquired increasing prominence in global development discourse in recent years'. It can be argued that this was given impetus in the Salamanca Statement of 1994 (UNESCO, 1994).

## The Salamanca Statement (1994)

The Salamanca Statement and Framework for Action (UNESCO, 1994) called for a broad approach to the inclusion of all marginalised groups of children in education, and claimed that inclusive learning is the most effective means of tackling discrimination, building inclusive societies, achieving education for all, and improving the efficiency and cost-effectiveness of the entire education system (Kuippis and Hausstatter, 2014). It put forward three justifications for inclusive learning:

- Educational: It is a way of producing higher-quality schools.
- Social: Inclusive learning is the basis of a just and non-discriminatory society.
- Economic: It is less costly to establish and maintain schools which educate all girls and boys, rather than funding a complex system of different types of schools.

The Statement also called for 'a major reform of the ordinary school' (UNESCO, 1994: iii–iv), arguing that inclusive learning 'has to form part of an overall educational strategy and, indeed, of new social and economic policies'.

## The United Nations Convention on the Rights of People with Disabilities (UNCRPD)

 Time to Reflect

Read Article 24 (Education) from the United Nations Convention on the Rights of People with Disabilities (available at: www.un.org/develop ment/desa/disabilities/convention-on-the-rights-of-persons-with-

*(Continued)*

disabilities/article-24-education.html). What are the key issues that strike you?

Refer to the story of Ron, the chief and the two children with microcephaly at the start of the chapter. How does that story relate to the rights set out in Article 24? Is the chief's decision in line with Article 24? Is Article 24 adequately relevant to such a situation?

The Salamanca Statement and the UNDRPD (Article 24) have been highly influential in the last two decades as they clearly move beyond the drive merely to an education for all, to a position of an education for all achieved by means of an inclusive framework. In other words, actively seeking to minimise educational provision that takes place in segregated spaces, and through an approach which 'accepts that learners have individual differences but sees pedagogically significant differences as located in the *interaction* between the learner and the school and therefore *within the teacher's influence and responsibility*' (emphasis added; Croft, 2010: 28).

## The UN Sustainable Development Goals (SDGs) (2016–2030)

The UN SDGs, of which there are 17, provide a global framework for development direction, policy and practice for the next decade. The UN states that the SDGs

> ... are an urgent call for action by all countries – developed and developing – in a global partnership. They recognize that ending poverty and other deprivations must go hand-in-hand with strategies that improve health and education, reduce inequality, and spur economic growth – all while tackling climate change and working to preserve our oceans and forests. (https://sustainabledevelopment.un.org/?menu=1300)

Whereas the previous Millennium Development Goals (2000–2015) were criticised for largely excluding the voices of people with disabilities, the SDGs have the theme of 'inclusive' development running through each. SDG 4 (Education) has ten targets, the fifth of which states:

> By 2030 ... ensure equal access to all levels of education and vocational training for the vulnerable, including persons with disabilities, indigenous peoples and children in vulnerable situations. (https://sustainabledevelopment.un.org/sdg4)

Thus, the issue of children with disabilities has now been placed firmly at the centre of the development agenda.

# Response: National policy

These various international standards and agreements mean little if they are not then translated into local policy and practice at the national level. Inevitably at this stage local historical, cultural, political and socio-economic factors influence the nature of that translation. There is little space in this chapter to pursue a great many examples at a country level, but as one example, Schuelka (2013: 99) notes how in the context of Bhutan, the education policy can be linked directly to a response by the government to the UNCRPD and its inclusive language, but that attitudes to disability remain rooted in Buddhist contexts of the concept.

Muthukrishna (2019) analyses the way in which South African policy has a very clear goal for inclusion for all – not just those with SEND but those marginalised for a variety of reasons. The author relates this deliberately broad approach to the recent history of the country when, under the apartheid regime, the majority black population were excluded from a good quality education by mere dint of their skin colour.

Naraian (2019) claims that inclusive education has been interpreted in a variety of ways around the world and that whilst that might reflect in part different sociocultural and economic circumstances it might also be due to the fact that many LMICs are reliant on large international organisations such as the UN and World Bank to help fund their education systems. This reliance means that they will reflect the priorities of such organisations, at least in the language used, even if the interpretation on the ground might be very different depending on the needs of the country.

# Response: School level

Having examined the response to various challenges of working toward a more inclusive educational experience at a policy level, we will consider some of the ways this is playing out in a practical basis at school level. As discussed previously (White et al., 2018) there is a dearth of good-quality research in LMICs with regard to what works well in improving educational experiences and outcomes for children with disabilities and other special needs. Price (2018: 2) notes that:

> One of the key difficulties surrounding inclusive education in developing countries is the lack of research about education in these countries. Although there has been an increase of research in the last 5 years, robust, empirical evidence for low- and middle-income countries is still lacking...

However, this gap is beginning to be filled with the small but increasing amount of research undertaken over the last decade. Some themes and strategies that are perhaps beginning to emerge are discussed briefly below.

At a broader community level, Community Based Rehabilitation (CBR) has been shown to be potentially beneficial in supporting the needs of people with disabilities generally and children in schools specifically (Lukersmith et al., 2013; White et al., 2018; WHO, 2010). Mariga et al. (2014: 77) describe how CBR evolved in nature from its start in the 1980s as a fairly technical rehabilitation response to disability into 'a broader means for developing the capacity of disabled people themselves to advocate for their own rights along with equity of access to education and basic services'. As well as working across various support services in the community and government, good CBR programmes also seek to challenge the societal and institutional prejudices pupils with disability may face when they try to enter the school system. (For an interesting video demonstrating these facets of CBR in a Nepalese context, search online for 'CBR for Inclusive Development – The Karuna Foundation Nepal'.)

There is also an increasing amount of material available free online to support policy makers, administrators and teachers to develop better inclusive practice (Hayes and Bulat, 2017). Indeed, there has been an explosion of such 'toolkits' and open access courses aimed at those working in LMICs often supported by various UN bodies. The effectiveness of these is rarely evaluated however and there is criticism that such material is often still ill-suited to the very basic needs of teachers, pupils and families and that they tend to promote a form of inclusion that reflects western beliefs that fail to reflect local culture (e.g. Le Fanu, 2015; Mukhopadhyay, 2015; Srivastava et al., 2015). Nevertheless, the fact that there is now good-quality information freely and widely available, coupled with the mushrooming expansion of connectivity via cheap smart phones across LMICs, has great potential for unlocking better support for children, their families and professionals.

There is a small but growing body of research on practices that are effective at pre-school and school level in LMICs. Disability Africa (2018: 4) note the importance of simple but structured play therapy early in the life of children with disabilities as a means of developing social and interactional skills and, just as importantly, breaking down societal prejudices. They also note that this is resource-efficient, a vital factor in environments that are often extremely poor. Likewise, early childhood intervention for specific impairments has also been shown to be effective. Lynch et al. (2014) describe the positive impact of working with parents and the local community in preparing children with visual impairment for school.

There is also evidence of the positive results of the targeted use of itinerant teachers to support students with particular disabilities in mainstream classrooms (Impact Initiative, 2017) and there is some evidence for well-planned peer-to-peer support as being effective as long as teachers do not over-rely on peer support and peers are provided with adequate direction for their task (Price, 2018).

---

 Key Points

- This chapter used data from the WHO 'World Report on Disability' (2011) and the UNESCO (2013) 'State of the World's Children Report: Disability' to explore the extent and nature of some of the challenges facing children with SEND in LMICs with regard to accessing education.
- It highlighted the way that the impact of disability is compounded by issues of poverty, negative societal attitudes and scarce resources.
- It discussed various developments at a global scale regarding policy statements and frameworks designed to encourage governments and other education providers to move to a model of inclusive education. Key amongst these has been the Salamanca Statement of 1994 and Article 24 of the United Nations Declaration on the Rights of People with Disabilities.
- It considered evidence that exists in the research literature that sheds light on good practice in supporting better inclusive practice such as working effectively with the wider community, the importance of early childhood intervention and the potential of peer-to-peer provision.

---

 Final Reflection Questions

- Explore the idea of 'intersectionality'. Why might disability be so closely linked to poverty? Develop your own response and then use your own research skills to find current literature on the issue. What are the other issues that disability tends to be related to?

*(Continued)*

- Internet access is developing rapidly in many poorer countries of the world. Much of this is through mobile phone technology and the costs of such connectivity can be relatively high. How might this impact the way in which information and ideas are shared in an online format?
- Create an information sheet that could be viewed on a phone on how to support children with a particular disability. Assume the reader has English as a second language and limited vocabulary. Test it on a colleague. How easy do they find it to access and understand?

# Further reading

Getting to grips with the various global frameworks that shape policy toward education for CYP with disability can be confusing. This chapter gives some useful insight from an author who has been closely involved:

Rose, P. (2019). Looking to the future: Including children with disabilities in the education sustainable development goal. In N. Singhal, P. Lynch and S. Johansson (eds), *Education and Disability in the Global South*. London: Bloomsbury, pp.21–40.

Here is a very different text. It was developed by Dr Patricia Lund through her work with people with albinism in Malawi. Note the simplicity of the language and the supporting pictures. It is available in various local languages. It is a good example of a resource relevant to the needs of the intended audience:

Lund, P., Massah, B., & Lynch, P. (2012). *Albinism in Malawi: Information for Teachers and Parents*. Blantyre, Malawi: The Albino Association of Malawi (TAAM). Available at: https://curve.coventry.ac.uk/open/file/5c501215-c908-ead9-1212-e9367731fd10/1/Albinism%20information%20for%20teachers%20and%20parents.pdf

Finding texts that focus in-depth on research from less-developed contexts can be challenging. This book (one in a series) does a good job at pulling together a variety of studies from around the world:

Mutua, K. and Sunal, C.V. (eds) (2012). *Advances in Research and Praxis in Special Education in Africa, Caribbean and the Middle East*. Charlotte, NC: InfoAge Publishing.

# 9

# PROFESSIONAL ROLES AND CONTEXTS

Joanne Smith

---

### Introduction

This chapter will explore the multidisciplinary context of working in a SEND environment and practices of educational inclusion. You will be introduced to the application of research and policy in practice, in a range of disciplinary contexts. This chapter will:

- Examine the different roles associated with working with children and adults with SEN and/or disabilities.
- Explore school roles and responsibilities, analysing the skills and attributes of specialist professionals.
- Focus on the importance of collaborative practice when working with Children and Young People (CYP) with SEN and/or disabilities and their families.

# The history of multi-agency working

From the mid-nineteenth century, health and social services worked together to try to reduce poverty in England. Moore (2008) identifies the Industrial Schools Act 1857 as the first drive towards child protection and connecting the state, the parents and the child. Dunlop (2009) recognises that local authorities have been made accountable for public health since 1858 and goes on to discuss a shift in social provision until 1939. During the post-war era the United Kingdom saw 'the adoption of state responsibility for social provision and an expanded role for central government' (Dunlop, 2009: 200).

By the 1980s, the foundations of multi-agency partnership working were laid. The Children Act 1989 established the statutory requirement for inter-agency collaboration and joint working in relation to CYP, requiring professionals to 'work together better'. The 1990s saw the development of multilateral partnerships where public, private and voluntary sector organisations joined together to tackle cross-cutting issues such as social exclusion, community safety and neighbourhood regeneration.

Partnership overload and fatigue began to occur, resulting in the need for practitioners from multi-agencies to begin to reflect upon where and when the partnership 'bandwagon' should stop. Since 1989 we have seen several government-funded initiatives aimed at promoting integrated services and more co-ordinated partnership working: Sure Start, Children's Fund, Youth Offending Teams and Connexions have all promoted multia-gency working.

Despite these initiatives there was a lack of information-sharing across agencies and services. Assessments to identify needs and subsequent provision seemed to be duplicated and there were poorly co-ordinated integrated activities across agencies. There was too much 'buck passing' and referring on of clients between agencies, a lack of continuity and inconsistent levels of service provision. Accountability – who is responsible for what – was unclear.

The Children Act (2004) required local authorities' (LAs') partnership arrangements via Children's Trusts to: identify the needs, circumstances and aspirations of CYP; agree the contribution each agency would make to meeting the Every Child Matters outcomes (DfES, 2003); improve information-sharing between agencies; and oversee arrangements for agencies to work collaboratively in the commissioning, delivery and integration of services (Cheminais, 2009: 1, 2).

The 'Aiming High' Green Paper (DfES, 2007) and 'Support and Aspiration' (DfE, 2011b) contributed towards major SEND reform leading to the new Code of Practice (DfE and DoH, 2014) explained further below.

Both papers suggested improving co-ordination between professionals from the education, health and care sectors.

# Current national policy: The SEND Code of Practice (DfE and DoH, 2014)

Organisations that must follow the SEND Code of Practice include: LAs; the governing bodies of schools, including non-maintained special schools, further education colleges and sixth form colleges; the proprietors of academies; the management committees of pupil referral units; independent schools and independent specialist providers; and all early years providers in the maintained, private, voluntary and independent sectors that are funded by the LA. The National Health Service and any trusts and groups associated with it must also adhere to the Code.

This gives all professionals who have a role in supporting CYP with SEND joint responsibility and accountability, as recommended by the DfES (2007) and DfE (2011b). The Code of Practice (DfE and DoH, 2014) puts emphasis on LAs to demonstrate how they support CYP with SEND through their 'local offer'.

Under the Care Act 2014 local authorities must provide an information and advice service on the adult care and support system. Local authorities must provide a range of short breaks for disabled children, young people and their families. The local offer must set out the support groups and others who can support parent carers of disabled children and how to contact them. Part 3 of the Children Act 1989 gives individuals with parental responsibility for a disabled child the right to an assessment of their needs by an LA. LAs must assess on the appearance of need, as well as on request, and must explicitly have regard to the well-being of parent carers in undertaking an assessment of their needs. Following a parent carer's needs assessment, the LA must decide whether the parent carer needs support to enable them to support their disabled child and, if so, decide whether to provide services under Section 17 of the Children Act 1989. Relevant services may include short breaks provision and support in the home.

As we explore the roles of professionals, we will need to consider their responses to the local offer.

# The concept of multi-agency working

Where practitioners from more than one agency work together jointly, sharing aims, information, tasks and responsibilities in order to intervene early to prevent problems arising which may impact on children's learning and achievement. Multiagency working involves the joint planning and delivery of co-ordinated services that are responsive to children and young people's changing needs. (Cheminais, 2009: 4)

Percy-Smith (2005) sees Multi-Agency Working (MAW) as more than one agency working together, a service provided by agencies acting in concert and drawing on pooled resources or budgets. Gasper (2010) describes it as multi-dimensional, with contributing factors being setting, staff, development stage, relationships, leadership, structure, attitude and expectations, whereas Siraj-Blatchford et al. (2007) recognise MAW as the adoption of the two concepts of partnership and integration and discusses the need for change in health services. Other terminology includes 'joined-up working', 'inter-agency', 'team around the child', 'multi-professional' and 'collaborative groups' (Atkinson et al., 2007: 99).

 Spotlight on Theory: Activity Theory (Engestrom, 1999)

Leadbetter (2005) explains activity theory in relation to MAW as each agency having their own 'activity systems' of rules, community, division of labour and mediating artefacts, but for there to be any meaningful joint-working, a new 'object' has to be agreed, despite the fact that these agencies may have different expectations or outcomes in mind for the child. Daniels et al. (2005) emphasise that this 'object' should not be confused with 'goals'. The object is the 'constantly reproduced purpose... that motivates and defines... goals and actions' (p.8).

Wenger et al. (2002, p.6) describe 'communities of practice' as agencies that meet because they find value in their practice, sharing information, insight and advice. They may create tools or develop a shared understanding and even a common sense of identity. It is not the community of practice that is new, but the need for organisations to become more intentional and systematic about managing knowledge. Knowledge is 'simply too valuable a resource to be left to chance'. The sharing of knowledge becomes an integral part of the agency's activities and interactions. Wenger encourages disagreements and debates and feels that controversy makes the community vital, effective and productive.

Gaskell and Leadbetter (2009) apply social identity theory (Turner and Brown, 1978) in relation to their study on educational psychologists and multi-agency working. They discovered an 'identity threat' as a response to the Every Child Matters agenda (DfES, 2003). These threats come under four classes – categorisation, distinctiveness, value and acceptance – which are further explored by Lewis and Crisp (2004). Gaskell and Leadbetter (2009) found that roles varied within multi-agency teams according to individual group members' areas of strength and expertise. Some Educational Psychologists (EPs) gained a stronger feeling of identity when working in a multi-agency team than they did within a group of EPs. Multi-agency work provided the EPs with opportunities to develop their skills, and the sense of value they felt contributed to their professional identity. Gaskell and Leadbetter (2009) suggested that multi-agency teams need to encourage a positive sharing and learning culture as well as retaining and strengthening (relevant) professional links.

We will continue to consider the implications of working in a multi-disciplinary team to support CYP with SEND as we explore some of the roles within education, health and care teams.

## Reflection Activity

What do professionals supporting those with SEND need in terms of skills/ attributes?

Add a skill/attribute on an individual sticky note.

Consider: Will it differ between roles? Why/why not? Similarities/differences?

Can you categorise all/most/some? With examples?

# School roles and responsibilities: Class teachers and teaching assistants

For the purpose of this section 'class teacher' is somebody who has Qualified Teacher Status (QTS) and is responsible for a class or group of children/young people. Refer to DfE (2019) 'Teachers standards' for further information on the teacher's role.

A class teacher should follow the graduated response (as described in Chapter 1) and be instrumental in identifying children who are having trouble in accessing the curriculum, despite receiving Quality-First Teaching (QFT). QFT includes teachers providing differentiation within the classroom which includes appropriate opportunities and resources. Teachers monitor and record the progress of the child as an ongoing process, including informing parents of areas of concern, and seek support from parents when required. The class teacher organises and differentiates the child's work and will keep records of this process for assessment by external agencies should this be required. For children experiencing emotional/behavioural difficulties, class teachers will keep evidence of the strategies used and will involve parents in a supportive role.

The role of the teaching assistant (TA) has shifted from the parent volunteer doing the photocopying, putting up displays and hearing children read, to a more supportive role in terms of learning support. The National Occupational Standards (TDA, 2010) say that TAs should know the rights of disabled CYP and those with special educational needs. This includes understanding the disabilities and/or special educational needs of CYP in their care and being able to contribute to the inclusion of CYP with disabilities and special educational needs. The TDA also suggest that TAs support disabled CYP and those with special educational needs to participate in the full range of activities and experiences.

Good practice dictates that good communication between the adults in the classroom is key to inclusive practice and better outcomes for children. The Teachers Standards state that teachers must:

> develop effective professional relationships with colleagues, knowing how and when to draw on advice and specialist support, deploy support staff effectively … and … take responsibility for improving teaching through appropriate professional development, responding to advice and feedback from colleagues. (DfE, 2019: 8)

Furthermore, communication between the adult supporting the child, whether that be the teacher or TA, and the external agencies involved is also important when sharing aims and information.

# School leadership: Headteachers, governors and SENCos

For the purpose of this section 'Headteachers' are those responsible for the day-to-day leadership of a school/similar institution.

Case study: Head Teacher A

There are two principle pathways where money comes in for SEND: the main school budget (for low attainment) and top-up funding for specific children. Schools subsidise initial support out of their main budget and use top-up funding for anything additional that may be needed (children with EHC plans). Where EHC plans are in place, we allocate further support, e.g. 1:1 if needed, additional interventions, as stated in EHC plans. All additional support is outlined in a location map. We invest heavily in quality-first teaching and inclusive practice, and resource staff training well (e.g. TAs trained in delivery of specific programmes). We also focus on early intervention and identify additional support in the early years – we utilise High Needs Block Funding to support children who are under 5.

SEND provision is monitored regularly by the Inclusion Manager and senior leaders. This is done through a range of monitoring activities. Feedback is given and actions reviewed. Regular meetings are held with parents and teachers to review children's progress, including IEP reviews and EHC plan reviews. The SEND information report and policy are updated annually. The governor for SEND visits the school each term.

As a maintained school, we utilise a range of services from the LwA Inclusion Support, e.g. speech and language, the complex communication team, behaviour support, the SEMH team, educational psychologists, advisory teachers for SEND, physiotherapists. Support action plan meetings are held at the start of each year which outline where support will be given and allocated. We use the LA to help train staff when needed and offer individual advice.

I ensure the accessibility plan is in place and regularly reviewed and updated. When needed, works are completed and adjustments made for children with disabilities. We work in connection with other agencies to help plan adjustments that need to be considered, e.g. physios.

## The role of the governor

Governing bodies should have a nominated SEND governor who oversees SEND provision and reports back to the governing body once a term. The SEND link governor should ensure the governing body is up to date about issues related to SEN and disability. They should ensure the school has a suitable and up-to-date SEN information report and policy and that this is published on the website and that the school has appointed a SENDCo and they have received appropriate training. The governor should meet regularly with the SENDCo to discuss the school's SEN provision, budget and resources and ensure that the school is meeting the needs of pupils with SEN and disabilities. The governor should ensure the school is making reasonable adjustments in line with the Equality Act (2010) and make sure SEN is considered in any budget discussions. They should attend training on the role of the SEN governor, as appropriate.

## The role of the SENCo

There are many books on the role of the SENCo that you can explore so for the purpose of this section we are going to briefly outline their roles within schools. Most SENCos have a teaching commitment too, and it is suggested that they should be part of the leadership team, but this is not always the case. Pearson and Ralph (2007) applied activity theory in their research into the identity of SENCos, using 'photo voice' methodology. The perceptions of others had an impact on the SENCo's enactment of their role, different groups within school saw the role of the SENCo differently and therefore complicated the development of the SENCo's identity. The area that was under-represented was the division of labour in relation to working with outside agencies.

SENCos are responsible for overseeing the day-to-day operation of the school's SEN policy, including co-ordinating provision for children with SEN and ensuring that the school keeps records of all pupils with SEN up to date. SENCos advise teachers on the graduated approach, providing SEN support and the deployment of the school's delegated budget and other resources to meet pupils' needs effectively. They liaise with parents of pupils with SEN, early years providers, other schools, educational psychologists, health and social care professionals, independent or voluntary bodies, and potential next providers of education to ensure a pupil and their parents are informed about options and that a smooth transition is planned. SENCos are usually the key point of contact with external agencies, especially the LA and its support services. They work with the Headteacher and school governors to ensure that the school meets its responsibilities under the Equality Act (2010) regarding reasonable adjustments and access arrangements. This includes updating reports to governors every term regarding SEN provision.

### Time to Reflect

Watch 'A Day in the Life of a SENCo' at www.youtube.com/watch?v=
YJTQKiOJ1GU and consider what key skills and attributes a SENCo
requires in order to support SEND effectively.

# Speech and language therapists

Speech and language therapists (SLTs) provide treatment, support and
care for children and adults who have difficulties with communication, or
with eating, drinking and swallowing; they are allied health professionals.
They work with parents, carers and other professionals, such as teachers,
nurses, occupational therapists and doctors. There are around 17,000
practising SLTs in the UK working in a wide variety of settings.

SLTs contribute to joint assessment, including joint target-setting and
joint planning, e.g. language unit curriculum, language-rich classrooms.
They work collaboratively with teachers and TAs in the delivery of programmes such as PECS. SLTs may attend case conferences, Team Around
the Child (TAC) meetings etc. They have a responsibility to inform of
safeguarding concerns when attending 'Look After Child' meetings. SLTs
liaise with educational and medical staff, and with parents and families.
They contribute to EHC plan assessments and may also deliver training to
setting staff, multi-disciplinary team staff, and parents – for example on
feeding and drinking strategies, or communication strategies and skills.

In 2014, 52% of speech and language therapy services reported cuts in
their budget or income (www.rsclt.org.uk). The results of these cuts at client
level are reduced support for clients, an increased wait for SLTs, less specialist input or even no service for some client groups. At service level the cuts
have an impact on workloads and coverage, an increase in complaints and
joint working with other services becomes less effective. The solution so far
has been top-up contracts, health promotion and training, and strategic
commissioning and planning of speech and language therapy services.

### Time to Reflect

Go to www.slcframework.org.uk/ and www.thecommunicationtrust.org.
uk/ – consider the barriers SLTs face in a multidisciplinary context.

# Occupational therapists

Occupational therapy assessment and treatment focuses on helping people with a physical, sensory, or cognitive disability to be as independent as possible in all areas of their lives. Occupational therapists (OTs) can help CYP with various needs to improve their cognitive, physical, sensory, and motor skills and enhance their self-esteem and sense of accomplishment. This can be done through grading and adapting occupational activities, promoting skill acquisition, modifying the environment, developing competence and confidence, and can be delivered across home, school and the community.

OTs understand brain development and recognise that early experiences shape the architecture of the brain. The brain doesn't stop developing but it slows down (neuroplasticity). OTs recognise that normal physical motor development is dependent on normal brain development.

OTs work with both acquired and developmental conditions. Acquired conditions may be birth injuries, the result of neglect, musculoskeletal injuries, brain injuries, or the result of cancer or infection. Developmental conditions could be conditions such as Autism Spectrum Condition (ASC), chromosome and genetic disorders, developmental coordination disorders and/or sensory processing disorders.

Skills and attributes of an occupational therapist include observational assessment regarding specifics on why a child is finding it difficult to learn. OTs are a link between the home environment and school. They may have specific intervention ideas and activities to enable the child to individually progress. They contribute towards potential provision recommendations and can suggest allocation of useful equipment.

In relation to multi-disciplinary working, OTs contribute to physical, psychological and social assessments. They look at the impact of different environments and make links with home and school. OTs can be part of the school team, the multi-disciplinary health team, and the social care team.

---

          Time to Reflect

Who else might an occupational therapist work with?

What other allied health professionals are you aware of?

You could investigate the role of the play therapist, or a physiotherapist.

# Sensory impairment team

LAs may employ qualified teachers to work with CYP with sensory impairments, including vision, hearing and multi-sensory. There is a team leader, which is a strategic role; team leaders may maintain a small caseload themselves. They have an overview of the whole sensory impairment team including budget control, team plan, eligibility criteria, data collection/outcomes, and future developments/recruitment. They act as a first point of contact regarding referrals and caseloads. The team may organise enrichment activities and social opportunities and may be involved with joint ventures with other disciplines we have explored.

A qualified teacher of vision impairment, teacher of the deaf, and qualified teacher of multi-sensory impairments must have QTS and mainstream teaching experience in any phase. They then do a two-year distance-taught mandatory training course 'on the job' – PGDip in Special Education (VI/HI/MSI) and Braille/BSL. Their roles and responsibilities include family support, functional assessments, reporting/advising, training, teaching, being a keyworker. An educational audiologist requires an additional qualification and is responsible for testing/loaning equipment/audits/review and liaison regarding needs.

A mobility/habilitation specialist also requires a two-year distance-taught 'on the job' qualification – the PGDip in Habilitation and Disabilities of Sight. Their roles and responsibilities include family guidance, early development, 'additional curriculum', training, peer awareness, mobility, symbols, crossings, routes, travel and independent living support.

Within the sensory impairment team there are also experienced, qualified TAs with specialist qualifications in British Sign Language or Braille. They may be responsible for additional curriculum delivery such as early signing, touch typing, transitions, Braille and tracking outcomes.

 Time to Reflect

Who might request input from the sensory impairment team?

What would this input look like?

# Behaviour support teams

For the purpose of this section we will look at an agency based in Worcestershire that also supports Caerphilly, Monmouthshire and

Herefordshire. There are similar agencies in other local areas that you may be able to research further. The purpose of the Behaviour Support Team (BST) is to support a child or young person with their behaviour needs, as well as work with parents, carers, families and school staff. They focus on building resilience and coping strategies rather than 'managing' the behaviour. 'Team Teach' is a strategy that some BSTs adopt which looks at triggers, stages of crisis and preventative strategies. As a last resort, those trained in Team Teach methods will use safe holding and positive handling (for more information see: www.teamteach.co.uk).

The BST meet every fortnight; they use a problem-solving approach and celebrate successes, encouraging communication, safety and mental well-being amongst the staff. Professional development includes theraplay training, drama/group work and role play. The BST can also offer support for children, young people and their families, regarding issues such as gender reassignment and self-harm. The BST can also offer mediation between school and parents when there has been a communication breakdown.

---

### Time to Reflect

What skills and attributes would you need to work in behaviour support?

---

# Educational psychologist

The role of the Educational Psychologist (EP) is to promote child development and learning through the application of psychology by working with individuals and groups of children, teachers and other adults in schools, families, other LA officers, health and social services and other agencies (DfEE, 2000). They work with CYP aged 0–25, supporting those experiencing barriers to education (learning difficulties, social and emotional problems, issues around disability, as well as more complex developmental disorders). EPs work at various levels: individual child, small group, parents/carers (case work), schools and early years providers and/or LAs and other agencies (systemic work) (https://careers.bps.org.uk/area/educational).

Many educational psychology services offer consultation as a model of service delivery which aims to bring about change for the individual child, through working at an organisational or whole-class level in schools (Wagner, 2016). EPs are therefore engaged in consulting with parents/carers, school staff, the child or young person, as well as working with other professionals. EPs often work directly or indirectly with a child or young person to gather information to inform their assessment. EPs support staff on how best to support children or young people. They are well-placed to be involved within various types of research, which can help to inform policy and enhance reflective practice within the profession (BPS, 2015). Training is often delivered to various services and educational providers.

EPs may work for the LA, either through core LA-funded work or 'traded' services. They also work for third sector organisations, social enterprises, private service providers, schools, colleges and other commissioners/purchasers. EPs are often self-employed or on occasion are employed by academic trusts and chains. They can be commissioned by parents. It is also important to point out that only they can undertake certain forms of assessment, for example when trying to obtain an EHC plan.

# Parent support: LA

LAs have built upon existing parent partnership services, now branded as 'SENDIASS' (Special Educational Needs and Disabilities Information and Support Services). They are a dedicated and easily identifiable service; they must be impartial, confidential, 'arms-length' and accessible. They offer impartial information, advice and support on all matters concerning SEND including health and social care, for CYP between the ages of 0 and 25. Young people can receive information, advice and support separately from parents. SENDIASS are not an advocacy service, they are an empowerment service which aims to represent the views of parents/carers, CYP, and feedback to the LA on non-curriculum issues.

---

      Case Study: Example of Casework, Low Level –
One or Two Involvements

Parent concerned that child is struggling in school, doesn't know what should be happening in school, who is involved etc.

SENDIASS advise parent to ask for a meeting with the SENCo to discuss concerns and ask the following questions:

*(Continued)*

- What additional provision/support your child receives.
- How this is being assessed.
- How it is being planned.
- How it is being delivered.
- How it is being reviewed.

We gave details of the outside support services that could be involved (e.g. EP, LST, BST, CCN) and how they could be involved.

We discussed realistic expectations and we explained how to pursue concerns if they are not happy with the response they have received.

## Time to Reflect

How do SENDIASS support the LA with the below objectives?

In response to the Children Act 2014, Section 19, Local Authorities MUST have regard for:

- the views, wishes and feelings of the child and his or her parent, or the young person.
- the importance of the child and parent or the young person participating as fully as possible in decisions.
- the importance of the child and parent or young person being provided with the information and support to enable participation in decisions.
- the need to support the child and parent or the young person to achieve the best possible educational and other outcomes.

# Parent support: The charity sector

There are charities that support parents and carers of CYP with SEND. Their aim is to keep the family together for short breaks and activities, giving support in numbers so that parents can take their children out, as a group, where they may not usually have the opportunity or confidence to do so on their own. The charities may work with professionals and families and the LA may consult with them.

## Case Study: Parent B's Perspective

It is difficult to challenge the professionals, even though you know your child better than anyone else; your views aren't always taken into account. Parents are the expert, especially if our children's conditions are rare. It is difficult as we are emotionally attached, but we ask that we are treated with respect as we do know what we are talking about. They (the professionals) need to consider how they communicate with our children, 'Do they feel safe? Do they like...?' Our children are not 'naughty' or 'making it up'. At primary school my son was treated as an individual, he didn't need a diagnosis. But when he entered secondary school the misunderstandings started, and he was bullied terribly. He started to withdraw from school. Peer awareness made a huge difference, a buddy system was set up and he finally started to achieve, his attendance improved, and he is now successfully studying at university. One professional can make all the difference. Even a good SENCo may not be able to keep the promises they make if the headteacher is not on board. It is so important that the school have a good relationship with parents and listen to our children's needs. Support to overcome these barriers together, asking not telling. Once we trust each other, anything is possible. If the communication breaks down, we (parents) stop listening too. Support us to support our children. The main barriers for successful SEND support are funding and the EHC plan process. We don't have a 'family conversation', we are just asked to fill the form in. We don't always know what we need to ask for. EHC plans are not reviewed as often as they should be or as carefully as they should be as needs change. Professionals don't always agree with each other and outcomes become confusing. A diagnosis or identification of need means that we have legal rights, but as our children turn 16, the parent does not always have the right to speak to professionals on their behalf.

## Time to Reflect

What can agencies do to support communication with parents? Investigate a parent support group in your area.

# Social care

Social workers aim to improve people's lives by helping with social and interpersonal difficulties, promoting human rights and well-being. Social workers protect children and adults with support needs from harm. From helping keep a family under pressure together to supporting someone with mental health problems, social work is a varied, demanding, often emotional and very rewarding career. The problems social workers deal with are often rooted in social or emotional disadvantage, discrimination, poverty or trauma. Social workers recognise the bigger picture affecting people's lives and work for a more equal and just society where human rights are respected and protected (BASW, 2014).

Social care responds to the Children Act (2004) Section 17, where a child needs support and intervention, or Section 47, concerned with experiencing significant risk of harm. This may result in a Child in Need Plan, and if a child is at risk or has been harmed there would be a Child Protection Conference. If there is an immediate risk of harm, the child would be removed from the family and the police have 72 hours to submit an interim care order.

Social workers always try to work with families and use a strengths-based model of practice that looks at signs of safety, what is working well and what we (the team including the family) are trying to achieve. Social care has a framework of assessment that looks at parenting capacity, family functioning and child development. Children's views are incorporated, where appropriate, from the age of 3 years old. For children with SEND, particularly those with speech, language and communication needs, or those with cognition and learning difficulties, it may be more challenging to acquire their views. Social workers aim to Achieve Best Evidence (ABE) through the Tell, Explain, Describe (TED) approach. Barriers to supporting SEND include an identified gap between identified SEND (DfE and DoH, 2014) and the criteria for 'children with disabilities' that social care may get involved with, exclusive to:

- Severe learning disabilities.
- Severe physical disabilities.
- Severe developmental delay in motor and/or cognitive functioning.
- Profound multiple disabilities.
- Severe sensory impairment (registered blind and/or profoundly deaf).
- Complex and severe health problems that arise from the disability that are life threatening; degenerative illness or organic disorder resulting in severe disability.

- A diagnosis of autism spectrum condition with an associated learning disability and where the condition severely affects day-to-day functioning.

It is very difficult for social care to use SEND as an indicator of harm. This relies on parental understanding and concentrates on the role of relationship-based practice. There needs to be a balance between advocating for the parent, and their reliance on the social worker, whose aim is to empower the parents.

---

    Spotlight on Theory: The Glass Effect

Rose (2012) discusses the glass effect: imagine the child as a glass, and within that glass are contained large stones which could be:

Inadequate housing

Parent drinking/drug reliance

Domestic abuse

Lack of food

Lack of warmth

Bullying at school

No help with homework

Learning difficulties.

In working together, the aim for the social worker and the parents is to 'reduce the stones'.

Consider what key attributes a social worker would need to facilitate this strategy.

---

# Barriers and enablers

Considerations regarding successful collaboration are that the best lead agency for each child could be different and there may be an unequal commitment to working with one another. Also each agency is organised differently, with their own priorities and sets of values, possibly even targets for the staff – some workers will have unacceptably large case-loads and be unable to give their attention to the problems in front of them, tending to jump to conclusions in order to find standard solutions.

### Spotlight on Research

Barnes (2008) found the barriers to multi-agency working were time, money, resources, information sharing, different cultures/systems/ boundaries, co-ordination, efficiency, individual personalities and professional challenges. Parker with Gordon (1998) identified an inability to merge budgets and agencies unable to delegate to each other (p.7). Limbric (2001) discusses unresolved contradictions in diagnosis, treatment and advice, unbalanced information, where professionals may be unaware of the other agencies involved, and a lack of opportunity to meet together, resulting in 'harmful effects of fragmentation of services' (p.7). Harrison et al. (2003) say there is a partnership 'fatigue' where we lose sight of the benefits and can only see the personal and professional costs to our agencies (p.72).

Key suggestions for effective multi-agency working in terms of SEND support are:

- Clear aims and objectives.
- Common working practice.
- Joint training.
- Monitoring and evaluation.
- Sharing resources.
- A flexible, consistent, fair and responsive approach.
- Adequate funding and time.
- Quality leadership.
- Equal partnerships.

### Key Points

We have:

- Examined some of the different roles associated with working with children and adults with SEN and/or disabilities.

- Explored school roles and responsibilities and started to analyse skills and attributes of specialist professionals.
- Identified the importance of collaborative practice when working with CYP with SEN and/or disabilities and their families.

## Final Reflection Questions

- How do leaders facilitate outcomes for CYP with SEND?
- What other roles can you explore in relation to supporting SEND?
- What is the child's/young person's experiences of the support they receive?

# Further reading

This article explores children's perspectives of SEND support including teaching assistance and accessibility:

Lewis, A., Davison, I., Ellins, J., Niblett, L., Parsons, S., Robertson, C. and Sharpe, J. (2007). The experiences of disabled pupils and their families. *British Journal of Special Education*, 34(4), 189–195.

Listen to Sir Andrew Carter discuss the keys to effective leadership in terms of SEND and inclusion:

YouTube (2017). *Successful Leadership with Sir Andrew Carter OBE*. Available at: www.youtube.com/watch?v=rLXyIDEDNiA (accessed 23 April 2020).

This article explores the theory behind possible multi-agency collaboration:

Greenhouse, P.M. (2013) Activity theory: A framework for understanding multi-agency working and engaging service users in change. *Educational Psychology in Practice*, 29(4), 404–415.

# 10

# BECOMING A SENDI PRACTIONER: PROFESSIONAL IDENTITY AND SELF-REFLECTION

Joanne Smith

## Introduction

This chapter focuses on you, the reader, on your values and what encourages you to develop an interest in working in SENDI. Having the motivation and drive to continue with a challenging career is important to enable you to progress in this rewarding practice. This chapter gives you an opportunity to reflect on what you have learnt so far regarding SENDI practice and encourages you to develop skills that can be used in the workforce. This chapter will help you to:

- Discover your own values and beliefs in relation to working to support those with SEND.
- Apply different models of reflection in relation to professional practice.
- Consider how your understanding of SENDI will influence your future career path.

# Who are you? Values and beliefs

**Values** play an important role in SENDI practice, and understanding our values gives us a strong personal and professional identity as well as self-belief.

---

    Time to Reflect

What do you believe to be your own core values?

What is important to you and why?

Do you know what has influenced your beliefs and values?

---

## What are values?

Within professional relationships, values can be described as an anchor, a moral compass, a contributor to making and sustaining healthy relationships, a framework for our thoughts, influencing standards and principles, supportive or destructive of developing relationships, judgements about importance in life, behaviours etc. It could be argued that values are what make us individual and diverse and form our characters. They also have the potential to improve or detract from our professional relationships.

Arthur (2010: 11) discusses values in relation to the concept of good characteristics (virtues) vs bad characteristics (vices) (see Table 10.1).

**Table 10.1** Summary of Arthur's characteristics

| Good (virtues) | Bad (vices) |
| --- | --- |
| Honesty | Dishonesty |
| Fairness | Injustice |
| Courage | Cowardice |
| Self-control | Intemperance |
| Kindness | Cruelty |
| Integrity | Unscrupulousness |
| Compassion | |

Source: Arthur (2010: 11)

> ## Time to Reflect
>
> Do you recognise these virtues and vices in yourself?
>
> Can you identify them in others?
>
> How are they demonstrated?
>
> What would you say are the key virtues to SENDI practice?

To understand what values are, we can look to ancient philosophers and their development of value-based systems. Arthur (2010) goes on to cite Plato (1961) and the three principles of the soul – reason, spirit and appetite – which we must develop to ensure morally appropriate conduct. The rational part of our soul (reason) is the part that seeks truth and wisdom. It is our conscience, what makes us aware; reason thinks and analyses, it weighs up the options and gauges what is best. Spirit is the part that seeks honour and victory. It gives us courage; spirit is what makes us angry at injustice and steels ourselves against adversity. Finally, appetite is concerned with pleasure and desires. It also provides us with comforts and temperance.

Aristotle (1941) is more concerned with a 'naturalistic' anthropology that looks at a functional construct of the soul based on human goals and purposes. Achieving these human endeavours serves to define a 'noble' life. Arthur (2010: 19) says that the goal of the virtuous character is not just doing what is morally right but feeling or wanting what is right.

Dr Stephenson discusses the concept of **social justice** in her discussion on inclusive leadership within the final chapter. Smith (2012) describes social justice as treating others according to what they are due/entitled to, implying that we should treat people differently according to their different needs. Smith cites Miller (2003) and their three concepts that we must a) treat people *consistently*, b) the treatment must be *relevant*, and c) the treatment must be *proportionate*. The decisions regarding what is 'right' or justified are subjective, depending on our values and judgements.

If we consider our values in relation to SENDI professions, there is a link between being and doing 'good' and wanting to make a difference. Our values influence our thoughts and subsequently our actions, they make us what and who we are. As SENDI practitioners we are driven by doing what we feel is 'right'. Chapter 11 goes on to explore how we justify those decisions.

Time to Reflect

Can you explain why you might choose a career in SENDI?

Would you associate this decision with your values? Why/why not?

## What forms our values?

Arthur (2010: 94) identifies the main influence of our values as our parents, then as we get older our friends and peer groups may be further influences. Prioste et al. (2017) discuss the vertical transmission of cultural values through the parent and child relationship. Family mythology constructs personal values in relation to the part of our identity that stabilises behavioural patterns, providing coherence and continuity to personal narratives. For instance, my mother and grandmother are teachers; my father is an active trade unionist. Growing up I developed the mindset that we can (and should) help others, especially those not as fortunate as ourselves. This has influenced my behaviour towards others; I recognise my compassion and need to construct positive experiences. This has led to a career in teaching, and has particularly supported my role in SENDI practice.

It is worth mentioning that the increase in life expectancy around the world has led to a longer co-existence of at least three family generations, providing further opportunity for close relationships and influences. Grandparents play a significant role in their grandchildren's lives and can be experienced storytellers who integrate history and family traditions into the cultural context. My grandmother still talks of her time in schools, working with 'parallel groups' of mixed age classes, how she would differentiate according to individual needs. Her insights have informed my own practice.

Other considerations relating to family values could be social and economic factors and country of origin. We may also associate our values with our religious beliefs. Roccas (2005) identified that people more committed to religion held values that expressed motivation to avoid uncertainty and change, rather than followings one's own desires or independent thoughts and actions. Roccas says that religious people place high importance on values relating to family security, forgiveness and obedience, rather than pleasure or an 'exciting life'. For more information on how religion and culture influence our values see Schwartz's value theory (Schwartz and Huismans, 1995).

Values at a cultural level are thought to reflect characteristics of a larger system or group (Fischer, 2006). If you are embedded in the group your values could be influenced by your social relationships, group identification, participation in the group's 'shared way of life' and striving towards shared goals. In SENDI practice, as explored in Chapter 9, professionals should keep the child or young person at the heart of what they do, the shared goal being to enable that child or young person to progress and achieve.

## Spotlight on Theory

Refer back to activity theory explored in Chapter 9 when considering the influence of professional and peer groups on your own values.

Arthur (2010) also recognises the role trusted managers, teachers and other role models (including those in the media) may play in the formation of our values. Kirk et al. (2016) discuss **empowerment** in relation to intrapersonal outcomes regarding individuals' sense of impact/voice, competence, meaningfulness and choice / self-determination. Empowerment processes are specific to the domain: we may be empowered at work in a different way to how we are empowered at home. Teachers (and other professions who may have a position of power) play an important role in empowering students if they demonstrate belief in their success and allow students to see them as 'human'. You may wish to refer to Dr Stephenson's discussions on ethical leadership in the final chapter when considering the role power positions have in SENDI practice.

Carr (2006) describes teachers' (and similar professions') values in relation to three types of 'norms':

*Technical norms* are evaluated as good or bad by reference to standards of efficiency/effectiveness such as the Teacher's Standards (DfE, 2019) described below. This ideology is represented by Aristotle's description as previously discussed.

*Deontic norms* are values that are underpinned by universal rules or imperatives. There is a distinctive conception of the profession and notions of ethical right or duty.

*Aretaic norms* are more concerned with types of person relating to the value and responsibility of professions (morals/virtues, as above).

These norms co-exist – if we consider them in relation to SENDI professions, there will be professional standards that we are expected to adhere to (the technical norms). Deontic norms are how we perceive our role to be, relating back to our behaviours and doing what is right (social justice). Finally, drive and motivation – what it is about us as people that encourages us to pursue a career in SENDI – underpin the aretaic norms.

 Time to Reflect

Consider the impact of our personal values on our professional practice.

Is there anything else that influences our values?

Values can increase **covert discrimination**:

> which involves subtle or passive acts of prejudice. Such actions are hard to prove, since they may be cloaked by rational or non-discriminatory reasons. These acts may be done intentionally, or even accidentally, in which case they may be a result of the perpetrator's subconscious beliefs. (Chavan, 2018)

We naturally associate ourselves with a group and may subconsciously develop positive beliefs for the group we belong to, while regarding everyone else as outsiders. After a while we may realise that we have such inherent prejudices. This can mean that whenever we encounter a person belonging to a minority group we try hard to avoid displeasing that individual, thus behaving in a subtly discriminatory way. If done intentionally, we might try to make it appear that our actions have a rational and non-discriminatory basis, to avoid being viewed as prejudicial (Chavan, 2018). For example: a group not talking to someone in class because they have a hearing impairment or the teacher talking to them in a loud voice and making gestures.

Discrimination is not only an individual problem, but also sits within structures of society; values can therefore perpetuate inequality. (Refer to Chapter 6 on equality and the final chapter regarding the social model of disability.) For instance, shared values regarding the historical integrity of a building might discriminate against wheelchair users, if the building only has stairs and we refuse to install any ramps or lifts.

**Stereotypes** can be broadly defined as 'shared beliefs about personality traits and behaviours of group members' (Fiedler and Bless, 2001: 123).

When stereotyping, we are categorising individuals into groups, according to their presumed common attributes. Asbrock et al. (2011) argue that stereotypes can function as cognitive schemas to facilitate social interactions with unknown individuals; as overgeneralisations of traits for a group in general. Consensually shared stereotypes within a culture can serve as social **norms** for behaviour toward the stereotyped group. These stereo-typical beliefs could influence our values and may also inform our **self-concept** in which widely held stereotypes about social groups can influence a person's view of themselves. For instance, boys are believed to have higher mathematical related self-concepts whereas girls have higher language related self-concepts (Retelsdorf et al., 2015).

Murugami (2009) identifies that people with disabilities may have low self-esteem, poor self-image and a negative self-concept. This could be because decisions are made, or activities are selected for them. She goes on to say 'it is difficult for persons with disabilities to cope with and overcome limitations, practical and emotional, that are caused by impairments without acquiring knowledge and gaining experience in confronting obstacles, meeting challenges, and engaging in activities that develop problem-solving strategies'. Therefore as SENDI practitioners it is important to consider how we might improve our service users' self-esteem, image and concepts.

---

 Time to Reflect

If we treat people with a disability in a certain way, through our stereo-typical views, are we creating a disabling environment? (Refer to Chapter 6.)

Consider the impact our behaviour has on other people's self-concept. Are we in danger of creating a self-fulfilling prophecy?

---

We must also consider how our emotions inform our values. An emotional experience is either pleasant or unpleasant, placing some intrinsic value (or disvalue) on the subject. Emotions arise because we care about someone, something or states of affairs; we value them. This is also considered as an evaluative belief or judgement (Todd, 2014). It would be very difficult to work in SENDI practice without having any emotional involvement, however there are professional standards we must consider, as discussed throughout this chapter.

## How do values work in practice?

Professions and organisations routinely develop their own set of values. For example, the University of Worcester's core values comprise of:

Making a difference to society.

Building relationships.

Developing leadership and delivering a distinctive education.

Engaging with the community.

Sustainable development and environmental management. (University of Worcester, 2019)

---

 **Time to Reflect**

What professional/organisational values are you familiar with?

---

## Values of teachers

Arthur (2010: 35) identifies how teachers are expected to act as role models in the classroom, demonstrating the characteristics they expect of their pupils. The teacher's standards (DfE, 2019: 2.1) state:

Teachers uphold public trust in the profession and maintain high standards of ethics and behaviour, within and outside school, by:

- treating pupils with dignity, building relationships rooted in mutual respect, and at all times observing proper boundaries appropriate to a teacher's professional position
- having regard for the need to safeguard pupils' well-being, in accordance with statutory provisions
- showing tolerance of and respect for the rights of others
- not undermining fundamental British values, including democracy, the rule of law, individual liberty and mutual respect, and tolerance of those with different faiths and beliefs
- ensuring that personal beliefs are not expressed in ways which exploit pupils' vulnerability or might lead them to break the law.

## Time to Reflect

Consider the following scenarios:

1) Max, aged 7, has just enrolled at the primary school where you are working. This is their first time at school because they are a member of a Traveller family which has previously home-schooled them. You have heard talk in the staff room and amongst children and parents in the playground that Max smells, cannot use a pencil and does not play nicely with the other children. Your knowledge of Max does not agree with these judgements.

Q. How would you respond in this situation?

(For more information about the Traveller, Gypsy and Roma communities, www.travellermovement.org.uk/)

2) A family living in poverty, receiving welfare benefits and accessing food banks purchase a 48" plasma TV.

Q. How do you feel? What do you do/say?

3) In the nursery where you work, 3-year-old Charlie is always tired, routinely swears (badly) in everyday speech and eats their lunch (including yoghurt) with their fingers.

Q. How do you feel? What do you do/say?

**Remember:** Self-awareness is essential in order to become a reflective practitioner. It is human nature to judge. However, an awareness of our biases enables us to make more informed choices about how we interact and use/misuse power. Consider what actions you may need to take if you feel you are being overly subjective.

Fisher and Byrne (2012) identify that traditionally roles in health and social care were associated with a 'rational' mindset, devoid of any emotion. However, they recognise that there is a current argument that being able to connect emotionally is the underpinning of 'care' roles. We need to have concrete emotions that are directed at particular people in specific contexts (p.80). The authors consider the interface between identity and professional motivation and recognise that they are shaped by emotions and values. They contest that professionals working in learning disability services may be significantly motivated by emotionally driven aspirations, interpreted as the desire to enhance service users' well-being and quality of life.

Being driven by our emotions and values can lead to reflexivity and criticality that can challenge official policies. Professionals who are committed to practice and to the people they work with have their values rooted within their affective lives and a holistic sense of identity.

# Where are you now? Positionality and identity

## Spotlight on Theory

Hogg et al. (1995) discuss the differences between identity theory and social identity theory:

> Identity theory (Stryker, 1968) explores social behaviour in terms of reciprocal relations between self and society. Our role identities have an impact on social behaviour; role identities are the distinct components of self for each of the role positions in society we occupy, e.g. wife, mother, daughter, teacher, village hall trustee. We develop self-meaning and self-definition from how others respond to our role identities.

> Social identity theory (Tajfel and Turner, 1979): the social categories such as nationality, sports team, institute we attend, into which we fall or feel we belong to, define who we are in terms of characteristics and attributes. Social identity can describe and prescribe what we might think, feel or do as a member of that group. Social identities are also self-evaluative in that members are strongly motivated to adopt behavioural strategies to achieve or maintain group comparisons that favour the group or the self.

## Time to Reflect

Write down all your role identities and consider how you behave differently in each role; how do people respond to you in these roles?

What are the positives and negatives of having a strong social identity?

Arthur (2010: 46) discusses the importance of Agency and Trust. Our current society is a service-orientated economy and therefore employees must have good personal and social skills (see further section on employability). Trust and confidence are key capabilities, where young people must rely on their own agency and motivation.

**Self-efficacy** and **self-regulation**: Bandura (2001) explores the part of the self that relates to our estimation regarding personal effectiveness. This relies on a socially interdependent effort, working in co-ordination with others, e.g. rules, social practices and sanctions that regulate human affairs. It is often difficult to trust others in case we become too dependent. Healthy self-reliant people are quite capable of relying on others when occasion demands (Arthur, 2010: 67). Trust in others facilitates the evolution and maintenance of self-conception, being able to absorb and learn from other people's reflected appraisals (Sennett, 1998: 146).

Students with high estimates of personal effectiveness display greater persistence, effort, motivation and interest in their education (Zimmerman, 1995). The higher the level of self-efficacy, the greater the individual's persistence in the face of difficulty. We will only benefit from success if we endure disappointment or accept failure. Being wrong is often part of the learning process (Arthur, 2010: 67).

# Goal orientation theory

Those who set learning goals tend to adopt a mastery orientation and focus on improving their ability, whereas those who set performance goals tend to focus on displaying their ability and are prone to adopt a helpless orientation if they fail to do so. (Brophy, 2010: 47)

This relates to the earlier discussion on Aristotle's naturalistic anthropology concerned with goals and purposes forming our character (McKeon, 1941). Brophy identifies that we adopt either a mastery or helpless orientation depending on the goals we set (see Table 10.2).

**Table 10.2** Fixed vs growth mindsets

| Mastery-oriented learners | Helpless-oriented learners |
|---|---|
| *Learning goals*: focus on developing competence in a task, 'mastering it' | *Performance goals*: focus on displaying ability rather on learning something new |
| Tend to seek out challenge, approaching mistakes as indication of need to change strategy | Vulnerable to helplessness when faced with difficulty |

*(Continued)*

**Table 10.2** (Continued)

| Mastery-oriented learners | Helpless-oriented learners |
| --- | --- |
| Tendency for a belief in incremental theory of intelligence – ability can be increased through effort (GROWTH MINDSET) | Tendency for a belief in entity theory of intelligence – ability is fixed and they have no control over it (FIXED MINDSET) |

---

**Time to Reflect**

Which learner are you? Do you have a growth mindset or fixed?

---

# What have you done? Reflecting on practice

Reflection is to 'analyse or evaluate one or more personal experiences and attempt to generalise from that thinking' (Cowan, 1998: 18). Reflection is a skill which can be learned and improved. Schon (1983) describes two types of reflection (see Table 10.3).

**Table 10.3** Summary of Schon's reflections

| Reflecting <u>on</u> action: | Reflecting <u>in</u> action: |
| --- | --- |
| • Occurs after an event<br>• The kind of thinking a professional engages in following an experience<br>• There is no single correct response to a situation or 'one size fits all' model<br>• Each situation and each case is unique | • The kind of thinking we all do as we are working, studying and living generally<br>• 'Thinking on your feet'<br>• No single response or action that will suit every situation<br>• Develops with practice |

Source: Schon (1983)

# Do the two relate? How/when?

Reflection serves the following purposes: it helps you analyse what happened, think through the event from several perspectives (see Brookfield's critical lenses below). Reflection enables you to identify the things that went well and identify areas for development. It helps you to build your professional knowledge and think about what you would do next time in a similar situation.

*Making sense of experience*: Cottrell (2003) identifies a difference between 'experience' and 'learning'. We may have an experience, yet we may not necessarily learn from it. *Standing back*: By taking a backward stance, we can see the experience from another perspective. *Repetition*: Reflection involves going over something, perhaps more than once, viewing it from several perspectives to ensure nothing has been missed. *Deeper honesty*: Reflection concerns striving for the truth. *'Weighing up'*: Being balanced in your judgement, accounting for all things rather than the obvious. *Clarity*: Reflecting can bring a sense of clarity, as if seeing a clear reflection in a mirror. *Understanding*: Being receptive to learning from the experience at a deeper level. *Making judgements* and drawing conclusions, while also identifying future directions.

---

### Time to Reflect

Can you apply Cottrell's model to your own experiences?

Keeping a reflective journal:

Using a blank notebook, write a question on each page and spend 5–10 minutes responding to each one.

- What have I learnt over the last 12 months? (What new skills, knowledge and insights have I gained?)
- What has been my biggest accomplishment to date?
- What might I do differently if given a second chance? Why?
- What have I done right?
- What am I particularly proud of?
- What am I most thankful for?
- Am I different this year than I was at this time last year? How so? What motivates me?
- What gives me energy?
- What am I striving for?

---

# Other models of reflection you may wish to engage with

- Rolfe (2001): What? So what? What next?

- Kolb's cycle (1984)
- Gibbs' reflective cycle (1998)

## Why is reflective practice so important?

Nicolas (2017) says we (practitioners) must be open to learning new ways of working. Reflective Practice (RP) allows us to identify themes and patterns so that we can continue or amend as we see fit. RP acknowledges our progress, successes, and personal development, and gives insight into our strengths and development needs. RP allows us to consider the impact of our behaviour(s) on others and gain feedback. Through RP we develop a greater understanding of how others' behaviour and styles may complement our own; we understand ourselves more in order to understand others.

Brookfield's 'lenses of reflection' (2005) questions assumptions about teaching and learning using four lenses: teachers' autobiographical experiences as learners, learners' eyes, colleagues' perceptions and educational literature.

### Reflection Activity

This is a paired activity. One of you tells a story from your placement/ own experience. The other one listens and completes the grid in Table 10.4. When the speaker has finished, ask further questions in order to add more detail to the grid. Together try to identify what sort of literature they may need to consider and what the relevant statutory documents may be.

**Table 10.4**   Reflection grid

| Self | Learners |
|------|----------|
| Colleagues / peers | Theory |

### Spotlight on Theory

Andragogy is teaching and learning with adults in mind (as opposed to pedagogy). Knowles (1980) discusses the importance of adult self-concept suggesting that you (adult learner) need to perceive yourself as responsible for your own learning. It is important that the learning has relevance to your own life; you need to know why you are learning certain things. Andragogy is often intrinsically motivated, i.e. we want to do an activity because of the inner-feelings and satisfaction it brings, we don't necessarily need any external inducement to undertake such activities. Andragogy recognises the importance of your own experiences.

It is important to consider what it is that motivates you on those difficult days, as SENDI practice can be challenging and at times emotionally overwhelming. But with these challenges come great rewards in being a part of a person's journey and enabling them to succeed.

## Where are you going? Career pathways

As identified in Chapter 9, careers in SENDI are not restricted to becoming a teacher (although this is a rewarding career in itself). It is therefore important to reflect on the characteristics, skills and attributes potential employers may be looking for in different professions.

Arthur (2010: 93, 94) says that students and new employees regard honesty as the primary quality they associate with good character. Other prominent words to support this view were: open, straightforward, genuine, and trustworthy. The second area regarding the perception of good character was capacity for friendship, helpfulness, trustworthy, courteous, generous, loyal, patient, empathetic. It is important to be a good listener, interested in others and attentive to their needs; also desirable is a willingness to work hard with others for what they believe in.

 Time to Reflect

Consider how these characteristics relate to the roles explored in Chapter 9. What would you consider to be the three most important characteristics for becoming a SENDI practitioner?

M. Allen (2011) summarises employability skills as:

*Personal attributes*

- A positive attitude: A 'can do' approach, good work ethic and a willing-ness to learn.
- Good personal presentation.
- Honesty and integrity.
- Reliability.
- Timekeeping and personal organisation.
- Team working, collaboration and co-operation.
- Flexibility.
- Commercial awareness and customer focus.

*Skills*

- Communication – oral and written.
- Numeracy.
- Computer literacy/IT skills.

M. Allen (2011) says that employability skills are concerned with what *any* employer looks for in *any* employee, beyond qualifications. Employability is not just about skills but is also concerned with capabilities and competencies.

---

### Key Points

- This chapter has enabled you, the reader, to reflect on your own values and beliefs.
- It has introduced you to potential models of reflective practice.
- Consider how these may inform current and future practice.

---

### Final Reflection Questions

- What attributes do you think this chapter has explored and how would you demonstrate them in practice?
- How could/will you use a reflection portfolio?
- What future careers could you pursue?

# Further reading

This book may give you insights into potential future careers in inclusive practices:

Gharabaghi, K. (2008). Values and ethics in child and youth care practice. *Child & Youth Services*, *30*(3–4), 185–209.

This article will give you further information on growth mindset:

Dweck, C.S. (2013) Self-theories: *Their Role in Motivation, Personality and Development*. Hoboken: Taylor and Francis.

For more information on how religion and culture influence our values:

Schwartz, S.H. and Huismans, S. (1995). Value priorities and religiosity in four Western religions. *Social Psychology Quarterly*, *58*, 88–107.

# 11

# RESEARCHING APPROACHES TO INCLUSIVE PRACTICE

Joanne Smith (with contributions from Dr Peter Gossman)

---

### Introduction

In this chapter we will be taking a broad overview of research into inclusive practice. We suggest you engage with further literature on research methods before starting an extended piece of research such as a dissertation. We are both producers and consumers of research, but rather than being a 'how to' guide or manual, this is more of a discussion about the role research plays in inclusive practice. This chapter will:

- Engage with the theory and practice of educational research within the fields of Special Educational Needs, Disabilities and Inclusion.
- Help you understand how research informs policy and practice in a range of appropriate contexts, roles and environments.
- Explore a range of methods for constructing a framework for a research enquiry, including consideration of ethical issues.

# Why do research?

Considering our reflections from Chapter 10 on values and beliefs, how can we prove what we believe is right? How can we demonstrate our points are *valid*?

**Intersubjectivity** has been used in social science to refer to agreement. There is 'intersubjectivity' between people if they agree on a given set of meanings or a definition of the situation. Scheff et al. (2006) define 'intersubjectivity' as 'the sharing of subjective states by two or more individuals'.

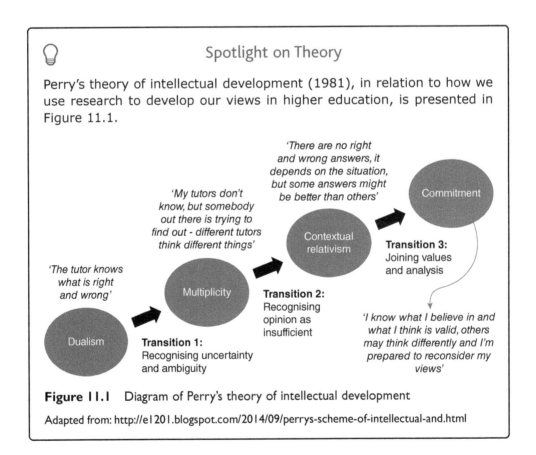

## Spotlight on Theory

Perry's theory of intellectual development (1981), in relation to how we use research to develop our views in higher education, is presented in Figure 11.1.

**Figure 11.1**   Diagram of Perry's theory of intellectual development

Adapted from: http://e1201.blogspot.com/2014/09/perrys-scheme-of-intellectual-and.html

As a student you will already be using literature to underpin your written arguments, and therefore embarking on some research to either validate your beliefs and views or reconsider them, identifying alternative standpoints.

Ichikawa and Steup (2018) describe a **justified true belief** as a 'sufficient' reason to believe a given proposition to be true. Basically:

X *knows* Y so Y is *true*.

X *believes* Y, X is *justified* in believing Y is true.

Most epistemologists have found it overwhelmingly plausible that what is false cannot be known, closely linked to the belief condition in that you can only know what you believe. Failing to believe something precludes knowing it.

---

### Time to Reflect

On what basis would you have sufficient reason (justification) to believe something to be true? In general? In research?

Are the requirements different? How would you validate this to be true?

---

# Methodology

The Enlightenment was a crucial period that established the argument that any truth and scientific knowledge cannot be achieved without a correct scientific method:

1. The scientist (or researcher) is confronted with a *problem* requiring explanation.
2. The scientist (or researcher) analyses the problem in the light of relevant *theory*.
3. From the theory, the scientist (or researcher) derives specific *hypotheses* to be tested.
4. Through *observation* or *experiment* the scientist (or researcher) tests out his or her hypothesis, using accurate *measurement*, under *controlled* conditions.
5. As a result, he or she obtains *data*.
6. The data is analysed to establish whether the hypothesis can be supported or refuted by the *fact* or *results*.
7. The hypothesis and theory are adjusted in the light of the results, and the findings are published.

(Morison, 1993)

## Spotlight on Theory

Can we use a 'natural scientific' approach to inclusive practice? Can we study people in the same way that we study atoms?

For example, in relation to inclusive practice research:

1) Problem: Fewer girls are identified with Autism than boys.
2) Theory: Autism is a 'male' trait.
3) Hypothesis: Boys display X traits, girls display Y.
4–5) Observation/data collection; the researcher observes a set number of boys and girls of similar age over a set period of time, recording behaviour traits seen. The researcher may also collect views from teachers/support staff/parents using either a questionnaire or interview.
6) Observations/views collected, themes identified; can the researcher back up their original hypothesis?
7) Hypothesis may be adjusted to say 'the evidence shows that boys do display X and girls display Y, however this is dependent on: (age/environment/stage of diagnosis)'.

**Epistemology** is the study of knowledge: How can we know 'Y' (something)?

**Paradigms** are a set of ideas and approaches, a distinctive set of values/beliefs, within the context of a viewpoint. As a researcher, your paradigm may either be positivist or interpretivist as described in Table 11.1 below.

**Table 11.1**   Positivist vs intepretivist paradigm

| **The Positivist Paradigm** | **The Interpretivist Paradigm** |
| --- | --- |
| Observe and test, controls, reduction | Interpret meanings-perceptions, understandings |
| One reality, context free | Ethnographical – studying groups of people |
| Empirical-physical, testable, practical | Exploring, investigating, flexible |
| Scientific, statistically rich | Information from within, acknowledges researcher and their situatedness |
| Objective/aloof – outside the situation (observe others) | |

Source: Contributed by Dr Peter Gossman

**Example:** when conducting research about a piece of music, the positivist might test how many beats per minute, whereas the interpretivist might ask how does it (the music) make you feel? The nature of research into inclusive practice lends itself more towards an interpretivist view as we are interested in people and social interactions, as explored in this book. The interpretivist paradigm also lends itself more to qualitative methods. However, before we look at data collection, we need to explore further the context of research and how it relates to both policy and practice.

# Research, policy, practice cycle

 Time to Reflect

What do we mean by practice?

Is it what we do/think we do?

How does it relate to SENDI research?

Some definitions of practice (noun):

The actual application or use of an idea, belief, or method, as opposed to theories relating to it.

'the principles and practice of teaching'

The carrying out or exercise of a profession, especially that of a doctor or lawyer.

'he abandoned medical practice for the Church'. (Oxford Living Dictionaries, 2020)

Within this chapter we are defining a **practitioner** as:

Anyone who works directly with children, young people and their families, whose primary role is to use a particular expertise or professional skill in order to help promote children and young people's well-being. (Cheminais, 2009: 138)

### Reflection Activity

Note down the types of policies the following practitioners may have to follow:

- Schoolteacher
- Social worker.
- Speech and language therapist.

Consider: How far do practitioners have to follow these policies? How far do practitioners shape these policies? How does this all relate to research?

We have explored the professional implications and the sense of duty we have in responding to certain policies within practice in previous chapters. Policies within settings may be shaped by the practitioners if they are given the opportunity to review those policies with the relevant leaders/managers. For instance, when reviewing the school behaviour policy, a headteacher may look at and discuss with school staff and mutually agree on any changes/interventions required. This relates to research if further evidence is required. For instance, the headteacher may not initially see the need to change the policy until they are presented with further evidence such as observations from the class teachers, or the SENCo may have received additional training in an intervention method that needs to be trialled.

# Practitioners as researchers

Skills, experience and the underlying common-sense core to the practice of social research... enables the interested practitioner to be directly involved in carrying out worthwhile studies. Involving practitioners in research... provides an obvious means of facilitating change. (Robson, 2002: 219)

Referring to previous discussions on motivation and values, SENDI practitioners have natural instincts to facilitate change. Reflecting on early experiences as a class teacher, with 33% of the children in my class having SEND and with only a shared teaching assistant, I felt I needed to research into methods to improve my pupils' experiences, including reading about and trialling communication tools for children with limited spoken English.

Clough and Nutbrown (2007) found that education students (HE) want their dissertation research to bring about change in: policy (e.g. *Education services can be very focused on 'educating the child'. I would like to highlight the issues around perspective, contribution and values of parents as a policy factor*); practice (e.g. *I hope the research will inform future practice in work with people with learning difficulties*); professional development; and stimulus for further research (pp.14–15).

Time to Reflect

What difference could your research make?

# Making the links between research, policy and practice

Anderson and Arsenault (1998) say research in education is a disciplined attempt to address or solve problems though the collection and analysis of primary data for the purpose of description, explanation, generalisation and prediction, whereas Blaxter et al. (2010) think research is a planned cautious systematic and reliable way of finding out and deepening understanding. Over the last 20 years there has been a growing recognition of the need for tighter links between research, practice and policy: '"Evidence informed" policy and practice has rapidly gained support and is coming to shape research agendas throughout the country' (Furlong and Oancea, 2005).

Traditionally it has been assumed that there is a clear distinction between the worlds of research and the worlds of policy and practice – that there are 'two communities'. On the one hand there is the world of research, based on explicit, systematic work aimed at the growth of theoretical knowledge. Practice and policy on the other hand are perceived as taking place in the 'real world', a world based on different forms of knowledge – on knowledge and on practical wisdom (Furlong and Oancea, 2005) (see Figure 11.2).

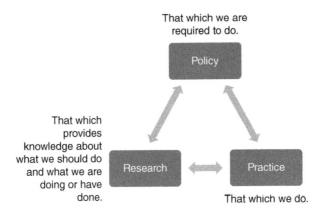

**Figure 11.2**   Research, policy, practice cycle

Source: Contributed by Gareth Dart

# Debates about nature and purpose

Unlike medicine, education is not a research-based profession. There is a need to grade evidence and the applicability of that evidence. Research needs to be linked to needs and needs to be contextualised (Hargreaves, 1997). Organisations must therefore cultivate wisdom and discretion about what constitutes evidence and how practitioners and leaders might use it to improve individual and organisational knowledge and self-knowledge as the basis for improvement. This involves making connections between wider research, practitioner research and evaluation in order to provide complementary information on which to base school improvement planning and activities (Durrant and Holden, 2006: 9).

 Case Study: Master's Research (as part requirement for an MA in Special and Inclusive Education)

'The role of the SENCo in a multiagency team' was born from personal experience as a SENCo and an increased frustration that 'external agencies' identified as supporting individual children did not appear to be working together with shared goals and outcomes for that child. The research explored whether other agencies shared these frustrations and looked into perceptions of the SENCo role. Data was gathered through an online focus group for SENCos and questionnaires to professionals from external agencies.

## Impact on practice

Improved confidence in leading multi-agency team meetings (agencies had identified SENCos as key links to school): 'The experience of being valued and offering a valid and beneficial contribution to MAW appears only to have positive effects on perceptions of professional identity' (Gaskell and Leadbetter, 2009: 105). Implementation of suggestions from both groups such as planning ahead and taking a leadership role.

## Impact on participants

Multi-Agency Working (MAW) became more streamlined, communication improved, actions for children became more effective. Guidelines introduced for new SENCos in the area on 'who to contact' regarding outside agencies. A module on partnership working for the National SENCo Award at the university was developed.

## Wider world impact?

The research was completed with regard to the new CoP from the Department for Education (2011b: 114). New EHC plans introduced from September 2014 in line with the Code of Practice (DfE and DoH, 2014) emphasised the key role of SENCos. The outcomes of the research continued to have an impact on practice and policy. The SENCo forum (2015) found the Code specifically requires local authorities to set out their 'offer' of services for pupils with SEND, but LAs can no longer afford to maintain their 'own' specialist support services (NASEN, 2015). SENCos have been concerned about enhancing their own further professional development and keeping up with changes in SEND legislation and requirements. The Code (DfE and DoH, 2014: 4.32) requires local authorities to set out in their 'local offer' arrangements for 'professional development to secure expertise at different levels'.

In relation to the research, policy, practice cycle: SENCos are taking account of evidence-based educational research in relation to 'personalising' teaching to meet the individual learning needs of a pupil, therefore conforming with the guidance of the CoP (DfE and DoH, 2014) – i.e. the concept of 'quality-first teaching' by classroom teachers, which encourages them to go beyond a 'one size fits all' approach to everyday practice. Currently prevailing pressures have constrained classroom teachers' scope for following this aspiration and SENCos are attempting to support teachers (Wedell, 2017): 'This is where the research evidence

*(Continued)*

informs but does not fully determine decision-making and practice' (Norwich, 2014).

The SENCo forum (NASEN, 2015) also identified budget constraints and alterations in provision and contrasting school policies towards those of their pupils who have SEND. Policies of recent governments have sent schools discordant messages – they have exhorted schools to adopt a 'personalised' approach to meeting pupils' individual learning needs, BUT the 'standards agenda' policies have demanded that schools should compete in the achievement of ever higher levels of attainment by their pupils. Schools are increasingly faced with a dilemma in how to allocate their remaining resources.

---

            Time to Reflect

Is there a tension between research and practice? Can research provide the link between the academic and the vocational (practical)? Can inclusive practice be based on research knowledge? Apart from research, what else informs/guides inclusive practices?

---

**Methods**: When discussing methodology, you will need to explain how the data was collected or generated in a way that is consistent with accepted practice in the field of study (adapted from Kallet, 2004). For example, if you are using a multiple-choice questionnaire, explain that it offered your respondents a reasonable range of answers to choose from. The method must be appropriate to fulfilling the overall aims of the study. For example, for larger-scale quantitative work you need to ensure that you have a large enough sample size to be able to generalise and make recommendations based upon the findings. In the social sciences, it is important to always provide enough information to allow other research-ers to *adopt or replicate* your methodology. This information is particularly important when a new method has been developed or an innovative use of an existing method is utilised.

Your methodology should have a clear connection with your research problem, ensuring that it addresses the problem. One of the most common deficiencies found in research papers is that the proposed methodology is not suitable to achieve the stated objective of your paper. *Describe the specific methods of data collection you are going to use*, such as surveys, interviews, questionnaires, observation and archival research. If you are analysing existing data, such as a data set or archival documents, describe how it was originally created or gathered and by whom. *Explain how you intend to analyse your results*. Will you use statistical analysis? Will you use specific theoretical perspectives to help you analyse a text or explain observed behaviours? Describe how you plan to obtain an accurate assessment of relationships, patterns, trends, distributions, and possible contradictions found in the data. Punch (2013) looks at qualitative versus quantitative approaches (see Figure 11.3).

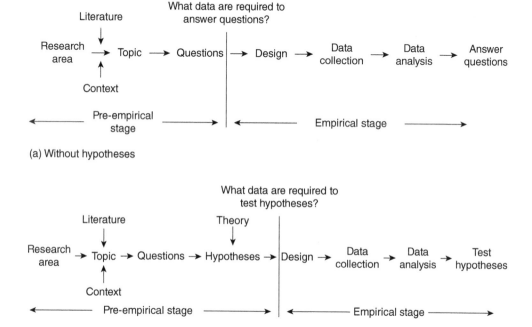

*Simplified model of research*

**Figure 11.3**   Punch's model of research

Source: Punch (2013: 68).

     Time to Reflect

Is your research qualitative or quantitative or a combination of both (mixed method)? Are you going to take a special approach? How does the approach fit the overall research design?

As researching into inclusive practice may be more qualitative, we present here two examples of qualitative research: **interviews** and **focus groups**.

# Interviews

Kvale (1996) defines qualitative research interviews as an 'attempt to understand the world from the subjects' point of view, to unfold the meaning of peoples' experiences, to uncover their lived world prior to scientific explanations'. Interviews for research or evaluation purposes differ in some important ways from other familiar kinds of interviews or conversations. Unlike conversations in daily life, which are usually recip-rocal exchanges, professional interviews involve an interviewer who is in charge of structuring and directing the questioning.

Interviews give opportunities for asking open-ended and probing questions (Cohen et al., 2011: 352). Interviews can encourage respondents to develop their own ideas, feelings, insights, expectations and attitudes, and in so doing allow them to say what they think with 'richness and spontaneity' (Opie, 2004: 111). In short, interviews are good for getting in-depth information without the narrow boundaries that are common in questionnaires. They also involve personal, face-to-face interaction between the interviewer and the respondent (see Opie, 2004 regarding stages in preparing for interviewing).

We need to use interviews carefully, bearing in mind the need for excellent interpersonal skills and careful and thorough preparation of the interview schedule (i.e. the questions). There is also the possibility of interviewer bias (the interviewer either affecting the responses, or a biased interpretation of or response towards what the interviewee is saying by the interviewer).

Time to Reflect

In what circumstances might you use interviews for your research?

Who would you interview?

Note three questions you might ask.

# Focus groups

*Key features*: Data generated by interaction between participants, who present own views and experiences AND hear from other people. The participants listen, reflect and consider own standpoint further, triggering additional material. It is NOT a collection of individual interviews; the researcher becomes a facilitator/moderator of the discussion presented (Ritchie et al., 2014).

*Advantages*: Focus groups enable a range of responses to be gained in a short space of time. [...] (In terms of data collection) [...] they are economical for the researcher to complete. They allow the observer to record respondents' views mediated through interaction. Focus groups provide rich responses that relate to the research questions. Hutchings and Archer (2001) suggest that a key advantage of focus groups 'lay in the opportunity they afford to tap into... jointly constructed discourse... [and]... interactions with each other' (p.72). This can be taken further where interaction elicits 'data and insights that would be less accessible without the interaction found in a group'. (Morgan, 1997: 2)

Focus groups enable rapid comparisons between responses: group discussions provide direct evidence about similarities and differences in participants' opinions and experiences as opposed to reaching such conclusions from post-hoc analyses of separate statements from each interviewee. They enable the group to control the focus of the discussions and so potentially facilitate material otherwise unanticipated. This has advantages in terms of 'idea generation' and again can produce a rich source of information. Focus groups offer a degree of control to the researcher to steer responses towards research questions, whilst also allowing group interaction that can be a 'valuable source of insights into complex behaviors and motivations' (Morgan, 1997).

---

 Time to Reflect

What are the disadvantages? How do they differ from interviews?
What factors might you need to consider?

---

# Ethics

Ethics is about right and wrong, the conduct of your work (in practice and in written work), respect for others, and balancing academic work and research with the rights and needs of others. Ultimately, ethics is about the responsibilities towards both yourself and others.

Never, never be afraid to do what's right, especially if the well-being of a person or animal is at stake. Society's punishments are small compared to the wounds we inflict on our soul when we look the other way.

---

### Time to Reflect

In practice how would you protect the following people/places in either discussions or writing?

- Josh (a child in a specialist setting).
- Josh's mum.
- Mrs Flynn (class teacher).
- The setting and its reputation.
- Your colleagues on your course.

Why is this so important?

What are the implications in practice if you do not follow ethical guidelines?

Any legal/professional/personal codes?

(Refer to the British Educational Research Association's Ethical Guidelines for Educational Research (2018)).

---

When our research involves children, vulnerable young people and vulnerable adults, Articles 3 and 12 of the UN Convention on the Rights of the Child apply. The best interests of the child must be the primary consideration along with children's rights to express their views (and therefore they should be facilitated to give fully informed consent). You must consider: voluntary informed consent; openness; the right to withdraw (how?); incentives; benefits to the participants; detriment arising from participation; privacy (anonymity, confidentiality and proper storage of data); and disclosure (safeguarding).

# General Data Protection Regulations (GDPR)

GDPR governs the processing (holding or using) of personal data in the UK. 'Personal data' is data about living people from which they can be identified. As well as data containing obvious 'identifiers' – such as name and date of birth – this includes some genetic, biometric and online data if unique to an individual. Data processing must be **lawful, fair** and **transparent**. Organisations that process personal data are accountable, yet we all have a role to play. All organisations involved in research must specify a lawful basis for processing personal research data. Consent is not likely to be a lawful basis for processing personal data for research purposes. There should be good ethical and legal reasons to seek consent. All applications for ethical approval must continue to engage with the core issue of informed consent. The new legislation sets out the information that should be provided to participants (referred to as a privacy notice).

But ethics is not just a formality and procedures in themselves are insufficient (Cohen et al., 2011: 76; Thomas, 2013: 151). There is always the potential that participants feel the researcher is 'getting a degree on our backs' (Delamont, 2016: 145). We aspire to 'non-exploitative and reciprocal' research (Benjamin, 2002: 30) and to 'tread lightly'.

---

 Time to Reflect

Who will the research benefit?

Whose time and effort will be involved? Who could suffer discomfort or stress?

What is the balance of costs and benefits?

---

You will need to ensure the setting and the person in charge ('gatekeeper') is fully informed about your research, and that you keep the gatekeeper and your supervisor informed of your research as you go along. Talk about your experiences and bring in everything that you can offer to the discussion, but be mindful of what you say. Listen when others talk about their experience, but be mindful of sensitivities and anonymity. Write about the setting and bring your professional experience into your work, but be mindful of what you write (sensitivities and anonymity). Recognise and identify 'bias': think about your own biases (being honest if your research doesn't find what you want it to) – being ethical extends to your write-up. It also extends to how you search the literature – if you do this with the intent to find what you want, it won't be balanced or fair. Ethics is about what you do and how you do it, and you owe it to the research/academic community to undertake your work with balance and fairness.

# Next steps

Ultimately your research needs to be something that sustains you; it must be a subject you are interested in. Start with a topic you are intrigued about and consider where you would take it next, what else you want to find out about it. When writing your research aims and objectives, remember the aims are what you hope to achieve; the objectives are how you will achieve the aims. For example:

Aim: To explore what is meant as 'dyslexic friendly practice'.

Objectives:

Interrogate recent and relevant literature to identify this term.

Collect views from teachers in both specialist and mainstream schools to draw similarities and differences in practice.

Drawing on both the literature and teachers' views, identify key implications for future practice.

Key Points

In this chapter we have:

- Explored the implications of undertaking research into inclusive practice.
- Gained an understanding of how your research may impact on future practice and policy.

Final Reflection Questions

- What other methods will you explore for future research designs?
- If you were to develop a piece of research to influence SEND policy and legislation what topic would you chose and why?
- Would you use a qualitative or quantitative approach in your research? Why would you use this approach?
- How can teachers be encouraged and supported to engage in practitioner research?

# Further reading

These chapters will provide you with further strategies to support you in structuring potential research projects:

Chapters 5 and 6 in: Thomas, G. (2013). *How to Do Your Research Project: A Guide for Students in Education and Applied Social Sciences* (2nd edn). Thousand Oaks: Sage.

This book demonstrates the relationship between research/policy and informed inclusive practice:

Mitchell, D. (2013) *What Really Works in Special and Inclusive Education: Using Evidence-Based Teaching Strategies*. London: Routledge.

This book will provide some insight into different research methods, giving you some informed comparisons of alternative methods:

Martin, D. (2014) *Doing a Successful Research Project: Using Qualitative or Quantitative Methods*. Basingstoke: Palgrave Macmillan.

# 12

# TOWARDS INCLUSION: RHETORIC AND REALITY

Joanne Smith and Dr Marie Stephenson

## Introduction

Inclusion has been roundly explored in previous chapters. But to gain a conclusive understanding of its importance in contemporary education we must also understand what basic principles underpin theory, as well as our role in promoting and embedding inclusion for all. This chapter will:

- Evaluate the definitions, theories, principles and models of inclusion explored so far and add a social justice lens.
- Identify your attitude and role as inclusion champions/advocates, and your responsibilities towards inclusive practice.
- Summarise and reflect upon current tools, practices and policies to support inclusion.

# Definitions, theories and models

The 'inclusion debate' has been a controversial concept in education since the recommendations of the Warnock report in 1978 (see Chapter 2). Further arguments involving what is appropriate regarding specialist versus mainstream education place demand on teachers and school leaders in terms of training, resources, confidence and competence. Reflecting on the inclusion framework identified in Chapter 1, we have seen a continuing emphasis on inclusion relating to provision for Children and Young People (CYP) with special educational needs/disability, not only in education but also in society as a whole.

## Time to Reflect

If a system, a school or 'pedagogy' is said to be inclusive, what does this mean?

What definitions or criteria are we using?

What is an inclusive school?

*The inclusive school is every school* – or rather, what every school should be. Inclusive schools are places of democracy, fairness and equality. Here all children flourish regardless of disadvantage. Inclusion is a whole-school approach in response to learners' voices and participation, positive teacher attitudes and pedagogy underpinned by visionary school leadership (Borg et al., 2011: 13–14). Educators listen, organise teaching and learning, provide access to information, the curriculum, and its assessment and give support. Borg et al. (2011: 17) advocate a holistic and coordinated approach with coherent interdisciplinary community services, where health, social and emotional needs are met through good working relationships, information sharing, timely support and parental engagement (see Chapters 6, 10 and 11). The bedrock principles of inclusion demand that learners are active participants in the life of the school and the community where they belong. *Truly* inclusive practice goes beyond the normal confines of the educational institution, involves all stakeholders, builds support networks, and comes up with innovative ways to realise the principles of social justice.

As inclusion advocates and champions, we are the agents of a positive ethos and learning culture. We understand the true nature of inclusion and make inclusive values and beliefs explicit in all aspects of educational practice (Borg et al., 2011). We stand with others, not above them, putting ourselves in the position of others by empathising, feeling and under-standing patterns of injustice (Vorhaus, 2006). We are critical and accountability partners, challenging the status quo and advocating for change. We are called to a social responsibility, because the concept of inclusion is not just a school concern but a societal one; we are part of the inclusion agenda, not separate from it (Attfield and Williams, 2003: 32).

How we treat others makes a statement about *our* attitudes. Therefore, we need to think very deeply about how we uphold 'inclusive' values; the way we demonstrate our commitment to equality, fairness, democracy and dignity. Courage is required to ask 'the hard questions regarding social class, race, gender and other areas of difference' which 'lead to the development of options related to important concepts such as oppression, power, privilege, authority, vice, language and empowerment' (Shapiro and Stefkovich, 2011: 15). We must develop a critical stance, to uncover disadvantage, inherent injustice and dehumanisation, we must make edu-cational experiences more responsive... for the common good and fuller participation and justice for individuals' (Starratt, 1991: 198–190).

# Differing interpretations of the concept of 'inclusion'

The term 'inclusion' is widely (even universally) used in education but lacks a universally accepted meaning. Here are some examples of differing (but often overlapping) meanings which could be attached to 'inclusion':

*Meaning 1: Inclusion as social justice and human right:* As explored in Chapter 2, there were broad social movements in the latter half of the 20th century, which included the civil rights and women's movements, other minority and indigenous voices and, from the 1970s, disability rights. Cole's (2012) book gives a good outline of this. Barton (2003) sees inclusion in terms of 'freedom and justice' (p.22), characteristic of the disability movement. From this point of view, inclusion is a means to an end, the end being an inclusive society, hence inclusion is radical and transformative. This view is also expressed in Martin Luther King's 'I Have a Dream' speech of 1963 (www.youtube.com/watch?v=3vDWWy4CMhE).

*Meaning 2: Associated with movement of pupils designated as having SEN into 'mainstream' schooling:* In 'pure' form this means every child attending their neighbourhood school, but this has probably only been adopted fully in a hand-ful of times and places. The UNESCO Salamanca Statement (1994) called upon countries to 'adopt the principle of inclusive education, enrolling all children in regular schools unless there are compelling reasons for doing otherwise' (UNESCO, 1994: ix). Salamanca was a key driver for inclusive education but can also be seen as ambiguous, referring, for example, to inclusive schools offering effective education to a 'majority' of children (Dyson, 1999: 37).

*Meaning 3: A philosophy of acceptance:* A 'framework within which all children – regardless of age, ability, gender, language, ethnic or cultural origin – are valued equally, treated with respect and provided with **equal opportunities** at school' (Thomas et al., 1998: 15). This concept is explored in Chapter 6 and encompasses all diverse characteristics. Achievement for All (Blandford, 2013) helps 'schools, early years settings and colleges to achieve, aspire, ensure access for all and accelerate progress regardless of background, challenge or need' (https://afaeducation.org/about-us/).

*Meaning 4: Inclusion as a feeling*: As a feeling of being valued. (Refer back to Chapter 10.) Slee (2011) cites Polk's view that 'for many children the experience of school is the daily experience of humility and pain' (Slee, 2011: 12). The Index for Inclusion (Booth et al., 2011) is a set of materials to guide schools through a process of inclusive school development. It is about building supportive communities and fostering high achievement for all staff and students, making everyone feel included.

There is also *Topping's (2012) 'expanding' model of inclusion*:

4 levels from children with SEN in mainstream school > children with SEN accessing mainstream curriculum with social and emotional integration > all children achieving and participating > all children, parents and community equally achieving and participating in lifelong learning. (p. 13)

           Time to Reflect

Which of the meanings and models of inclusion do you relate to the most?

How do we apply these meanings to inclusive educational practice?

# Rhetoric or reality?

Clough and Corbett point out that the term 'inclusive education' implies 'many different strong forms of belief, many different local struggles and a myriad of forms of practice' (2011: 6). For example, some see provision of special and mainstream schools or groupings within schools as part of an overall inclusive education system. From some 'full inclusionist' or 'disability studies' perspectives, this is certainly not inclusive (Ballard, 1999). Slee's (2006) view is that imprecise terms permit 'all manner of thinking, discourse and activity to pass itself off as inclusive' (p.111).

In schooling of pupils with 'SEN', the term 'integration' was internationally used from the 1960s (see Chapter 2), replaced by the term 'inclusion' during the 1990s. Integration implies the minority group may join the majority; inclusion may be taken to mean a more equal relationship. In Figure 12.1 the coloured dots represent the minority group.

 Spotlight on Theory: Integration vs Inclusion

Vislie (2003) questions whether the terminology meant a linguistic shift or a new agenda. She says that integration had two strategies, one focusing on reform in special education, the other related to the reformulation of regular education. She also states that inclusion is a 'broader vision' as it covers more issues. She cites Farrell (2000) who describes inclusion as the quality of education offered to pupils with SEND in integrated settings. Ainscow (2000) took the notion of inclusion a stage further to describe the way mainstream schools should cater for all their pupils, and also used phrases such as 'inclusive schools for all' without specific reference to pupils with SEND.

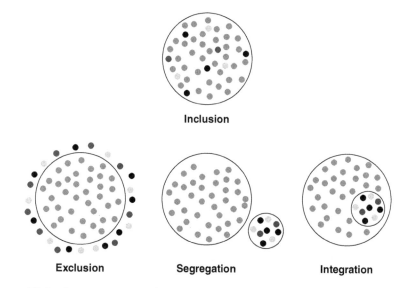

**Figure 12.1**   Integration vs inclusion

Time to Reflect

What is your understanding of inclusion?

How far has inclusion been achieved? (Your understanding or that of others.)

Are most children/young people successfully 'included'?

# A 'special' pedagogy for learners with 'special' or 'additional' educational needs

We return to the debate introduced by Dr Sewell in Chapter 4 of whether effective teaching for those with SEND is effective teaching for all? Or do specific SEND conditions require specialist interventions?

Hanks (2011: 17–19) has a useful approach, based on the analogy of choosing, in a relaxed and reflective mood, from a restaurant menu:

*Choose from the basics* including, for example:

1. Clear unambiguous explanations.
2. Clarity and careful sequencing of tasks.
3. Ask students what would help.

*Then choose from 'menus'* For dyspraxia, for example:

1. Consider word processing to replace writing for some tasks.
2. Consider sloping writing surfaces, writing on alternate lines.
3. Allow time and pre-planning for learners to express themselves rather than 'on the spot' responses.

Remember: in response to the new Code of Practice (DfE and DoH, 2014) local authorities must publish their 'local offer' stating what schools and settings should be providing for each dimension of need. In turn, schools and settings should also publish their 'school offer' providing a clear outline of what/how they support SEND. Take time to explore your local authority and familiar school offers to secure your understanding of what this looks like, and consider how it is applied in practice. See Behan (2017: 34–61) on inclusive classroom models.

Wearmouth (2016) stresses that English schools should frame their teaching and learning for all students around the National Curriculum Inclusion Statement (DfE, 2015) that:

1. Teachers should set high expectations for every pupil, including planning and assessment for those with low levels of prior attainment.
2. They should take account of their duties under equal opportunities legislation (see Chapter 6).
3. Lessons should be planned so there are no barriers to any pupil achieving.
4. With the right teaching, many disabled pupils will have little need for additional resources beyond the aids they use for daily life.

Wearmouth suggests that teachers should concentrate on 'quality-first teaching' strategies, improving the learning environment and increasing the range of approaches rather than assuming each individual may need something different (2016: 100) (refer back to Chapter 6 regarding reasonable adjustment duty). Wearmouth recognises however that there may be students who cannot work on the same learning objectives as the rest of the class, but it may be more appropriate to 'track back' and choose earlier objectives from the learning progression that is linked to the whole-class topic (p.110). Teachers may also prioritise one set of learning needs over others at certain times, for instance missing a Spanish lesson in order to concentrate on key vocabulary spelling strategies. It is recognised that this is a difficult balance and judgement for practitioners to make, and it should be based on their understanding and assessment of these individuals.

# Inclusive educational practice: Current policy

 Time to Reflect

Look at: *Local Area SEND Inspections: One Year On* (found at: www.gov.uk/government/publications/local-area-send-inspections-one-year-on).

What do local SEND inspections mean for the individual schools and therefore the learner? What is working well in terms of inclusive practice and what is not?

Although there are local SEND inspections for local authorities as explored above, when looking at school reports there is no separate judgement for special educational needs (SEN) provision under the school inspection framework (www.gov.uk/government/collections/education-inspection-framework).

SEN provision forms part of whole-school inspections. However: 'Inspectors will evaluate evidence of the impact of the curriculum, including on the most disadvantaged pupils. This includes pupils with SEND,' (Ofsted, 2019: 24). Inspectors will also gather evidence on how well pupils with SEND are prepared for the next stage of education and their adult lives (p.48) (refer back to the Equality and Human Rights Commission (2018) report: *Is Britain Fairer?*).

### Time to Reflect

What are your experiences of inclusive practice so far, especially in relation to the Code of Practice (DfE and DoH, 2014)? Look up a recent school inspection report and identify how effective and inclusive the provision of education is in meeting the needs of learners.

# So how can we monitor/evaluate inclusive practice?

Fredrickson and Cline (2015: Chapter 9) discuss the effectiveness of the learning environment in response to legislation, research and principles of effective learning. They refer to Kyriakides and Creemers' 'Dynamic model of educational effectiveness' (2012: 405) to demonstrate the tiered approach from national/regional policy – school policy/evaluation – quality of teaching outcomes.

# School evaluation and audits

Schools and settings use a variety of methods to evaluate and audit inclusive practice, such as the Index for Inclusion (Booth and Ainscow, 2011) and Achievement for All (Blandford, 2013) as previously mentioned. There are also 'disability-friendly' audits and approaches such as the 'Inclusive teaching observation checklist' (Table 8.1) and 'Whole school needs analysis' (Appendix B9), both from Wearmouth (2016). These are SENCo/school leadership tools for observing/analysing inclusive practice. You can also refer to books such as *The Dyslexia-Friendly Primary School* (Pavey, 2007):

> The self-evaluation/audit tool does not address the professional teaching of reading. It seeks to take a social model approach in moving the emphasis away from child deficit and toward the improvement of the learning setting. For this reason, it does not focus on individual learning characteristics. (p.77)

You may also wish to look at the SSAT Engagement Profile and Scale; this scale 'allows educators to focus on the child's engagement as a learner and create personalised learning pathways. It prompts student-centred reflection on how to increase the learner's engagement leading to deep learning' (http://complexneeds.org.uk/modules/Module-3.2-Engaging-in-learning---key-approaches/All/downloads/m10p040c/engagement_chart_scale_guidance.pdf).

---

 **Time to Reflect**

Consider how inclusion has become a normalising force by critiquing the purpose of interventions (as a way of eradicating difference). What is the role of interventions in creating 'othering'?

---

When we evaluate, we always judge against a standard. So, assessing how far inclusion has been achieved will depend on what we mean by inclusion. If we are assessing inclusion as being about children attending mainstream school, then we need to assess numbers and data such as exclusion figures. If inclusion is about quality of experience, then we need to try to assess quality too. Think about the sources of evidence you could use in relation to inclusion in your own or your setting's practice. Remember to include references to different definitions and types of evidence.

## Inclusive school leadership: The missing link?

Throughout this book we have argued that inclusion is an individual responsibility across all levels and roles, but arguably, the key responsibility lies with those who lead the school. School leaders must foster 'new meanings about diversity; promoting inclusive practices within schools; and build new connections between schools and communities' (Riehl, 2000: 55). By focusing on social justice, leaders can redress marginalisation, inequality and divisive action. They do this through practices such as democratic decision-making to transform inequitable arrangements (Wang, 2018). According to Attfield and Williams (2003) inclusive leaders are not daunted by the challenges they face and understand the key role they play in recognising, developing and instigating an inclusive culture and environment. They understand that commitment and hard work are a prerequisite.

Inclusive leaders possess a set of characteristics which support effective leadership, a moral conscience and judgement to enable ethical decision-making. The most important characteristic is trust (Stephenson, 2017), and this has added significance for the inclusive leader. Diverse, marginalised and under-represented pupils, their parents and carers and the community need to see that their trust is not misplaced. Inclusive leaders are expected to demonstrate *how* they uphold equality, fairness, democracy and dignity throughout the school and direct activities. Inclusive school leaders will draw on skills such as motivating staff, strategic decision-making, systemic, structural and cultural change, but as can be seen throughout this book, the inclusive leader faces higher challenges and deeper demands.

For a school to be truly inclusive, the focus must be on the whole school, working toward a 'new inclusive rationale' (Powers et al., 2001: 108). Notably, 'whole school' *means whole school*. We have talked at length throughout the book about the practices that support inclusion, and the impact upon pupils and families, but we must not forget that this extends to the staff. School leaders must value diversity amongst their staff, encourage collegiality and support innovation (Borg et al., 2011: 16). Inclusive leaders must provide a 'positive ethos and a learning culture by making their vision and inclusive values and beliefs explicit in all aspects of school life' (Borg et al., 2011: 16). These principles must be evident in all school policies, plans, and practices to ensure mutually supportive working relationships (see Chapters 6, 9 and 10). Support such as this from the inclusive leader is a crucial indicator of staff attitudes to inclusion (Lindqvist and Nilholm, 2014).

The most significant way of influencing the behaviour in a school is to lead by example (Stephenson, 2017). Inclusive leaders show concern for others, and are altruistically orientated on an individual, organisational and societal level. They know how to listen, observe and respond (Shapiro and Stefkovich, 2011: 18); they go beyond what law and justice require and take responsibility collectively as a human being, educator, administrator and citizen (Starratt, 1991). They are expert communicators and create the conditions necessary for dialogue regarding inclusion. They develop others and foster a caring and productive learning environment. Let us not forget that although leading a school is a big responsibility, it is also enjoyable. Whilst school leadership is thought to be challenging and exciting (Lindqvist and Nilholm, 2014), inclusive leadership is highly rewarding and satisfying because of its transformative nature. Inclusive school leaders, practitioners and those in the community of support have the power to make life-altering decisions which lift others.

You may also wish to refer to Chapter 10 in relation to the role of the headteacher and the governor in leading inclusive practice.

---

 ### Key Points

- This chapter has encouraged you to evaluate the definitions, theories, principles and models of 'inclusion' explored so far including considerations of social justice.
- You have reflected upon individual attitudes and roles as inclusion champions/advocates, and on your responsibilities towards inclusive practice.
- In evaluating current tools, practices and policies to support inclusion, it is anticipated that you will feel more equipped and prepared to embark on further roles and research in the area of SEND/inclusion.

---

 ### Final Reflection Questions

- What are your current aspirations in terms of your own (inclusive) practice?
- What else needs to be done regarding the future of SEND policy? (Return to our original challenge at the end of Chapter 1.)
- How will you advocate/champion inclusive practice in others?

---

# Further reading

This article provides you with some insight into whether a 'special pedagogy' is necessary:

Hornby, G. (2015). Inclusive special education: Development of a new theory for the education of children with special educational needs and disabilities. *British Journal of Special Education*, *42*(3), 234–256.

These chapters further support arguments for an inclusive society:

Chapter 4 of Fredrickson, N. and Cline, T. (2015). *Special Educational Needs, Inclusion and Diversity* (3rd edn). Maidenhead: Open University Press.

And Part 1 of Peer, L. and Reid, G. (2016). *Special Educational Needs: A Guide for Inclusive Practice* (2nd edn). London: Sage.

This article discusses developments in inclusive education since the introduction of the Salamanca Statement in 1994, and identifies future implications:

Kiuppis, F. and Hausstatter, R.T. (eds) (2014). *Inclusive Education Twenty Years after Salamanca*. New York: Peter Lang Publishing.

# GLOSSARY

**Ancient Greece** was a civilisation and period in history dated between 323 BCE and 30 BCE.

**Ancient Rome** was a civilisation and period in history dated between 753 BCE and 476 AD.

**Applied Behaviour Analysis (ABA)** is the application of the principles of operant conditioning to change behaviour.

**Asperger's Syndrome** is a form of autism that influences how a person communicates and understands the world.

**Assistive technology** is any piece of technology that improved daily functioning for disabled people.

**Asylums** are a form of institution for the care of people who have mental ill health.

**Auditory processing skills** are the cognitive ability to comprehend and respond to auditory information.

**Barrier to learning** occurs when access to typical educational provision is hindered by a learning difficulty or disability.

**British Sign Language** is a form of sign language commonly used in Great Britain.

**Calculation dysfluency** is the opposite of calculation fluency, where mathematical calculations can be completed with accuracy and speed. Instead, completing calculations can take a long time with a high error rate.

**Charity model of disability** postulates that disability occurs 'within' a person and should inspire pity as its occurrence is viewed as a tragedy.

**Children in Need** is where a child is deemed at risk of harm by the Local Authority and the family is given support by Social Services.

**Cognitive flexibility** is the cognitive ability to shift attention between competing tasks.

**Community model of disability** occurs when responsibility for supporting a disabled person is adopted by the community around them.

**Controlled (experimental) conditions** occur during an experiment when all confounding variables are held constant.

**Counting difficulties** occur when an individual has difficulty with counting numbers forwards and backwards.

**Covert discrimination** is discrimination that occurs in a subtle and concealed way but is still as harmful as overt discrimination.

**Data** is information gathered about the world, usually through observation, that can be numerical, visual and language based.

**Disability** is defined by the Equality Act (2010) as occurring if a person has a physical or mental impairment that significantly impacts engagement with regular daily activities for a substantial amount of time.

**Disability Civil Rights** are fundamental human rights equally afforded to disabled peoples.

**Disability Civil Rights Movement** originated in the USA in the 21st century with a view to protest for the promotion of Disability Civil Rights.

**Discrimination** is unjust and unfair treatment of others based on a protected characteristic (Equality Act, 2010) and/or aspect of their personhood.

**Early Intensive Behavioural Intervention (EIBI)** is a therapy for individuals with Autism Spectrum Condition that applied the principles of operant conditioning.

**Empowerment** can be the authority or power given to an individual to act. It can also be the process of becoming stronger and more confident, such as claiming one's rights.

**Epistemology** is the philosophical study of knowledge and 'truth'.

**Equal opportunities** are the right to be treated fairly regarding opportunities, such as job interviews and exams, regardless of the possession of protected characteristics.

**Ethnic group** is a community or population made up of people from the same culture or descent.

**Evidence-Based Practice (EBP)** is the considered use of all relevant evidence when deciding on a course of treatment or action for an individual.

**Evidence-Informed Practice (EIP)** is the considered use of all relevant evidence when deciding on a course of treatment or action for an individual, with a deemphasis on a heighted importance of scientific experimental evidence.

**Executive functioning difficulties** are characterised by a collection of cognitive difficulties that influence planning, organisation and problem-solving.

**Experiment** is a procedure of controlled observation of phenomena to test a hypothesis.

**Externalising behaviours** are symptoms of mental ill health that can be readily observed, such as aggressive behaviour.

**Fine motor skills** involve the use and coordination of small muscle groups to complete a movement.

**Focus groups** are a method of collecting data for research where multiple participants are interviewed together.

**Functional communication** occurs when an individual can spontaneously communicate their needs and wants to others without additional prompting or support.

**Graduated response** occurs in education when increasing levels of intensity of SEND support occur in a planned manner.

**Gross motor skills** involve the movement and coordination of large muscle groups to complete a movement.

**Hyperactivity** is characterised by a person experiencing unusually high levels of activity.

**Hyper reactivity to sensory stimuli** is where a person has sensory sensitivities that make certain sensory stimuli unpleasant.

**Hypo reactivity to sensory stimuli** is where a person has sensory sensitivities that make certain sensory stimuli pleasant.

**Hypothesis/hypotheses** is formed of a proposed reason for a phenomenon based on initial information and used to guide further investigation.

**Ideographic** an ideographic psychological approach is concerned with the personal experience of an individual and does not seek generalisable claims about behaviour.

**Impairment** is to be in possession of a physical or mental difference which means one's body or mind does not function in the same way as the perceived norm.

**Impulsivity** involves behaviour that is engaged in without prior thought or planning.

**Inattention** is characterised by an inability to focus on a situation or task when required to do so.

**Inclusion** is involving all people equally in an opportunity or activity regardless of personal characteristics.

**Inclusive education** is an extension of the concept of inclusion where all people are given equal access to educational opportunities regardless of personal characteristics.

**Inclusive pedagogy** is an educational theory focusing on inclusive educational practice.

**Inclusive practice** is the practice of putting the concept of inclusion into practical effect.

**Individual provision map** is similar to an individual education plan in that it details the educational provision that a child is entitled to as a result of their special educational needs and disability that is different from and/or additional to that which is typically made available.

**The Industrial Revolution** is a historical period in Great Britain that occurred predominantly in the 19th Century, characterised by the rapid development of technology and industry.

**Inhibitory control** is an executive cognitive function to reduce the influence of distracting behaviours and thoughts so that thinking and behaviour can be directed towards goal completion.

**Innate number sense** refers to an innate ability for the brain to be able to differentiate between quantities.

**Institutions** are organisations that serve a societal function, such as health, educational, social, political, religious etc.

**Integration** occurs when disabled individuals and those who have special educational needs receive their education in the same context as others but are not deemed to be fully included.

**Internalising behaviours** are symptoms of mental ill health that cannot be readily observed as they occur within the person, such as anxious thought patterns.

**Intersubjectivity** occurs when two or more people have a shared common agreement for a definition of an object.

**Intervention** occurs when a plan of action specific to an individual's needs is implemented to alleviate some undesirable state or condition.

**Interviews** are a research method where qualitative data is obtained through asking participants questions about the topic being studied.

**Justified true belief** is a sufficient reason to believe a given proposition is true.

**Looked after children (LAC)** are children who are under the care of the Local Authority.

**Low- and middle-income countries** the United Nations defines low income countries as those with less than $1,036 gross national income per capita and middle income countries as those with between $1,036 and $12,615 gross national income per capita.

**Low-tech** is a form of assistive technology that does not require much technical speciality.

**Makaton** is a form of alternative communication that utilises symbols.

**Mapping of number representations** is the ability to assign the correct numerical symbol to its corresponding quantity.

**Measurement** occurs during a research study when changes in chosen phenomena are systematically observed.

**Medical model of disability** posits that disability occurs 'within' a person and is organic in origin.

**Medieval period** was a period in history dated between 476–1453 AD.

**Mesopotamia** was an ancient historical region dated between 3100 BCE–539 BCE.

**Mid-tech to high-tech** is a category of assistive technology that involves a high level of technology.

**Modernism** is a philosophical movement that emerged at the beginning of the 20th Century characterised by the application of reason and scientific enquiry.

**Neurodiversity** refers to a movement which focuses on viewing people with Autistic Spectrum Condition, and other conditions, as possessing differences and strengths rather than as disordered.

**Neurotypical** refers to individuals perceived as having normative neurological development and abilities and who haven't experienced developmental difference.

**Nomothetic** a nomothetic psychological approach is concerned with understanding generalisations about behaviour that can be applied to all people.

**Norms** are a collection of set societal standards that act as a guide for behaviour and cultural practices.

**No-tech** is a category of assistive technology that requires no technology.

**Number sense** refers to a child's innate ability to understand numbers, their sizes and relationships, such as being able to recognise the difference between smaller and larger quantities.

**Number skills** is a broad term that refers to the basic set of skills that enable accurate processing of number.

**Observation** in the context of a research study is making a formal inquiry of the study's phenomena by collecting and analysing data.

**Orthographic working memory difficulties** occur when a person has difficulty processing and utilising visual information to complete an action or task.

**Paradigms** are a set of ideas and approaches, a distinctive set of values/beliefs, within the context of a viewpoint.

**Participatory design** in the context of assistive technology involves involving the opinions and experiences of the device user in technology development.

**Phonological processing skills** is the possession of the cognitive ability to accurately process units of language to aid verbal understanding.

**Place–value** is the understanding that each digit corresponds to a number.

**Positive psychology** is a psychological paradigm concerned with studying what contributes to wellbeing and a successful human experience.

**Practitioner** is a term used to denote a professional qualified to work in a role.

**Protected characteristics** are outlined in the Equality Act (2010). They are age, disability, gender reassignment, race, religion or belief, sex, sexual orientation, marriage and civil partnership and pregnancy and maternity.

**Provision mapping/individual provision map** provide details of provision that a learner with special educational needs shall receive.

**Randomised Controlled Trials (RCTs)** are a form of scientific experiment that aims to reduce bias by randomly allocating participants to groups and giving them different treatments or interventions.

**Reasonable adjustments** are changes to work, educational and social environments that enable people with a disability to equally participate.

**Re-authoring** is a term used in Narrative Therapy to denote when a person creates an alternative narrative for their lived experience.

**(Research) methods** are the way in which data is collected or generated.

**Results** are the outcomes of collecting and analysing research data.

**Segregation** is the physical separation of a group of individuals from society.

**Self-concept** is the collection of beliefs a person holds about themself which enables self-awareness.

**Self-efficacy** is the collection of beliefs a person holds about their ability to complete a set course of action.

**Self-regulation** is also known as emotional regulation and is the ability to recognise and effectively respond to the full range of human emotions.

**Single-case research design** is a form of experimental design where the subject serves as their own control rather than using another person or group as a comparison.

**Social construct** is a term that refers to the presumed socially constructed nature of reality. Within this framework a social construct is a concept or idea created and accepted by people in a given society.

**Social justice** is the notion of fair and just relations and distribution of resources and opportunities between all members of a society.

**Social model of disability** places the cause of disability external to the individual, as a function of how the physical and social environment is designed.

**Social norms** are cultural products of acceptable individual and group behaviour as created and generally agreed upon within a particular society.

**Special Educational Needs (SEN)** is where an individual may require educational provision that is additional and different from what is typically available, to successfully learn.

**Statement of Special Educational Needs**  was a legal process and document that outlined a learner's special educational needs and additional educational entitlements.

**Statementing process** was the assessment process that led to the issuing of a Statement of Special Educational Needs.

**Statutory protection**  is a legal requirement that an institution must follow.

**Stereotypes**  are a set of over-generalised assumptions about a group of people accompanied with the expectation that these assumptions can be applied all group members.

**Strategies**  are the implementation of a discrete instructional actions as part of wider teaching practice.

**Subitising**  is the ability to accurately judge the number of an array of items without counting.

**Symptoms**  are differences within the body and mind from normal functioning which indicate the presence of a disease or condition.

**Technology**  is the application of science and knowledge to develop useful tools and appliances.

**Theory**  can be a set of principles on which the practice of an activity is based, e.g. a theory of Education. It can also be an idea used to account for a situation or justify a course of action.

**Triad of impairments**  refers to the three difficulties of Autism Spectrum Condition developed by Lorna Wing.

**Verbal processing**  includes a range of cognitive abilities associated with distinguishing, understanding and responding to verbal stimuli.

**Virtual Reality (VR)**  is a computer simulated experience that seeks to mimic the world or create a new world experience.

**Visual magnocellular functions**  are part of the major neural pathways within the brain associated with vision.

**Visual processing skills**  involve the cognitive ability to identify, classify and respond appropriately to visual sensory stimuli.

# REFERENCES

Aaron, P.G. (1997). The impending demise of the discrepancy formula. *Review of Educational Research*, *67*(4), 461–502.

Abdulkarim, W.F., Abdulrauf, M.S. and Elgendy, A.A. (2017). The effect of a multi-sensory program on reducing dyspraxia and dysgraphia among learning disabled students in Rafha. *Journal of Educational Sciences & Psychology*, *7*(1), 51–65.

Adelman, H.S. and Taylor, L. (2007). Systemic change for school improvement. *Journal of Educational and Psychological Consultation*, *17*(1), 55–77.

Aghebati, A., Gharraee, B., Shoshtari, M.H. and Gohari, M.R. (2014). Triple P Positive Parenting Program for mothers of ADHD children. *Iranian Journal of Psychiatry and Behavioral Sciences*, *8*(1), 59.

Ainscow, M. (2000). *Reaching out to all learners: The development of an inclusive pedagogy*. Paper presented at International Seminar, Hedmark University College, Hamar, Norway, 29 June.

Al Jabery, M., Al Khateeb, J. and Zumberg, M. (2012). 'Current Special Education Programs in the Hashemite Kingdom of Jordan.' In K. Mutua and C.V. Sunal (eds), *Advances in Research and Praxis in Special Education in Africa, Caribbean and the Middle East*. Charlotte, NC: InfoAge Publishing.

Al Ju'beh, K. (2015). *Disability Inclusive Development Toolkit*. Bensheim: CBM. Available at: www.cbm.org/article/downloads/54741/CBM-DID-TOOLKIT-accessible.pdf (accessed 23 April 2020).

Albano, A.M., Chorpita, B.F. and Barlow, D.H. (2003). Childhood anxiety disorders. In E.J. Mash and R.A. Barkley (eds), *Child Psychopathology* (2nd edn). New York: Guilford Press, pp.279–329.

Aldrich, R. (1982). *An Introduction to the History of Education*. London: Hodder & Stoughton.

Allan, J. (2003). Productive pedagogies and the challenge of inclusion. *British Journal of Special Education*, *30*(4), 175–179.

Allen, G.E. (2011). Eugenics and modern biology: Critiques of eugenics, 1910–1945. *Annals of Human Genetics*, *75*(3), 314–325.

Allen, M. (2011). *Employability, What Are Employees Looking For?* Available at: www.jobs.ac.uk/careers-advice/interview-tips/1515/employability-what-are-employers-looking-for (accessed 23 April 2020).

Alves, C.C.D.F., Monteiro, G.B.M., Rabello, S., Gasparetto, M.E.R.F. and Carvalho, K.M.D. (2009). Assistive technology applied to education of students with visual impairment. *Revista Panamericana de Salud Pública*, *26*, 148–152.

American Psychiatric Association (2013). *Diagnostic and Statistical Manual of Mental Disorders* (5th edn) (DSM-5). Philadelphia, PA: American Psychiatric Association.

Anderson, G.L. and Arsenault, N. (1998). *Fundamentals of Educational Research* (2nd edn). London: Falmer Press.

Archer, T. and Kostrzewa, R.M. (2012). Physical exercise alleviates ADHD symptoms: Regional deficits and development trajectory. *Neurotoxicity Research*, *21*(2), 195–209.

Arthur, J. (2010). *Citizens of Character: New Directions in Character and Values Education*. Exeter: Imprint Academic.

Asbrock, F., Nieuwoudt, C., Duckitt, J. and Sibley, C. G. (2011). Societal stereotypes and the legitimation of intergroup behavior in Germany and New Zealand. *Analysis of Social Issues and Public Policy*, *11*(1), 154–179.

Atkinson, M., Jones, M. and Lamont, E. (2007). *Multi-Agency Working and its Implications for Practice: A Review of the Literature*. Reading: CfBT Education Trust.

Attachment Aware Schools (2020). *Attachment Aware Schools*. Available at: www.bathspa.ac.uk/schools/education/research/attachment-aware-schools/ (accessed 3 February 2020)

Attfield, R. and Williams, C. (2003). Leadership and inclusion: A special school perspective. *British Journal of Special Education*, *30*(1), 28–33.

Au, A., Lau, K.M., Wong, A.H.C., Lam, C., Leung, C., Lau, J. and Lee, Y.K. (2014). The efficacy of a group Triple P (Positive Parenting Program) for Chinese parents with a child diagnosed with ADHD in Hong Kong: A pilot randomised controlled study. *Australian Psychologist*, *49*(3), 151–162.

Avalos, H., Melcher, S.J. and Schipper, J. (2007). *This Abled Body: Rethinking Disabilities in Biblical Studies*. Atlanta, GA: The Society of Biblical Literature.

Bain, R. (1937). Technology and state government. *American Sociological Review*, *2*(6), 860–874.

Ballard, K. (1999). *Inclusive Education: International Voices on Disability and Justice*. Abingdon: Psychology Press (Taylor and Francis).

Bandura, A. (2001). Social cognitive theory: An agentic perspective. *Annual Review of Psychology*, *52*(1), 1–26.

Barnes, C. and Mercer, G. (2003). *Disability*. Cambridge: Polity Press.

Barnes, P. (2008). Multi-agency working: What are the perspectives of SENCo and parents regarding its development and implementation? *British Journal of Special Education*, *35*(4), 230–240.

Barnyak, N.C. and McNelly, T.A. (2016). The literacy skills and motivation to read of children enrolled in Title I: A comparison of electronic and print nonfiction books. *Early Childhood Education Journal*, *44*(5), 527–536.

Bartelet, D., Vaessen, A., Blomert, L. and Ansari, D. (2014). What basic number processing measures in kindergarten explain unique variability in first-grade arithmetic proficiency? *Journal of Experimental Child Psychology*, *117*, 12–28.

Barton, L. (2003). *Professorial Lecture: Inclusive Education and Teacher Education: A Basis for Hope or a Discourse of Delusion?* London: Institute of Education.

BASW (2014). *The Code of Ethics for Social Work*. Available at: www.basw.co.uk/about-basw/code-ethics (accessed 23 April 2020).

Beck, A.T., Emery, G. and Greenberg, R.L. (2005). Anxiety Disorders and Phobias: A Cognitive Perspective. New York: Basic Books.

Behan, D. (2017). *Taking Sides: Clashing Views in Special Education* (8th edn). New York: McGraw Hill Education.

Benjamin, A.S. and Tullis, J. (2010). What makes distributed practice effective? *Cognitive Psychology*, *61*(3), 228–247.

Benjamin, S. (2002). *The Micropolitics of Inclusive Education: An Ethnography*. Buckingham: Open University Press.

Bertilsdotter, H., Kourti, M., Jackson-Perry, D., Brownlow, C., Fletcher, K., Bendelman, D. and O'Dell, L. (2019). Doing it differently: Emancipatory autism studies within a neurodiverse academic space. *Disability & Society*. doi: https://doi.org/10.1080/09687599.2019.1603102.

Bhopal, K. (2011). 'This is a school, it's not a site': Teachers' attitudes towards Gypsy and Traveller pupils in schools in England, UK. *British Educational Research Journal*, *37*(3), 465–483.

Bhowmick, A. and Hazarika, S.M. (2017). An insight into assistive technology for the visually impaired and blind people: State-of-the-art and future trends. *Journal on Multimodal User Interfaces*, *11*(2), 149–172.

Biederman, J., Monuteaux, M.C., Doyle, A.E., Seidman, L.J., Wilens, T.E., Ferrero, F., Morgan, C.L. and Faraone, S.V. (2004). Impact of executive function deficits and attention-deficit/hyperactivity disorder (ADHD) on academic outcomes in children. *Journal of Consulting and Clinical Psychology*, *72*(5), 757.

Bigozzi, L., Tarchi, C., Pinto, G. and Donfrancesco, R. (2016). Divergent thinking in Italian students with and without reading impairments, *International Journal of Disability, Development and Education*, *63*(4), 450–466.

Blandford, S. (2013). *Achievement For All: Raising Aspirations, Access and Achievement*. London: Bloomsbury Educational.

Blaxter, L., Hughes, C. and Tight, M. (2010). *How To Research* (4th edn)., 4th edn, Maidenhead: McGraw Hill Open University Press.

Booth, T. and Ainscow, M. (2011). *The Index for Inclusion*. Bristol: CSIE.

Borg, G., Hunter, J., Sigurjonsdóttir, B. and D'Alessio, S. (2011). *Key Principles for Promoting Quality in Inclusive Education: Recommendations for Practice*. Brussels: European Agency for Development in Special Needs Education.

Bouck, E. (2015). *Assistive Technology*. Thousand Oaks, CA: Sage.

BPS (2015). *The Child & Family Clinical Psychology Review*. Available at: www.bps.org.uk

Bracken, S. and Novak, K. (2019). *Transforming Higher Education through Universal Design for Learning: An International Perspective*. London: Routledge.

Bravo, L. (2014). Neuroscience and education: Current state of research on dyslexia/Neurociencias. *Estudios de Psicología*, *35*(1), 1–28.

British Dyslexia Association (2019). *Defining Dyslexia*. Available at: www.bdadyslexia.org.uk/dyslexic (accessed 23 April 2020).

British Educational Research Association (2018). *Ethical Guidelines for Educational Research*. Available at: www.bera.ac.uk/researchers-resources/publications/ethical-guidelines-for-educational-research-2018 (accessed 23 April 2020).

Brookfield, P. (2005). Critically reflective practice. *Journal of Continuing Education in the Health Professions*, *18*(4), 197–205.

Brophy, J.E. (2010). *Motivating Students to Learn* (3rd edn). New York: Routledge.

Brown, C. and Zhang, D. (2016). Is engaging in evidence-informed practice in education rational? What accounts for discrepancies in teachers' attitudes towards evidence use and actual instances of evidence use in schools? *British Educational Research Journal*, *42*(5), 780–801.

Browning, K. (2018). An early review of the new SEN/disability policy and legislation: Where are we now? Impact of the legislation on the SENCo role and school practices. *Journal of Research in Special Educational Needs*, *18*(3), 169–173.

Bryant, B.R., Bryant, D.P., Shih, M. and Seok, S. (2010). Assistive technology and supports provision: A selective review of the literature and proposed areas of application. *Exceptionality*, *18*(4), 203–213.

Buron, K.D. and Curtis, M. (2012) *The Incredible 5-Point Scale: The Significantly Improved and Expanded Second Edition*. Shawnee Mission, Kansas: AAPC Publishing.

Caligari, M., Godi, M., Guglielmetti, S., Franchignoni, F. and Nardone, A. (2013). Eye tracking communication devices in amyotrophic lateral sclerosis: Impact on disability and quality of life. *Amyotrophic Lateral Sclerosis and Frontotemporal Degeneration, 14*(7–8), 546–552.

Cancer, A., Manzoli, S. and Antonietti, A. (2016). The alleged link between creativity and dyslexia: Identifying the specific process in which dyslexic students excel, *Cogent Psychology, 3*(1), 1–13.

Cappella, E., Frazier, S.L., Atkins, M.S., Schoenwald, S.K. and Glisson, C. (2008). Enhancing schools' capacity to support children in poverty: An ecological model of school-based mental health services. *Administration and Policy in Mental Health and Mental Health Services Research, 35*(5), 395.

Carl, E., Stein, A.T., Levihn-Coon, A., Pogue, J.R., Rothbaum, B., Emmelkamp, P., Asmundson, G.J., Carlbring, P. and Powers, M.B. (2019). Virtual reality exposure therapy for anxiety and related disorders: A meta-analysis of randomized controlled trials. *Journal of Anxiety Disorders, 61*, 27–36.

Carr, D. (2006). Professional and personal values and virtues in education and teaching. *Oxford Review of Education, 32*(2), 171–183.

Carroll, M. (2018). *Infancy and Earliest Childhood in the Roman World: 'A Fragment of Time'*. Oxford: Oxford University Press.

Castro, S., Grande, C. and Palikara, O. (2019). Evaluating the quality of outcomes defined for children with Education, Health and Care plans in England: A local picture with global implications. *Research in Developmental Disabilities, 86*, 41–52.

Charach, A., Carson, P., Fox, S., Ali, M.U., Beckett, J. and Lim, C.G. (2013). Interventions for preschool children at high risk for ADHD: A comparative effectiveness review. *Pediatrics, 131*(5), e1584–e1604.

Chavan, A. (2018). *Understanding Overt and Covert Discrimination*. Opinion Front. Available at: https://opinionfront.com/covert-overt-discrimination (accessed 23 April 2020).

Cheminais, R. (2009). *Effective Multi Agency Partnerships*. London: Sage.

Cheminais, R. (2010). *Rita Cheminais' Handbook for New SENCOs*. London: Sage.

Childs, P. (2016). *Modernism*. London: Routledge.

Clapton, J. and Fitzgerald, J. (1997). The history of disability: A history of 'otherness'. *New Renaissance Magazine, 7*(1), 1–3.

Clarke, P.A. and Rose, L.M. (2013). Mental states, bodily dispositions and table manners: A guide to reading 'intellectual disability' from Homer to Late Antiquity. In C. Laes, C.F. Goodley and L.M. Rose (eds), *Disabilities in Roman Antiquity: Disparate Bodies A Capite ad Calcem*. Boston, MA: Brill.

Climie, E.A. and Mastoras, S.M. (2015). ADHD in schools: Adopting a strengths-based perspective. *Canadian Psychology/Psychologie Canadienne, 56*(3), 295–300.

Clough, P. and Corbett, J. (2011). *Theories of Inclusive Education*. London: Chapman/Sage.

Clough, P. and Nutbrown, C. (2007). *A Student's Guide to Methodology* (2nd edn). London: Sage.

Cohen, L., Manion, L., Morrison, K. and Bell, R. (2011). *Research Methods in Education* (7th edn). London: Routledge.

Cole, B. (2012). *Mother-Teachers: Insights into Inclusion*. London: Fulton.

Collins, M.T. (1995). History of deaf-blind education. *Journal of Visual Impairment & Blindness, 89*(3), 210–212.

Cooper, J.O., Heron, T.E. and Heward, W.L., (2007). *Applied Behaviour Analysis*. New York: Pearson.

Corker, M. and Shakespeare, T. (2002). *Disability/Postmodernity: Embodying Disability Theory*. London: Bloomsbury Publishing.

Cottrell, S. (2003). *Skills for Success: The Personal Development Planning Handbook*. Basingstoke: Palgrave.

Cowan, J. (1998). *On Becoming an Innovative University Teacher*. Buckingham: Open University Press/The Society for Research into Higher Education (SRHE).

Cowne, E., Frankl, C. and Gerschel, L. (2018). *The SENCo Handbook: Leading and Managing a Whole School Approach*. Abingdon: Routledge.

Creemers, B. and Kyriakides, L. (2013). Using the dynamic model of educational effectiveness to identify stages of effective teaching: An introduction to the special issue. *Journal of Classroom Interaction, 48*(2), 4–10.

Croft, A. (2010). Including disabled children in learning: Challenges in developing countries. *CREATE Research Monograph 36*, University of Sussex, Brighton.

Csikszentmihalyi, M. (1990). *Flow: The Psychology of Optimal Experience*. New York: Harper & Row.

Cummins, J. (2014). *Biliteracy, Empowerment, and Transformative Pedagogy*. Available at: www.researchgate.net/publication/241492125_ Biliteracy_Empowerment_and_Transformative_Pedagogy (accessed 23 April 2020).

Curran, H. (2015). *SEND reforms 2014 and the narrative of the SENCO: Early impact on children and young people with SEND, the SENCO and the school*. Paper presented at the BERA Annual Conference, Queen's University, Belfast, Northern Ireland, 15–17 September.

Dalley, S. (1998). *Myths from Mesopotamia: Creation, the Flood, Gilgamesh, and Others*. New York: Oxford University Press.

Daniels, H., Brown, S., Edwards, A., Leadbetter, J., Martin, D., Middleton, D., Parsons, S., Popova, A. and Warmington, P. (2005). *Studying Professional Learning for Inclusion*.

Davis, K. (2008). Intersectionality as buzzword: A sociology of science perspective on what makes a feminist theory successful. *Feminist Theory*, *9*(1), 67–85.

DCSF (2007). *Social and Emotional Aspects of Learning for Secondary Schools*. Nottingham: Department for Children, Schools and Families Publications.

DCSF (2008). *Bercow Review of Services for Children and Young People (0-19) with Speech, Language and Communication Needs*. Nottingham: Department for Children, Schools and Families Publications.

DCSF (2009). *Report to the Secretary of State on the Lamb Inquiry Review of SEN and Disability Information*. Nottingham: Department for Children, Schools and Families Publications.

DCSF (2010). *Salt Review: Independent Review of Teacher Supply for Pupils with Severe, Profound and Multiple Learning Difficulties (SLD and PMLD)*. Nottingham: Department for Children, Schools and Families Publications.

de Oliveira, R.F. & Wann, J.P. (2010). Integration of dynamic information for visuomotor control in young adults with developmental coordination disorder, *Experimental Brain Research*, *205* (3), 387–394.

Dehaene, S. and Cohen, L. (2007). Cultural recycling of cortical maps. *Neuron*, *56*, 384–398.

Delamont, S. (2016). *Fieldwork in Educational Settings: Methods, Pitfalls and Perspectives* (3rd edn). London: Routledge.

DeMatteo, D., Batastini, A., Foster, E. and Hunt, E. (2010). Individualizing risk assessment: Balancing idiographic and nomothetic data. *Journal of Forensic Psychology Practice*, *10*(4), 360–371.

Derrington, C. and Kendall, S. (2008). Challenges and barriers to secondary education: The experiences of young Gypsy traveller students in English secondary schools. *Social Policy and Society*, *7*(1), 119–128.

DfE (2011a). *SEAL National Strategies*. Available at: https://webarchive. nationalarchives.gov.uk/20110221192111/http://nationalstrategies. standards.dcsf.gov.uk/inclusion/behaviourattendanceandseal/seal (accessed 23 April 2020).

DfE (2011b). *Support and Aspiration: A New Approach to Special Educational Needs and Disability: A Consultation* (Green Paper; Cm8027). London: HMSO.

DfE (2013) Children and Faimilies Bill 2013: Contextual information and Responses to Pre-Legislative Scruitiny. Available at: https://assets. publishing.service.gov.uk/government/uploads/system/uploads/ attachment_data/file/219658/Children_20and_20Families_20Bill_2020 13.pdf (accessed 18 May 2020).

DfE (2015). *Research on Funding for Young People with Special Educational Needs* (RR470). London: DfE.

Dfe (2017). Children looked after in England (including adoption), year ending 31 March 2017. Available at: https://assets.publishing.service. gov.uk/government/uploads/system/uploads/attachment_data/ file/664995/SFR50_2017-Children_looked_after_in_England.pdf

DfE (2019). *The Teachers Standards*. Available at: www.gov.uk/govern ment/publications/teachers-standards (accessed 23 April 2020).

DfE and DoH (2014). *The SEND Code of Practice: 0–25*. Available at: www.gov.uk/government/publications/send-code-of-practice-0-to-25 (accessed 23 April 2020).

DfEE (2000). *Educational Psychology Services (England)*: Current Role, Good Practice and Future Directions: The Research Report London: HMSO.

DfES (2001) *Special Educational Needs Code of Practice*. Available at: https://www.gov.uk/government/publications/special-educational-needs-sen-code-of-practice (accessed 18 May 2020).

DfES (2003). *Every Child Matters*. Norwich: The Stationery Office.

DfES (2007). *Aiming High for Disabled Children*. Norwich: The Stationery Office.

Disability Africa (2018). *The Case for Inclusion: A New Approach to Disability in Low- and Middle-Income Countries*. Guildford: Disability Africa.

D'Mello, A.M. and Gabrieli, J.D.E. (2018). Cognitive neuroscience of dyslexia. *Language, Speech & Hearing Services in Schools*, *49*(4), 798–809.

Döhla, D., Willmes, K. and Heim, S. (2018). Cognitive profiles of developmental dysgraphia. *Frontiers in Psychology*, 9, 2006.

Dunlop, J.M. (2009). Social policy devolution: A historical review of Canada, the United Kingdom, and the United States (1834–1999). *Social Work in Public Health*, *24*(3), 191–209.

DuPaul, G.J., Weyandt, L.L. and Janusis, G.M. (2011). ADHD in the classroom: Effective intervention strategies. *Theory into Practice*, *50*(1), 35–42.

Durrant, J. and Holden, G. (2006). *Teachers Leading Change: Doing Research for School Improvement*. London: Sage.

Dyson, A. (1999). Inclusion and inclusions: Theories and discourses in inclusive education. In H. Daniels and P. Garner (eds), *Inclusive Education*. London: Kogan Page, pp.36–53.

Dyspraxia Foundation (2019). *What is Dyspraxia?* Available at: https://dyspraxiafoundation.org.uk/about-dyspraxia/dyspraxia-glance/ (accessed 23 April 2020).

Education for All (EFA) (2015). *Education for All 2000–2015: Achievements and Challenges* (EFA Global Monitoring Report). Paris: UNESCO. Available at: http://unesdoc.unesco.org/images/0023/002322/232205e.pdf (accessed 23 April 2020).

Edyburn, D.L. (2004). Rethinking assistive technology. *Special Education Technology Practice*, *5*(4), 16–23.

Ek, U., Fernell, E., Westerlund, J., Holmberg, K., Olsson, P., Gillberg, C., Gothenburg University, Institute of Neuroscience and Physiology, Department of Psychiatry and Neurochemistry, and Sahlgrenska Academy (2007). Cognitive strengths and deficits in schoolchildren with ADHD. *Acta Pædiatrica*, *96*(5), 756–761.

Ekins, A. (2012). *The Changing Face of Special Educational Needs: Impact and Implications for SENCOs and their Schools*. London: Routledge.

Engel, G.L. (1977). The need for a new medical model: A challenge for biomedicine. *Science*, *196*(4286), 129–136.

Engeström, Y. (1999) Innovative learning in work teams: Analysing cycles of knowledge creation in practice. In Y. Engestrom et al. (eds), *Perspectives on Activity Theory*. Cambridge: Cambridge University Press, pp.377–406.

Equality and Human Rights Commission (2018). *Is Britain Fairer?* Available at: www.equalityhumanrights.com/en/publication-download/britain-fairer-2018 (accessed 23 April 2020).

Ervin, R.A., DuPaul, G.J., Kern, L. and Friman, P.C. (1998). Classroom-based functional and adjunctive assessments: Proactive approaches to intervention selection for adolescents with attention deficit hyperactivity disorder. *Journal of Applied Behavior Analysis*, *31*(1), 65–78.

Evidence-Based Medicine Working Group (1992). Evidence-based medicine: A new approach to teaching the practice of medicine. *Jama*, *268*(17), 271–275.

Eyler, J.R. (2016). *Disability in the Middle Ages: Reconsiderations and Reverberations*. Abingdon: Routledge.

Farmer, T.W. and Xie, H. (2007). Aggression and school social dynamics: The good, the bad, and the ordinary. *Journal of School Psychology*, *45*(5), 461–478.

Farrell, P. (2000). The impact of research on developments in inclusive education. *International Journal of Inclusive Education*, *4*(2), 153–162.

Feifer, S.G. (2001). *Subtypes of language-based dysgraphias*. Handout from Learning of the Brain: Using Brain Research To Leave No Child Behind workshop, Hyatt Regency. Boston, MA.

Fiedler, K. and Bless, H. (2001). Social cognition. In M. Hewstone and W. Stroebe (eds), *Introduction to Social Psychology: A European Perspective*. Malden, MA: Blackwell, pp.115–149.

Fischer, R. (2006). Congruence and functions of personal and cultural values: Do my values reflect my culture's values? *Personality and Social Psychology Bulletin*, *32*(11), 1419–1431.

Fisher, P. and Byrne, V. (2012). Identity, emotion and the internal goods of practice: A study of learning disability professionals. *Sociology of Health & Illness*, *34*(1), 79–94.

Fisher, P. and Goodley, D. (2007). The linear medical model of disability: Mothers of disabled babies resist with counter-narratives. *Sociology of Health & Illness*, *29*(1), 66–81.

Fleischer, D. (2001). *The Disability Rights Movement*. Philadelphia, PA: Temple University Press.

Florian, L. (2015). Inclusive pedagogy: A transformative approach to individual differences but can it help reduce educational inequalities? *Scottish Educational Review*, *47*(1), 5–14.

Florian, L. and Linklater, H. (2010). Preparing teachers for inclusive education: Using inclusive pedagogy to enhance teaching and learning for all. *Cambridge Journal of Education*, *40*(4), 369–386.

Flynn, N. (2019). Facilitating evidence-informed practice, *Teacher Development*, *23*(1), 64–82.

Fredrickson, N. and Cline, T. (2015). *Special Educational Needs, Inclusion and Diversity* (3rd edn). Maidenhead: Open University Press.

Furlong, J. and Oancea, A. (2005). Assessing quality in applied and practice-based educational research: a framework for discussion. Oxford: Oxford Department of Educational Studies.

Garland, R. (1995). *The Eye of the Beholder: Deformity and Disability in the Graeco-Roman World*. Ithaca, New York: Cornell University Press.

Gaskell, S. and Leadbetter, J. (2009). Educational psychologists and multi-agency working: Exploring professional identity. *Educational Psychology in Practice*, *25*(2), 97–111.

Gasper, M. (2010). *Multi-Agency Working in the Early Years: Challenges and Opportunities*. London: Sage.

Geurts, H.M., Pol, S.E., Lobbestael, J. and Simons, C.J. (2020). Executive functioning in 60+ autistic males: The discrepancy between experienced challenges and cognitive performance. *Journal of Autism and Developmental Disorders*, *50*, 1380–1390.

Gibbs, G. (1998). *Learning by Doing: A Guide to Teaching and Learning Methods*. Oxford: Further Education Unit, Oxford Polytechnic.

Gibbs, J., Appleton, J. and Appleton, R. (2007). Dyspraxia or developmental coordination disorder? Unravelling the enigma. *Archives of Disease in Childhood*, *92*(6), 534–539.

Gillan, N. (2019). Social Anxiety in Adult Autism. Doctorate Thesis. University of Exeter: Exeter. Available at: https://ore.exeter.ac.uk/repository/bitstream/handle/10871/35444/GillanN.pdf?sequence=4&isAllowed=y (accessed 19 May 2020).

Gliksman, Y. and Henik, A. (2019). Enumeration and alertness in developmental dyscalculia. *Journal of Cognition*, *2*(1), 5.

Goldacre, B. (2013). *Building Evidence into Education*. Available at: http://media.education.gov.uk/assets/files/pdf/b/ben%20goldacre%20paper.pdf (accessed 23 April 2020).

Goleman, D. (1996). *Emotional Intelligence: Why It Can Matter More Than IQ*. London: Bloomsbury Publishing.

Gottman, J.M., Katz, L.F. and Hooven, C. (1996). Parental meta-emotion philosophy and the emotional life of families: Theoretical models and preliminary data. *Journal of Family Psychology*, *10*, 243–268.

Gottman, J.M., Katz, L.F. and Hooven, C. (2013). *Meta-Emotion: How Families Communicate Emotionally*. Abingdon: Routledge.

Gough, D., Maidment, C. and Sharples, J. (2018). *UK What Works Centres: Aims, Methods and Contexts*. London: EPPI-Centre, Social Science Research Unit, UCL Institute of Education, University College London.

Gray, C. (1994). *Social Stories*. Arlington, TX: Future Horizons.

Green, R.M., Travers, A.M., Howe, Y. and McDougle, C.J. (2019). Women and autism spectrum disorder: Diagnosis and implications for treatment of adolescents and adults. *Current Psychiatry Reports*, *21*(4), 22.

Gresham, F.M. (2004). Current status and future directions of school-based behavioral interventions. *School Psychology Review*, *33*(3), 326.

Gunn, K.C. and Delafield-Butt, J.T. (2016). Teaching children with autism spectrum disorder with restricted interests: A review of evidence for best practice. *Review of Educational Research*, *86*(2), 408–430.

Haertel, G.D. and Means, B. (eds) (2003). *Evaluating Educational Technology: Effective Research Designs for Improving Learning*. New York: Teachers College Press.

Hallam, S. (2009). An evaluation of the social and emotional aspects of learning (SEAL) programme: Promoting positive behaviour, effective learning and well-being in primary school children. *Oxford Review of Education*, *35*(3), 313–330.

Halperin, J.M. and Healey, D.M. (2011). The influences of environmental enrichment, cognitive enhancement, and physical exercise on brain development: Can we alter the developmental trajectory of ADHD? *Neuroscience & Biobehavioral Reviews*, *35*(3), 621–634.

Hamm, B. and Mirenda, P. (2006). Post-school quality of life for individuals with developmental disabilities who use AAC. *Augmentative and Alternative Communication*, *22*(2), 134–147.

Hanks, R. (2011). *Common SENse for the Inclusive Classroom: How Teachers Can Maximise Existing Skills to Support Special Educational Needs*. London: Jessica Kingsley Publishers.

Hannen, E. and Woods, K. (2012). Narrative therapy with an adolescent who self-cuts: A case example. *Educational Psychology in Practice*, *28*(2), 187–214.

Hargreaves, D.H. (1997). In defence of evidence-based teaching. *British Educational Research Journal*, *23*, 405–419.

Harrison, R., Mann, G., Murphy, M., Taylor, A. and Thompson, N. (2003). *Partnership Made Painless: A Joined Up Guide to Working Together*. Lyme Regis: Russell House Publishing.

Hart, S.L. and Banda, D.R. (2010). Picture exchange communication system with individuals with developmental disabilities: A meta-analysis of single subject studies. *Remedial and Special Education*, *31*(6), 476–488.

Hartnett, D.N., Nelson, J.M. and Rinn, A.N. (2004). Gifted or ADHD? The possibilities of misdiagnosis. *Roeper Review*, *26*(2), 73–76.

Hayes, A.M. and Bulat, J. (2017). *Disabilities Inclusive Education Systems and Policies Guide for Low-and Middle-Income Countries* (occasional paper; RTI Press Publication OP-0043-1707, RTI International). Available at: www.rti.org/rti-press-publication/disabilities-inclusive-education-systems-and-policies-guide-low-and-middle-income/fulltext.pdf (accessed 23 April 2020).

Haynes, R.B., Sackett, D.L., Gray, J.M.A., Cook, D.F. and Guyatt, G.H. (1996). Transferring evidence from research into practice: The role of clinical care research evidence in clinical decisions. *ACP Journal Club*, *125*(3), A14–A16

Hersh, M. and Johnson, M.A. (2010). *Assistive Technology for Visually Impaired and Blind People*. Berlin: Springer Science & Business Media.

Hill, L.J., Williams, J.H., Aucott, L., Thomson, J. and Mon-Williams, M. (2011). How does exercise benefit performance on cognitive tests in primary-school pupils? *Developmental Medicine & Child Neurology*, *53*(7), 630–635.

Hoath, F.E. and Sanders, M.R. (2002). A feasibility study of enhanced group Triple P Positive Parenting Program for parents of children with attention-deficit/hyperactivity disorder. *Behaviour Change*, *19*(4), 191–206.

Hoffmann, S. (2016). Human rights and history. *Past & Present*, *232*(1), 279–310.

Hogg, M.A., Terry, D.J. and White, K.M. (1995). A tale of two theories: A critical comparison of identity theory with social identity theory. *Social Psychology Quarterly*, *58*(4), 255–269.

Holland, J., Pell, G. and KIDS. (2018). Children with SEND and the emotional impact on parents. *British Journal of Special Education*, *45*(4), 392–411.

Hollocks, M.J., Lerh, J.W., Magiati, I., Meiser-Stedman, R. and Brugha, T.S. (2019). Anxiety and depression in adults with autism spectrum disorder: A systematic review and meta-analysis. *Psychological Medicine*, *49*(4), 559–572.

Honeyman, K. (2016). *Childhood and Child Labour in Industrial England: Diversity and Agency, 1750–1914*. London: Routledge.

Howgego, C., Miles, S. and Myers, J. (2014). *HEART Topic Guide: Inclusive Learning*. Available at: www.heart-resources.org/wp-content/uploads/2014/09/Inclusive-Learning-Topic-Guide.pdf (accessed 23 April 2020).

Hsy, J. (2016). Symptom and surface: Disruptive deafness and medieval medical authority. *Journal of Bioethical Inquiry*, *13*(4), 477–483.

Humphrey, N., Lendrum, A. and Wigelsworth, M. (2010). *Social and Emotional Aspects of Learning (SEAL) Programme in Secondary Schools: National Evaluation*. Department for Education. Available at: www.gov.uk/government/publications/social-and-emotional-aspects-of-learning-seal-programme-in-secondary-schools-national-evaluation (accessed 23 April 2020).

Hutchings, M. and Archer, L. (2001). 'Higher than Einstein': Constructions of going to university among working-class non-participants. *Research Papers in Education*, *16*(1), 69–91.

Hutchinson, T.E., White, K.P., Martin, W.N., Reichert, K.C. and Frey, L.A. (1989). Human-computer interaction using eye-gaze input. *IEEE Transactions on Systems, Man, and Cybernetics*, *19*(6), 1527–1534.

Ichikawa, J. and Steup, M. (2018). The analysis of knowledge. In E.N. Zalta (ed.), *The Stanford Encyclopedia of Philosophy*. Available at: https://plato.stanford.edu/archives/sum2018/entries/knowledge-analysis/ (accessed 23 April 2020).

Impact Initiative (ed.) (2017). *Disability and Education, ESRC-DFID Research for Policy and Practice*. Brighton: IDS. Available at: https://opendocs.ids.ac.uk/opendocs/handle/20.500.12413/13460 (accessed 23 April 2020).

Ingram, K., Lewis-Palmer, T. and Sugai, G. (2005). Function-based intervention planning: Comparing the effectiveness of FBA function-based and non-function-based intervention plans. *Journal of Positive Behavior Interventions*, *7*(4), 224–236.

Inter-Agency Commission (1990) *World Conference on Education for All,* New York.

Jaarsma, P. and Welin, S. (2012). Autism as a natural human variation: Reflections on the claims of the neurodiversity movement. *Healthcare Analysis, 20*(1), 20–30.

Jacobsen, T. (1987). *The Harps that Once…: Sumerian Poetry in Translation.* New Haven, CT: Yale University Press.

Jeffries, S.A. (2007). *Education Related Learning Difficulties and Working Memory Functioning.* Guildford: University of Surrey.

Jensen, S.L.B. (2016). *The Making of International Human Rights: The 1960s, Decolonization, and the Reconstruction of Global Values.* New York: Cambridge University Press.

Johnstone, C.L. (2012). *Listening to the Logos: Speech and the Coming of Wisdom in Ancient Greece.* Columbia, SC: University of South Carolina Press.

Kallet, R.H. (2004). How to write the methods section of a research paper. *Respiratory Care, 49,* 1229–1232.

Kamali Arslantas, T., Yıldırım, S. and Altunay Arslantekin, B. (2019). Educational affordances of a specific web-based assistive technology for students with visual impairment. *Interactive Learning Environments.* doi: https://doi.org/10.1080/10494820.2019.1619587.

Kandalaft, M.R., Didehbani, N., Krawczyk, D.C., Allen, T.T. and Chapman, S.B. (2013). Virtual reality social cognition training for young adults with high-functioning autism. *Journal of Autism and Developmental Disorders, 43*(1), 34–44.

Kapp, S.K., Gillespie-Lynch, K., Sherman, L.E. and Hutman, T. (2013). Deficit, difference, or both? Autism and neurodiversity. *Developmental Psychology, 49*(1), 59.

Kazdin, A.E. (2000). *Psychotherapy for Children and Adolescents: Directions for Research and Practice.* New York: Oxford University Press.

Kelly, N. (2007). Deformity and disability in Greece and Rome. In A. Hector, S.J. Melcher and J. Schipper (eds), *This Abled Body: Rethinking Disability in Biblical Studies.* Atlanta, GA: Society of Biblical Literature.

Killu, K., Marc, R. and Crundwell, A. (2016). Students with anxiety in the classroom: Educational accommodations and interventions. *Beyond Behavior, 25*(2), 30–40.

Kirk, C., Lewis, R., Brown, K., Karibo, B. and Park, E. (2016). The power of student empowerment: Measuring classroom predictors and individual indicators. *Journal of Educational Research, 109*(6), 589–595.

Knowles, G. and Lander, V. (2011). *Diversity, Equality and Achievement in Education.* London: Sage.

Knowles, M.S. (1980). *The Modern Practice of Adult Education: Andragogy versus Pedagogy*. New York: Association Press.

Kolb, D.A. (1984). *Experiential Learning: Experience as the Source of Learning and Development*. Englewood Cliffs, NJ: Prentice Hall.

Kosc, L. (1974). Developmental dyscalculia. *Journal of Learning Disabilities*, *7*(3), 164–177.

Kucian, K. and von Aster, M. (2015). Developmental dyscalculia. *European Journal of Pediatrics*, *174*(1), 1–13.

Kuippis, F. and Hausstatter, R.S. (2014). *Inclusive Education Twenty Years after Salamanca*. New York: Peter Lang.

Kvale, S. (1996). *InterViews*: An Introduction to Qualitative Research Interviews. London: Sage.

Lamb, B. (2018). The SEND reforms and parental confidence: Are the reforms achieving greater parental confidence in the SEND system? *Journal of Research in Special Educational Needs*, *18*(3), 157–182.

Lamb-Parker, F., LeBuffe, P., Powell, G. and Halpern, E. (2008). A strength-based, systemic mental health approach to support children's social and emotional development. *Infants & Young Children*, *21*(1), 45–55.

Lane, K.L., Kalberg, J.R. and Shepcaro, J.C. (2009). An examination of the evidence base for function-based interventions for students with emotional and/or behavioral disorders attending middle and high schools. *Exceptional Children*, *75*(3), 321–340.

Lane, P., Spencer, S. and Jones, A. (2014). *Gypsy, Traveller, Roma: Experts by Experience. Reviewing UK Progress on the European Union Framework for National Roma Integration Strategies*. Essex: Anglia Ruskin University. Available at: www.Gypsy-traveller.org/wpcontent/uploads/2015/03/FFT_Inclusion-of-Gypsy-Traveller-health-needs-in-JSNA_FINAL.pdf (accessed 23 April 2020).

Laurillard, D. and Butterworth, B. (2016). Investigating dyscalculia from the lab to the classroom: A science of learning perspective. In J. Horvath and J. Hattie (eds), *From the Laboratory to the Classroom: Translating the Science of Learning for Teacher*. Abingdon: Routledge.

Lawson, J. and Silver, H. (2013). *A Social History of Education in England*. London: Routledge.

Le Fanu, G. (2013). Reconceptualising inclusive education in international development. In L. Tikly and A. Barrett (eds), *Education, Equality and Social Justice in the Global South*. London: Routledge.

Le Fanu, G. (2015). Imagining disability? Conceptualizations of learners with disabilities and their learning in the pedagogic manuals of international development agencies. *International Journal of Educational Development*, *40*, 267–275.

Leadbetter, J. (2005). Activity theory as a conceptual framework and ana-
    lytical tool within the practice of educational psychology. *Educational &
    Child Psychology*, *22*(1), 18–29.

Leamy, M., Bird, V., Le Boutillier, C., Williams, J. and Slade, M. (2011).
    Conceptual framework for personal recovery in mental health:
    Systematic review and narrative synthesis. *The British Journal of
    Psychiatry*, *199*(6), 445–452.

Lendrum, A., Humphrey, N. and Wigelsworth, M. (2013). Social and emo-
    tional aspects of learning (SEAL) for secondary schools: Implementation
    difficulties and their implications for school-based mental health pro-
    motion. *Child and Adolescent Mental Health*, *18*(3), 158–164.

Levene, A. (2008). Children, childhood and the workhouse: St Marylebone,
    1769–1781. *The London Journal*, *33*(1), 41–59.

Lewis, A. and Crisp, R.J. (2004). Measuring social identity in the profes-
    sional context of provision for pupils with special needs. *School
    Psychology International*, *4*, 404–421.

Lewis, A. and Norwich, B. (2004). *Special Teaching for Special Children?
    Pedagogies for Inclusion: A Pedagogy for Inclusion?* London: McGraw
    Hill Education.

Lewis, M. and Rudolph, K.D. (eds) (2014). *Handbook of Developmental
    Psychopathology*. Berlin: Springer Science & Business Media.

Lewis, T.J., Hudson, S., Richter, M. and Johnson, N. (2004). Scientifically
    supported practices in emotional and behavioral disorders: A proposed
    approach and brief review of current practices. *Behavioral Disorders*,
    *29*(3), 247–259.

Limbric, P. (2001). *The Team around the Child: Multi-Agency Service
    Coordination for Children with Complex Needs and their Families*.
    Worcester: Interconnections

Lindner, P., Miloff, A., Zetterlund, E., Reuterskiöld, L., Andersson, G. and
    Carlbring, P. (2019). Attitudes toward and familiarity with virtual reality
    therapy among practicing cognitive behavior therapists: A cross-
    sectional survey study in the era of consumer VR platforms. *Frontiers
    in Psychology*, *10*, 176.

Lindqvist, G. and Nilholm, C. (2014). Promoting inclusion? 'Inclusive' and
    effective head teachers' descriptions of their work. *European Journal of
    Special Needs Education*, *29*(1), 74–90.

Lockiewicz, M., Bogdanowicz, K. and Bogdanowicz, M. (2013). Psychological
    resources in adults with developmental dyslexia. *Journal of Learning
    Disabilities*, *47*, 543–555.

Love, J.R., Carr, J.E., Almason, S.M. and Petursdottir, A.I. (2009). Early
    and intensive behavioral intervention for autism: A survey of clinical
    practices. *Research in Autism Spectrum Disorders*, *3*(2), 421–428.

Lukersmith, S., Hartley, S., Kuipers, P., Madden, R., Llewellyn, G. and Dune, T. (2013). Community-based rehabilitation (CBR) monitoring and evaluation methods and tools: A literature review. *Disability and Rehabilitation*, *35*(23), 1941–1953.

Lupton, D. and Seymour, W. (2000). Technology, selfhood and physical disability. *Social Science & Medicine*, *50*(12), 1851–1862.

Lynch, P., Lund, P. and Massah, B. (2014). Identifying strategies to enhance the educational inclusion of visually impaired children with albinism in Malawi. *International Journal of Educational Development*, *39*, 216–224.

Mackenzie, G. (2018). Building resilience among children and youth with ADHD through identifying and developing protective factors in academic, interpersonal and cognitive domains. *Journal of ADHD and Care*, *1*(1), 14–31.

Mariga, L., McConkey, R. and Myezwa, H. (2014). *Inclusive Education in Low-Income Countries: A Resource Book for Teacher Educators, Parent Trainers and Community Development Workers*. Cape Town: Atlas Alliance and Disability Innovations Africa.

Maskey, M., Rodgers, J., Grahame, V., Glod, M., Honey, E., Kinnear, J., Labus, M., Milne, J., Minos, D., McConachie, H. and Parr, J.R. (2019). A randomised controlled feasibility trial of immersive virtual reality treatment with cognitive behaviour therapy for specific phobias in young people with autism spectrum disorder. *Journal of Autism and Developmental Disorders*, *49*(5), 1912–1927.

Mathisen, A. (2015). So that they may be useful to themselves and the community: Charting childhood disability in an eighteenth-century institution. *Journal of the History of Childhood and Youth*, *8*(2), 191–210.

Maughan, B., Rowe, R., Messer, J., Goodman, R. and Meltzer, H. (2004). Conduct disorder and oppositional defiant disorder in a national sample: Developmental epidemiology. *Journal of Child Psychology and Psychiatry*, *45*(3), 609–621.

McCulloch, G. (2011). *The Struggle for the History of Education*. Abingdon: Routledge.

McKeon, R. (1941) *The Basic Works of Aristotle*. New York: Random House.

McNaughton, D. and Bryen, D.N. (2007). AAC technologies to enhance participation and access to meaningful societal roles for adolescents and adults with developmental disabilities who require AAC. *Augmentative and Alternative Communication*, *23*(3), 217–229.

Mik-Meyer, N. (2016). Othering, ableism and disability: A discursive analysis of co-workers' construction of colleagues with visible impairments. *Human Relations*, *69*(6), 1341–1363.

Miller, D. (2003). *Political Philosophy: A Very Short Introduction*. Oxford: Oxford University Press.

Mintz, J. and Wyse, D. (2015). Inclusive pedagogy and knowledge in special education: Addressing the tension. *International Journal of Inclusive Education*, *19*(11), 1161–1171.

Mistry, M. and Sood, K. (2015). *English as an Additional Language in the Early Years: Linking Theory to Practice*. London: Taylor and Francis.

Mitra, S., Posarac, A. and Vick, B. (2013). Disability and poverty in developing countries: A multidimensional study. *World Development*, *41*, 1–18.

Mitra, S. and Sambamoorthi , U. (2014). Disability prevalence among adults: Estimates for 54 countries and progress toward a global estimate, *Disability* and *Rehabilitation*, *36*(11), 940–947, DOI: 10.3109/09638288.2013.825333

Moll, K., Göbel, S.M., Gooch, D., Landerl, K. and Snowling, M.J. (2016). Cognitive risk factors for specific learning disorder: Processing speed, temporal processing, and working memory. *Journal of Learning Disabilities*, *49*(3), 272–281.

Moore, M. (2008). Social control or protection of the child? The debates on the Industrial Schools Acts 1857–1894. *Journal of Family History*, *33*(4), 359–387.

Morgan, D. (1997). *Focus Groups as Qualitative Research*. London: Sage.

Morison, M. (1993). *Methods in Sociology*. London: Longman.

Morrish, I. (2013). *Education Since 1800*. London: Routledge.

Mukhopadhyay, S. (2015). West is best? A post-colonial perspective on the implementation of inclusive education in Botswana. *KEDI Journal of Educational Policy*, *12*(1), 19–39.

Murphy, J.W. (2005). Social norms and their implication for disability. In J.W. Murphy and J.T. Pardeck (eds), *Disability Issues for Social Workers and Human Services Professionals in the Twenty-First Century*. London: Routledge.

Murugami, M. (2009). Disability and identity. *Disability Studies Quarterly*, *29*(4). Available at: http://dsq-sds.org/article/view/979/1173 (accessed 23 April 2020).

Muthukrishna, A. (2019). The practice architectures of inclusive education in two African contexts. In N. Singhal, P. Lynch and S. Johansson (eds), *Education and Disability in the Global South*. London: Bloomsbury, pp.166–182.

Naraian, S. (2019). Diversifying theoretical commitments for a transnational inclusive education: Lessons from India. In N. Singhal, P. Lynch and S. Johansson (eds), *Education and Disability in the Global South*. London: Bloomsbury, pp.90–107.

NASEN (2014a). *SEN Support and the Graduated Response*. Available at: www.nasen.org.uk/resources/resourrces.sen-support-and-the-graduated-approach-inclusive-practice.html (accessed 23 April 2020).

NASEN (2014b). Tracking progress and managing provision: A quick guide to promoting the achievement of all pupils by tracking progress and evaluating the impact of provision. Available at: https://nasen.org.uk/uploads/assets/6e05fa97-d48a-4c12-969e488ab8eb8ed1/tracking-progress.pdf (accessed 23 April 2020).

NASEN (2015) 'Points from the SENCo-Forum', *British Journal of Special Education*, *42*(2), pp. 217–219.

National Autistic Society (2019). *What is Autism?* Available at: www.autism.org.uk/about/what-is.aspx (accessed 23 April 2020).

National Health Service (2019). *Overview: Developmental Coordination Disorder (Dyspraxia) in Children*. Available at: www.nhs.uk/conditions/developmental-coordination-disorder-dyspraxia/ (accessed 23 April 2020).

Nejedly, M. (2017). Earning their keep: Child workers at the Birmingham Asylum for the Infant Poor, 1797–1852. *Family & Community History*, *20*(3), 206–217.

Nelson, J. and Campbell, C. (2017). Evidence-informed practice in education: Meanings and applications. *Educational Research*, *59*(2), 127–135.

Neudorf, J., Ekstrand, C., Kress, S., Neufeldt, A. and Borowsky, R., (2019). Interactions of reading and semantics along the ventral visual processing stream. *Visual Cognition*, *27*(1), 1–17.

Nevo, I. and Slonim-Nevo, V. (2011). The myth of evidence-based practice: Towards evidence-informed practice. *British Journal of Social Work*, *41*(6), 1176–1197.

Newcomer, L.L. and Lewis, T.J. (2004). Functional behavioral assessment: An investigation of assessment reliability and effectiveness of function-based interventions. *Journal of Emotional and Behavioral Disorders*, *12*(3), 168–181.

Newman, I. (2019). When saying 'Go read it again' won't work: Multisensory ideas for more inclusive teaching and learning, *Nurse Education in Practice*, *34*, 12–16.

Ng, Q.X., Ho, C.Y.X., Chan, H.W., Yong, B.Z.J. and Yeo, W.S. (2017). Managing childhood and adolescent attention-deficit/hyperactivity disorder (ADHD) with exercise: A systematic review. *Complementary Therapies in Medicine*, *34*, 123–128.

NICE (2018). *Attention Deficit Hyperactivity Disorder: Diagnosis and Management*. Available at: www.nice.org.uk/guidance/ng87 (accessed 23 April 2020).

Nicholas, H. (2017). Professional developments in counselling psychology. In V. Galbraith (ed.), *Counselling Psychology: Topics in Applied Psychology*. Oxford: Routledge, pp.210–215.

Norcross, J., Beutler, L. and Levant, R. (2006). *Evidence-Based Practice in Mental Health: Debate and Dialogue on the Fundamental Questions*. Washington, DC: American Psychological Association.

Norwich, B (2014) 'Context, interests and methodologies', *Research in Special Needs and Inclusive Education: The interface with policy and practice*. London University, 19th November 2013. London: SEN Policy Research Forum, pp. 7–11.

Ofsted (2010). *The special educational needs and disability review: A statement is not enough*. Available at: https://www.gov.uk/government/publications/special-educational-needs-and-disability-review

Ofsted (2014). *Gypsy, Roma and Traveller Pupils: Supporting Access to Education*. Available at: www.gov.uk/government/case-studies/gypsy-roma-and-traveller-pupils-supporting-access-to-education (accessed 23 April 2020).

Ofsted (2019) *The education inspection framework*. Available at: www.gov.uk/government/collections/education-inspection-framework

Øien, I., Fallang, B. and Østensjø, S. (2015). Everyday use of assistive technology devices in school settings. *Disability and Rehabilitation Assistive Technology*, *11*(8), 630–636.

O'Neill, T., Light, J. and Pope, L. (2018). Effects of interventions that include aided augmentative and alternative communication input on the communication of individuals with complex communication needs: A meta-analysis. *Journal of Speech, Language, and Hearing Research*, *61*(7), 1743–1765.

Opie, C. (2004). *Doing Educational Research*. London: Sage.

Orlemanski, J. (2016). Literary genre, medieval studies, and the prosthesis of disability. *Textual Practice*, *30*(7), 1253–1272.

O'Tool , M.P. (2010). Disability and the suppression of historical identity: Rediscovering the professional backgrounds of the blind residents of Hospital des Quinze-Vingts. In J.R. Eyler (eds), *Disability in the Middle Ages: Reconsiderations and Reverberations*. Ashgate: Routledge.

Oxford Living Dictionaries (2020). Practice. Available at: https://en.oxforddictionaries.com/definition/practice (accessed 23 April 2020).

Park, S. (2018). *International Organisations and Global Problems: Theories and Explanations*. London: Cambridge University Press.

Parker, C. with Gordon, R. (1998). *Pathways to Partnership: Legal Aspects of Joint Working in Mental Health*. London: The Sainsbury Centre for Mental Health.

Parsons, S. and Mitchell, P. (2002). The potential of virtual reality in social skills training for people with autistic spectrum disorders. *Journal of Intellectual Disability Research*, *46*(5), 430–443.

Paul, J.M., Gray, S.A., Butterworth, B.L. and Reeve, R.A. (2019). Reading and math tests differentially predict number transcoding and number fact speed longitudinally: A random intercept cross-lagged panel approach. *Journal of Educational Psychology*, *111*(2), 299.

Pavey, B. (2007). *The Dyslexia-Friendly Primary School*. London: Paul Chapman Publishing.

Payne, S. (2015). How is life experienced by teenagers with dyspraxia? *An interpretative phenomenological analysis*. Unpublished PhD thesis, Coventry: Coventry University.

Pearman, T. (2010). *Women and Disability in Medieval Literature*. New York: Palgrave Macmillian.

Pearson, S. and Ralph, S. (2007). The identity of SENCos: Insights through images. *Journal of Research in Special Educational Needs*, *7*(1), 36–45.

Pedro, A. and Goldschmidt, T. (2019). Managing dyspraxia: Pre-school teachers' perceptions, experiences and strategies. *Journal of Psychology in Africa*, *29*(2), 182–186.

Peer, L. and Reid, G. (2016). *Special Educational Needs: A Guide for Inclusive Practice* (2nd edn). London: Sage.

Percy-Smith, J. (2005). *Definitions and Models: What Works in Strategic Partnerships for Children*. Ilford: Barnado's.

Perry, W.G. Jr. (1981). Cognitive and ethical growth: The making of meaning. In A.W. Chickering and Associates (eds), *The Modern American College*. San Francisco, CA: Jossey-Bass, pp.76–116.

Peskin, M., Wyka, K., Cukor, J., Olden, M., Altemus, M., Lee, F.S. and Difede, J. (2019). The relationship between posttraumatic and depressive symptoms during virtual reality exposure therapy with a cognitive enhancer. *Journal of Anxiety Disorders*, *61*, 82–88.

Pitchforth, J., Fahy, K., Ford, T., Wolpert, M., Viner, R.M. and Hargreaves, D.S. (2019). Mental health and well-being trends among children and young people in the UK, 1995–2014: Analysis of repeated cross-sectional national health surveys. *Psychological Medicine*, *49*(8), 1275–1285.

Plato (1961). Republic. In E. Hamilton and H. Cairns (eds), *Plato: The Collected Dialogues*. Princeton: Princeton University Press.

Polanczyk, G.V., Willcutt, E.G., Salum, G.A., Kieling, C. and Rohde, L.A. (2014). ADHD prevalence estimates across three decades: An updated systematic review and meta-regression analysis. *International Journal of Epidemiology*, *43*(2), 434–442.

Politis, Y., Olivia, L., and Olivia, T. (2019). Empowering autistic adults through their involvement in the development of a virtual world. *Advances in Autism*, *5*(4), 303–317.

Pontifex, M.B., Saliba, B.J., Raine, L.B., Picchietti, D.L. and Hillman, C.H. (2013). Exercise improves behavioral, neurocognitive, and scholastic performance in children with attention-deficit/hyperactivity disorder. *Journal of Pediatrics*, *162*(3), 543–551.

Powers, S., Rayner, S. and Gunter, H. (2001). Leadership in inclusive education: A professional development agenda for special education. *British Journal of Special Education*, *28*(3), 108–112.

Preston, D. and Carter, M. (2009). A review of the efficacy of the picture exchange communication system intervention. *Journal of Autism and Developmental Disorders*, *39*(10), 1471–1486.

Price, R.A. (2018). *Inclusive and Special Education Approaches in Developing Countries* (K4D Helpdesk Report 373). Brighton: Institute of Development Studies.

Prioste, A., Narciso, I., Gonçalves, M.M. and Pereira, C. (2017). Values' family flow: Associations between grandparents, parents and adolescent children. *Journal of Family Studies*, *23*(1), 98–117.

Pritchard, D.G. (1963). The development of schools for handicapped children in England during the nineteenth century. *History of Education Quarterly*, *3*(4), 215–222.

Punch, K.F. (2013). *Introduction to Social Research: Quantitative and Qualitative Approaches* (3rd edn). London: Sage.

Rabiee, A., Samadi, S.A., Vasaghi-Gharamaleki, B., Hosseini, S., Seyedin, S., Keyhani, M., Mahmoodizadeh, A. and Ranjbar Kermani, F. (2019). The cognitive profile of people with high-functioning autism spectrum disorders. *Behavioral Sciences*, *9*(2), 20.

Rapp, B., Purcell, J., Hillis, A.E., Capasso, R. and Miceli, G. (2016). Neural bases of orthographic long-term memory and working memory in dysgraphia. *Brain: A Journal of Neurology*, *139*(2), 588–604.

Ravenberg, B. and Söderström, S. (2017). *Disability, Society and Assistive Technology*. Abingdon: Routledge.

Reeve, R.A., Gray, S.A., Butterworth, B.L. and Paul, J.M. (2018). Variability in single digit addition problem-solving speed over time identifies typical, delay and deficit math pathways. *Frontiers in Psychology*, *9*. doi: 10.3389/fpsyg.2018.01498.

Reichow, B. (2012). Overview of meta-analyses on early intensive behavioral intervention for young children with autism spectrum disorders. *Journal of Autism and Developmental Disorders*, *42*(4), 512–520.

Reichow, B., Hume, K., Barton, E.E. and Boyd, B.A. (2018). *Early Intensive Behavioral Intervention (EIBI) for Increasing Functional Behaviors and Skills in Young Children with Autism Spectrum Disorders (ASD)*.

Available at: www.cochrane.org/CD009260/BEHAV_early-intensive-behavioral-intervention-eibi-increasing-functional-behaviors-and-skills-young (accessed 23 April 2020).

Rekkedal, A.M. (2012). Assistive hearing technologies among students with hearing impairment: Factors that promote satisfaction. *Journal of Deaf Studies and Deaf Education*, *17*(4), 499–517.

Retelsdorf, J., Schwartz, K. and Asbrock, F. (2015). 'Michael can't read!' Teachers' gender stereotypes and boys' reading self-concept. *Journal of Educational Psychology*, *107*(1), 186–194.

Retief, M. and Letsosa, R. (2018). Models of disability: A brief overview. *HTS Teologiese Studies (Theological Studies)*, *74*(1), 1–8.

Richards, R. (2019). *Dysgraphia: A Student's Perspective on Writing*. Available at: www.readingrockets.org/article/dysgraphia-students-perspective-writing (accessed 23 April 2020).

Riehl, C.J. (2000). The principal's role in creating inclusive schools for diverse students: A review of normative, empirical, and critical literature on the practice of educational administration. *Review of Educational Research*, *70*(1), 55–81.

Ritchie, J., Lewis, J., McNaughton Nicholls, C. and Ormston, R. (2014). *Qualitative Research Practice* (2nd edn). London: Sage.

Rix, J., Hall, K., Nind, M., Sheehy, K. and Wearmouth, J. (2009). What pedagogical approaches can effectively include children with special educational needs in mainstream classrooms? A systematic literature review. *Support for Learning*, *24*(2), 86–94.

Robson, C. (2002). *Real World Research* (2nd edn). Oxford: Blackwell.

Roccas, S. (2005). Religion and value systems. *Journal of Social Issues*, *61*(4), 747–759.

Rodgers, A. and Dunsmuir, S. (2015). A controlled evaluation of the 'FRIENDS for Life' emotional resiliency programme on overall anxiety levels, anxiety subtype levels and school adjustment. *Child and Adolescent Mental Health*, *20*(1), 13–19.

Rohwerder, B. (2015). *Disability Inclusion: Topic Guide*. Birmingham: GSDRC, University of Birmingham.

Rolfe, G. (2001). *Learning by Doing: A Guide to Teaching and Learning Methods*. Oxford: Oxford Polytechnic, Further Education Unit.

Rones, M. and Hoagwood, K. (2000). School-based mental health services: A research review. *Clinical Child and Family Psychology Review*, *3*(4), 223–241.

Rose, D. (2000). Universal design for learning. *Journal of Special Education Technology*, *15*(3), 45–49.

Rose, J. (2009). *Identifying and Teaching Children and Young People with Dyslexia and Literacy Difficulties*. London: Her Majesty's Stationary Office.

Rose, L. (2006). Deaf and dumb in Ancient Greece. In L. Davis (eds), *The Disabilities Studies Reader*. London: Routledge.

Rose, R. (2012). *Life Story Therapy with Traumatised Children: A Model for Practice*. London: Jessica Kingsley.

Rose, P. (2019). Looking to the future: Including children with disabilities in the education sustainable development goal. In N. Singhal, P. Lynch and S. Johansson (eds), *Education and Disability in the Global South*. London: Bloomsbury, pp.21–40.

Rotzer, S., Loenneker, T., Kucian, K., Martin, E., Klaver, P. and Von Aster, M. (2009). Dysfunctional neural network of spatial working memory contributes to developmental dyscalculia. *Neuropsychologia*, *47*(13), 2859–2865.

Saban, M.T. and Kirby, A. (2019). Empathy, social relationship and co-occurrence in young adults with DCD. *Human Movement Science*, *63*, 62–72.

Sackett, D.L., Rosenberg, W.M.C., Gray, J.A.M., Haynes, R.B. and Richardson, W.S. (1996). Evidence-based medicine: What it is and what it isn't. *British Medical Journal*, *312*, 71–72.

Sasso, G.M., Conroy, M.A., Stichter, J.P. and Fox, J.J. (2001). Slowing down the bandwagon: The misapplication of functional assessment for students with emotional or behavioral disorders. *Behavioral Disorders*, *26*(4), 282–296.

Schaeffer, C.M., Bruns, E., Weist, M., Stephan, S.H., Goldstein, J. and Simpson, Y. (2005). Overcoming challenges to using evidence-based interventions in schools. *Journal of Youth and Adolescence*, *34*(1), 15–22.

Scheff, T., Phillips, B.S. and Kincaid, H. (2006). *Goffman Unbound! A New Paradigm for Social Science (The Sociological Imagination)*. Boulder, CO: Paradigm Publishers.

Schon, D. (1983). *The Reflective Practitioner*. New York: Basic Books.

Schuelka, M.J. (2013). A faith in humanness: Disability, religion and development. *Disability & Society*, *28*(4), 500–513.

Schwartz, S.H. and Huismans, S. (1995). Value priorities and religiosity in four Western religions. *Social Psychology Quarterly*, *58*, 88–107.

Scotch, R.K. (1989). Politics and policy in the history of the disability rights movement. *The Milbank Quarterly*, *67* (Supplement Part 2), 380–400.

Seligman, M.E.P. (2002). *Authentic Happiness: Using the New Positive Psychology to Realize your Potential for Lasting Fulfilment*. New York: Free Press.

Seligman, M.E.P., Ernst, R.M., Gillham, J., Reivich, K. and Linkins, M. (2009). Positive education: Positive psychology and classroom interventions. *Oxford Review of Education*, *35*(3), 293–311.

Sen, A. (1999). *Development as Freedom*. Oxford: Oxford University Press.

Sennett, R. (1998). *The Corrosion of Character: The Personal Consequences of Work in the New Capitalism*. New York: Routledge.

Shakespeare, T. (2006). *Disability Rights and Wrongs*. London: Routledge.

Shapiro, J.P. and Stefkovich, J.A. (2011). *Ethical Leadership and Decision Making in Education: Applying Theoretical Perspectives to Complex Dilemmas*. New York: Routledge.

Shaywitz, B., Shaywitz, S., Blachman, B., Pugh, K., Fulbright, R., Skudlarski, P., Mencl, W., Constable, T., Holahan, J., Marchione, K., Fletcher, J., Lyon, R. and Gore, J. (2004). Development of left occipito-temporal systems for skilled reading in children after a phonologically based intervention. *Biological Psychiatry*, 55, 926–933.

Singhal, N. (2019). Researching disability and education: Rigour respect and responsibility. In N. Singhal, P. Lynch and S. Johansson (eds), *Education and Disability in the Global South*. London: Bloomsbury, pp.41–57.

Siraj-Blatchford, I., Clarke, K. and Needham, M. (2007). *The Team around the Child: Multi-Agency Working in the Early Years*. Stoke on Trent: Trentham Books.

Slee, R. (2006). Limits to and possibilities for educational reform. *International Journal of Inclusive Education*, 10(2–3), 109–119.

Slee, R. (2011). *The Irregular School: Exclusion, Schooling and Inclusive Education*. London: Routledge.

Smith, E. (2012). *Key Issues in Education and Social Justice*. London: Sage.

Smith, R.O. (2000). Measuring assistive technology outcomes in education. *Diagnostique*, 25(4), 273–290.

Smith, T., Scahill, L., Dawson, G., Guthrie, D., Lord, C., Odom, S., Rogers, S. and Wagner, A. (2007). Designing research studies on psychosocial interventions in autism. *Journal of Autism and Developmental Disorders*, 37(2), 354–366.

Snowling, M.J. (2013). Early identification and interventions for dyslexia: A contemporary view. *Journal of Research in Special Educational Needs*, 13(1), 7–14.

Snowling, M.J. and Hulme, C. (2011). Evidence-based interventions for reading and language difficulties: Creating a virtuous circle. *British Journal of Educational Psychology*, 81(1), 1–23.

Srivastava, M., de Boer, A. and Pijl, S.J. (2015). Inclusive education in developing countries: A closer look at its implementation in the last 10 years. *Educational Review*, 67(2), 179–195.

Stahr, B., Cushing, D., Lane, K. and Fox, J. (2006). Efficacy of a function-based intervention in decreasing off-task behavior exhibited by a student with ADHD. *Journal of Positive Behavior Interventions*, *8*(4), 201–211.

Stallard, P., Simpson, N., Anderson, S., Carter, T., Osborn, C. and Bush, S. (2005). An evaluation of the FRIENDS programme: A cognitive behaviour therapy intervention to promote emotional resilience. *Archives of Disease in Childhood*, *90*(10), 1016–1019.

Stanford, B. and Reeves, S. (2009). Making it happen: Using differentiated instruction, retrofit framework, and universal design for learning. *Teaching Exceptional Children Plus*, *5*(6), 6.

Stapleton, D.C., O'Day, B.L., Livermore, G.A. and Imparato, A.J. (2006). Dismantling the poverty trap: Disability policy for the twenty-first century. *The Milbank Quarterly*, *84*(4), 701–732.

Starratt, R.J. (1991). Building an ethical school: A theory for practice in educational leadership. *Educational Administration Quarterly*, *27*(2), 185–202.

Steinberg, E.A. and Drabick, D.A. (2015). A developmental psychopathology perspective on ADHD and comorbid conditions: The role of emotion regulation. *Child Psychiatry & Human Development*, *46*(6), 951–966.

Stephenson, M.E. (2017). *Ethical Decision-Making: Learning from Prominent Leaders in Not-for-Profit Organisations*. Doctoral thesis at University of Worcester.

Storey, C., McDowell, C. and Leslie, J.C. (2017). Evaluating the efficacy of the ©Headsprout reading program with children who have spent time in care. *Behavioral Interventions*, *32*(3), 285–293.

Story, M.F. (1998). Maximizing usability: The principles of universal design. *Assistive Technology*, *10*(1), 4–12.

Story, M. F. (2001). 'Principles of universal design.' In W. F. E. Preiser., and K. H. Smith (Eds.) Universal Design Handbook. London: McGraw Hill.

Stryker, S. (1968). Identity salience and role performance: The importance of symbolic interaction theory for family research. *Journal of Marriage and the Family*, *30*, 558–564.

Stuart-Hamilton, I. (2007). *Dictionary of Psychological Testing, Assessment and Treatment*. London: Jessica Kingsley.

Sulzer-Azaroff, B., Hoffman, A.O., Horton, C.B., Bondy, A. and Frost, L. (2009). The Picture Exchange Communication System (PECS): What do the data say? *Focus on Autism and Other Developmental Disabilities*, *24*(2), 89–103.

Swain, J. and French, S. (2000). Towards an affirmation model of disability. *Disability & Society*, *15*(4), 569–582.

Tafti, M.A., Hameedy, M.A. and Baghal, N.M. (2009). Dyslexia, a deficit or a difference: Comparing the creativity and memory skills of dyslexic and nondyslexic students in Iran. *Social Behavior and Personality: An International Journal*, *37*(8), 1009–1016.

Tajfel, H. and Turner, J. (1979). An integrative theory of intergroup conflict. In W.G. Austin and S. Worchel (eds), *The Social Psychology of Intergroup Relations*. Monterey: Brooks-Cole, pp.33–47.

Tavassoli, T., Miller, L.J., Schoen, S.A., Brout, J.J., Sullivan, J. and Baron-Cohen, S. (2018). Sensory reactivity, empathizing and systemizing in autism spectrum conditions and sensory processing disorder. *Developmental Cognitive Neuroscience*, *29*, 72–77.

TDA (2010). *Unit 18: Support Children and Young People with Disabilities and Special Educational Needs*. Available at: www.ocr.org.uk/images/75537-level-2-unit-18-support-children-and-young-people-with-disabilities-and-special-educational-needs.pdf (accessed 23 April 2020).

Thomas, G. (2013). *How to Do Your Research Project: A Guide for Students in Education and Applied Social Sciences* (2nd edn). Thousand Oaks: Sage.

Thomas, G. and Loxley, A. (2007). *Deconstructing Special Education and Constructing Inclusion* (2nd edn). Berkshire: McGraw Hill.

Thomas, G., Walker, D. and Webb, J. (1998). *The Making of the Inclusive School*. London: Routledge.

Todd, C. (2014). Emotion and value. *Philosophy Compass*, *9*(10), 702–712.

Topping, K. (2012). Conceptions of inclusion: Widening ideas. In C. Boyle and K. Topping (eds), *What Works in Inclusion?* Berkshire: Open University Press, pp.9–18.

Traveller Movement (2016). *Conference Report*. Available at: www.grthm-london.org.uk/2016/02/16/the-traveller-movement-conference-report/ (accessed 23 April 2020).

Trembath, D., Iacono, T., Lyon, K., West, D. and Johnson, H. (2014). Augmentative and alternative communication supports for adults with autism spectrum disorders. *Autism*, *18*(8), 891–902.

Trussell, R.P. (2008). Promoting school-wide mental health. *International Journal of Special Education*, *23*(3), 149–155.

Turner, J.C. and Brown, R. (1978). Social status, cognitive alterations and intergroup relations. In H. Tajfel (ed.), *Differentiation between Social Groups: Studies in the Social Psychology of Intergroup Relations*. London: Academic Press.

UNESCO (1994). *The Salamanca Statement and Framework for Action on Special Needs Education*. Paris: UNESCO. Available at: www.unesco.org/education/pdf/SALAMA_E.PDF (accessed 23 April 2020).

UNESCO (2000). *Education for All*. Paris: UNESCO.

UNESCO (2013). *Schooling for Millions of Children Jeopardized by Reductions in Aid* (Policy Paper 09; Education for All Global Monitoring Report). Paris: UNESCO. Available at: http://unesdoc.unesco.org/images/0022/002211/221129E.pdf (accessed 23 April 2020).

UNESCO (2015). *Education for All 2000–2015: Achievements and Challenges*. Paris: UNESCO.

UNICEF (2013). *State of the World's Children: Children with Disabilities*. New York: UNICEF. Available at: www.unicef.org/sowc2013/report.html (accessed 23 April 2020).

UNICEF (2014). *Strengthening Statistics on Children with Disabilities: UNICEF's Work and Planned Activities*. New York: Data and Analytics Section, UNICEF. Available at: www.un.org/disabilities/documents/events/2014_summary_strengthening_statistics_shildren_with_disabilities.pdf (accessed 23 April 2020).

United Nations (1948). *Universal Declaration of Human Rights*. Geneva: UN General Assembly.

United Nations (1989). *Convention on the Rights of the Child*. Geneva: UN General Assembly.

United Nations (1994). *The UNESCO Salamanca Statement*. Geneva: UN General Assembly.

United Nations (2006). *Convention of the Rights of Persons with Disabilities*. Geneva: UN General Assembly.

United Nations (2019). *Universal Declaration of Human Rights*. Available at: www.un.org/en/universal-declaration-human-rights/ (accessed 23 April 2020).

University of Worcester (2019). *Our Values*. Available at: www.worcester.ac.uk/about/job-opportunities/our-values.aspx (accessed 23 April 2020).

Van Hoorn, J.F., Maathuis, C.G.B. and Hadders-Algra, M. (2013). Neural correlates of paediatric dysgraphia. *Developmental Medicine and Child Neurology*, *55*, 65–68.

Van Luit, J.E.H. and Toll, S.W.M. (2018). Associative cognitive factors of math problems in students diagnosed with developmental dyscalculia. *Frontiers in Psychology*, *9*, 1907.

Velikonja, T., Fett, A.K. and Velthorst, E. (2019). Patterns of nonsocial and social cognitive functioning in adults with autism spectrum disorder: A systematic review and meta-analysis. *JAMA Psychiatry*, *76*(2), 135–151.

Vislie, L. (2003). From integration to inclusion: Focusing global trends and changes in the western European societies. *European Journal of Special Needs Education*, *18*(1), 17–35.

Von Aster, M.G. and Shalev, R.S. (2007). Number development and developmental dyscalculia. *Developmental Medicine & Child Neurology*, *49*(11), 868–873.

Vorhaus, J. (2006). Respecting profoundly disabled learners. *Journal of Philosophy of Education*, *40*(3), 313–328.

Wagner. P (2016) Consultation as a framework for practice. In B. Kelly, L>M> Woolfson and J. Boyle (eds), *Frameworks for Practice in Educational Psychology* (2nd edn). London: Jessica Kingsley, pp.194–215.

Wallace-Hadrill, A. (1988). The social structure of the Roman house. *Papers of the British School at Rome*, *56*, 43–97.

Walls, N.H. (2007). The origins of the disabled body: Disability in Ancient Mesopotamia. In H. Avalos, S.J. Melcher and J. Schipper (eds), *This Abled Body: Rethinking Disabilities in Biblical Studies*. Atlanta, GA: The Society of Biblical Literature, pp.13–31.

Wang, F. (2018). Social justice leadership – Theory and practice: A case of Ontario. *Educational Administration Quarterly*, *54*(3), pp.470–498.

Wapling, L. and Downie, B. (2012). *Beyond Charity: A Donor's Guide to Inclusion – Disability Funding in the Era of the UN Convention on the Rights of Persons with Disabilities*. Boston: Disability Rights Fund. Available at: www.disabilityrightsfund.org/files/beyond_charity._a_donors_guide_to_inclusion.pdf (accessed 23 April 2020).

Warnock, M. (1978). *Special Education Needs: Report of the Committee of Enquiry into the Education of Handicapped Children and Young People*. London: HM Stationery Office.

Weare, K. (2000). *Promoting Mental, Emotional and Social Health: A Whole School Approach*. Hove: Psychology Press.

Wearmouth, J. (2016). *Effective SENCO: Meeting the Challenge*. Maidenhead: Open University Press.

Webb, S.A. (2001). Some considerations on the validity of evidence-based practice in social work. *British Journal of Social Work*, *31*, 57–79.

Wedell, K. (2015). Points from the SENCo-Forum. *British Journal of Special Education*, *42*, 444–447.

Wedell, K. (2017). Points from the SENCo-Forum: The implications of research findings for SENCos' support for individual children. *British Journal of Special Education*, *44*, 112–114.

Welsh, M.C. and Pennington, B.F. (1989). Assessing frontal lobe functioning in children: Views from developmental psychology. *Developmental Neuropsychology*, *4*, 199–230.

Wenger, E., McDermott, R. and Snyder, W. (2002). *A Guide to Managing Knowledge: Cultivating Communities of Practice*. Boston, MA: Harvard Business School Press.

White, H., Saran, A., Polack, S. and Kuper, H. (2018). *Rapid Evidence Assessment of 'What Works' to Improve Social Inclusion and Empowerment for People with Disabilities in Low- and Middle-Income Countries.* International Centre for Evidence in Disability, London School of Hygiene and Tropical Medicine and Campbell Collaboration. Available at: https://assets.publishing.service.gov.uk/government/uploads/system/uploads/attachment_data/file/727792/Social_empowerment_Rapid_Review_Full_Report.pdf (accessed 23 April 2020).

White, M. and Epston, D. (1990). *Narrative Means to Therapeutic Ends.* New York: W.W. Norton.

Whooley, O. (2010). Diagnostic ambivalence: Psychiatric workarounds and the Diagnostic and Statistical Manual of Mental Disorders. *Sociology of Health & Illness, 32*(3), 452–469.

Wigal, S.B., Emmerson, N., Gehricke, J.G. and Galassetti, P. (2013). Exercise: Applications to childhood ADHD. *Journal of Attention Disorders, 17*(4), 279–290.

Williams, G. (1993). Chronic illness and the pursuit of virtue in everday life. In A. Radley (ed.), *Worlds of Illness. Biological and Cultural Perspectives on Health and Disease.* London:Routledge.

Williams-Fortune, T. (2020). *What Research Says about Immersion.* Available at: http://carla.umn.edu/immersion/documents/Immersion Research_TaraFortune.html#_edn9 (accessed 23 April 2020).

Wilson, A.J. and Dehaene, S. (2007). Number sense and developmental dyscalculia. *Human Behavior, Learning, and the Developing Brain: Atypical Development, 2,* 212–237.

Wing, L. (1981). Language, social, and cognitive impairments in autism and severe mental retardation. *Journal of Autism and Developmental Disorders, 11*(1), 31–44.

Winter, M. (2019). *Scribbling Out Dysgraphia: Beating Learning Disabilities with Adaptive Study Methods.* Available at: www.learningscientists.org/blog/2016/7/26-1 (accessed 23 April 2020).

Wolf, M. and Katzir-Cohen, T. (2001). Reading fluency and its intervention. *Scientific Studies of Reading, 5*(3), 211–239.

Woodward, J. and Rieth, H. (1997). A historical review of technology research in special education. *Review of Educational Research, 67*(4), 503–536.

World Bank (2007). *People with Disabilities in India: From Commitments to Outcomes.* Washington, DC: World Bank.

World Bank (2018). *World Development Report 2018: Learning to Realize Education's Promise.* Washington, DC: World Bank.

World Health Organization (WHO) (1992). *The ICD-10 Classification of Mental and Behavioural Disorders: Clinical Descriptions and Diagnostic Guidelines*. Geneva: WHO.

World Health Organization (WHO) (2001). *International Classification of Functioning, Disability and Health*. Geneva: WHO.

World Health Organization (WHO) (2004). Promoting Mental Health: Concepts, Emerging evidence, Practice. Summary Report. Available at: https://www.who.int/mental_health/evidence/en/promoting_mhh.pdf (accessed 01 October 2020).

World Health Organization (WHO) (2010). *Community-Based Rehabilitation: CBR Guidelines*. Geneva: WHO.

World Health Organization (WHO) (2011). *World Report on Disability*. Geneva: WHO. Available at: http://whqlibdoc.who.int/publications/2011/9789240685215_eng.pdf (accessed 23 April 2020).

World Health Organization (WHO) (2014). *The ICD-10 Classification of Mental and Behavioural Disorders: Clinical Descriptions and Diagnostic Guidelines*. Geneva: WHO.

Wyn, J., Cahill, H., Holdsworth, R., Rowling, L. and Carson, S. (2000). MindMatters: A whole-school approach promoting mental health and wellbeing. *Australian & New Zealand Journal of Psychiatry*, *34*(4), 594–601.

Yates, M. and Slattery, T.J. (2019). Individual differences in spelling ability influence phonological processing during visual word recognition. *Cognition*, *187*, 139–149j.

Zimmerman, M.A. (1995). Psychological empowerment: Issues and illustrations. *American Journal of Community Psychology*, *23*, 581–599.

# Acts and legislation

Butler Education Act (1944). Available at: www.parliament.uk/about/living-heritage/transformingsociety/livinglearning/school/overview/educationact1944/ (accessed 23 April 2020).

Care Act (2014). Available at: http://www.legislation.gov.uk/ukpga/2014/23/contents/enacted (accessed 18 May 2020).

Children Act (1989). Available at: http://www.legislation.gov.uk/ukpga/1989/41/contents (accessed 18 May 2020).

Children Act (2004). Available at: www.legislation.gov.uk/ukpga/2004/31/pdfs/ukpga_20040031_en.pdf (accessed 23 April 2020).

Children and Families Act (2014). Available at: http://www.legislation.gov.uk/ukpga/2014/6/contents/enacted (accessed 15 May 2020)

Chronically Sick and Disabled Person's Act (1970). Available at: www.legislation.gov.uk/ukpga/1970/44/pdfs/ukpga_19700044_en.pdf (accessed 23 April 2020).

Disability Discrimination Act (1995). Available at: www.legislation.gov.uk/ukpga/1995/50/pdfs/ukpga_19950050_en.pdf (accessed 23 April 2020).

Disability Discrimination Act (2005). Available at: www.legislation.gov.uk/ukpga/2005/13/contents (accessed 23 April 2020).

Education Act (1880). Available at: www.educationengland.org.uk/documents/acts/1880-elementary-education-act.html (accessed 23 April 2020).

Education Act (1972). Available at: www.legislation.gov.uk/ukpga/1972/44/enacted (accessed 23 April 2020).

Education Act (1981). Available at: http://www.legislation.gov.uk/ukpga/1981/60/enacted (accessed 15 May 2020).

Elementary Education (Blind and Deaf Children) (1893). Available at: https://api.parliament.uk/historic-hansard/acts/elementary-education-blind-and-deaf-children-act-1893 (accessed 18 May 2020).

Elementary Education of Defective and Epileptic Children's Act (1899). Available at: https://api.parliament.uk/historic-hansard/acts/elementary-education-defective-and-epileptic-children-act-1899 (accessed 23 April 2020).

Equality Act (2010). Available at: www.legislation.gov.uk/ukpga/2010/15/contents (accessed 23 April 2020).

Forster Education Act (1870). Available at: www.parliament.uk/about/living-heritage/transformingsociety/livinglearning/school/overview/1870educationact/ (accessed 23 April 2020).

Industrial Schools Act (1857). Available at: https://api.parliament.uk/historic-hansard/lords/1860/aug/16/industrial-schools-act-1857-amendment (accessed: 18 May 2020).

Public Sector Bodies (Websites and Mobile Applications) Accessibility Regulations (2018). Available at: www.legislation.gov.uk/uksi/2018/852/pdfs/uksi_20180852_en.pdf (accessed 23 April 2020).

Race Relations Act (1976). Available at: http://www.legislation.gov.uk/ukpga/1976/74/enacted (accessed 18 May 2020).

Special Educational Needs Disability Act (2001). Available at: http://www.legislation.gov.uk/ukpga/2001/10/contents (accessed 18 May 2020).

The Handicapped Pupils and Special Schools Regulations (1959). Available at: https://www.legislation.gov.uk/uksi/1959/365/made (accessed 23 August 2020).

# INDEX